HUMAN ASPECTS OF
UNEMPLOYMENT AND RELIEF

THE UNIVERSITY OF NORTH CAROLINA
SOCIAL STUDY SERIES

UNDER THE GENERAL EDITORSHIP OF HOWARD W. ODUM. BOOKS MARKED WITH *
PUBLISHED IN COÖPERATION WITH THE INSTITUTE FOR RESEARCH IN SOCIAL SCIENCE.

The University of North Carolina Press, Chapel Hill, N. C.; The Baker and Taylor Co., New York; Oxford University Press, London; The Maruzen Company, Tokyo; Edward Evans & Sons, Ltd., Shanghai; D. B. Centen's Wetenschappelijke Boekhandel, Amsterdam.

HUMAN ASPECTS OF UNEMPLOYMENT AND RELIEF

WITH SPECIAL REFERENCE TO THE EFFECTS OF THE DEPRESSION ON CHILDREN

By

JAMES MICKEL WILLIAMS, Ph.D.

CHAPEL HILL
THE UNIVERSITY OF NORTH CAROLINA PRESS
1933

To Those Who Have Fought for Constructive Relief

AND

To My Comrades in this Research

L. N. W. and H. N. W.

FOREWORD

ONE OF THE most pertinent questions that can be asked about our commonwealth today is: How have the depression and the methods of relief affected the unemployed and those dependent on them? The eleven million or more men in this country, who, in 1932, were able and willing to work but could not get work had many more than this number dependent on them, of whom more than fourteen million were children under sixteen. What have been the effects on their families and especially on the children of the inability of these eleven million men to carry their responsibilities?

The emphasis in this volume is on the effects of unemployment on the children of the unemployed. This interest in the children is not due to pity but to the fact that the children are truly the America of the future. On their physical and mental health and morale depend the possibilities before the country, and in part the future of the world as well.

I am indebted to a number of individuals and agencies for assistance of various kinds. The following federal and state departments have contributed material for the research: the United States Children's Bureau; the United States Public Health Service; the New York State Department of Social Welfare; the New York State Child Welfare Board; the Division of Junior Placement of the New York State Department of Labor; the New York State Department of Health; the New York State Department of Mental Hygiene; the New York State Department of Corrections; the New York State Department of Education. Various county and city agencies also furnished material, including public welfare departments, police departments, health departments, county tuberculosis sanatoriums, psychopathic hospitals, juvenile courts, child clinics, schools, and nursing agencies.

The following national and state organizations also have contributed: the Child Welfare League of America; the New York Child Labor Committee; the Family Welfare Association of America; the National Organization for Public Health Nursing; the Health Nursing Service of the American Red Cross; the American Public Health Association; the American Child Health Association; the National Tuberculosis Association; the National Probation Association; the New York State Charities Aid Association; the New York State Conference of Social Workers; the American Association of Social Workers; the American Public Welfare Association; the National Conference of Jewish Social Work; the Bureau of Jewish Social Research; the Church Mission of Help, and other church organizations; the Girls' Service League; the Committee of Fourteen of New York City; the Big Brothers' and Big Sisters' Federation; the Boys' Clubs of America; the National Education Association; the National Association of Community Chests and Councils; the National Council of the Young Men's Christian Association; the National Council of the Young Women's Christian Association.

I have had the use of confidential reports of welfare agencies and councils of large cities, these reports prepared by experts and based on answers to questionnaires by hundreds of nurses, social workers and others. But most of all I am indebted to the social workers of public and private welfare offices, to the practicing physicians, public health nurses, clinical workers, visiting teachers, probation officers, and members of the staffs of psychopathic hospitals who, though overwhelmed with work, went over many cases of children and youth with me and helped me to follow up typical ones for the information I needed. Welfare work cannot be understood merely from knowing its legal and administrative side; one must see welfare practices through the eyes of those who do the work.

I have discussed the material in this book with public welfare officials and their staffs, with members of the New York State Temporary Emergency Relief Administration and the New York State Department of Social Welfare, with the workers of family welfare societies and children's agencies, with juvenile court judges and probation officers, and with university teachers of political science and sociology. Some of these people have read parts or the whole of the manuscript and I have profited by their criticisms and suggestions so that the result represents, to a considerable degree, the thinking of workers in different cities and in various fields.

We have stated our facts with candor and with a view to their relative importance in the total picture. Some readers may think that we have over-stated some facts but one of the best seasoned experts, who has been in child welfare work in his city for over twenty years, exclaimed, after he had read the manuscript: "It is not a bit over-done. I know that you have not made it as bad as it is." Another said: "Maybe this book will give the public some realization of the needs so that they will give us more intelligent support, but certainly the half has not been told." It cannot be told. It must be seen day by day, week after week, to realize its significance.

Some of the material in this book was published in a pamphlet, "Children and the Depression," which was written for the American Public Welfare Association with the understanding that the material would also be used in this book.

The publication of this volume was made possible by subscriptions of men and women engaged in public welfare work.

For assistance in the proof reading I am indebted to Miss Mary E. McCormick, instructor in English and to Miss Eleanor H. Graves, instructor in economics in Hobart College, also to Mrs. R. C. Collison and Margaret F. Parrott, Esther F. Patrick and Dorothy H. Bolin of Geneva.

JAMES M. WILLIAMS.

Geneva, N. Y.

TABLE OF CONTENTS

INTRODUCTION

THIS BOOK originated in an investigation of the effect of unemployment and welfare practices in five cities of New York. The investigation was begun in the spring of 1931 and, as time permitted, was carried on throughout that year and into the summer of 1932.

It is probable that conditions are better in up-state New York than in other sections of the country.[1] The public welfare law of New York is one of the most advanced in the country, and this state was the first to provide state aid during the present emergency.[2] A description of conditions in New York is therefore fairly certain to be no exaggeration of the state of affairs throughout the country. In those regions where people depend on staple crops or where rapid changes have occurred in recent years, worse conditions may be found.

It is true, of course, that in some sections of the country there is much chronic poverty and, strangely enough, where this is true the people often are not conscious of it. For this reason, if for no other, there will undoubtedly be readers of this volume who will say: Conditions such as these certainly do not exist in my community. Only recently I secured information about an almost entirely rural county in the southern United States in which the county welfare officer was allowed for a time to provide work-relief from county funds. During the few weeks while this work was given, it was often said that "only niggers and po' white trash" were asking for relief (other citizens were too proud to apply). In this county one family out of every ten is eating only now and then. Government flour made up with water and a little hoarded or borrowed salt and soda constitutes the basis of subsistence. Able-bodied men, both white and black, weakened by hunger but anxious to work, were willing to walk six miles to and from a job to earn fifty cents a day. Yet the opinion of the "solid" citizens is that "niggers" who apply for relief are not any good and

---

[1] "How the Cities Stand," *Survey*, Apr. 15, 1932, p. 71.

[2] See Chapter IX.

the whites are trash. A southern white woman, a university graduate whose husband had been out of work for several months but who was being taken care of by her husband's parents, expressed the opinion that public relief was unnecessary and wasteful and pauperizing. Her opinion is typical of a large class, though notable exceptions may be found here and there.

It would be difficult to believe the truth of testimony like this from the South were it not confirmed repeatedly by my own observation in New York and that of correspondents in New England and the Middle West.

All the evils suffered in depression are found to some degree in prosperity, but they are then accepted as inevitable results of "a changing order" or as due to the residue of families that have proved unfit in the struggle for existence, while in depression the number afflicted is so enormously increased that the future of the country is imperiled and the failure of the economic system is plain. The injury to society in prosperity is as truly institutional in its causes as it is in depression, but these ultimate causes are then ignored, while in depression they cannot be ignored.

The injuries are due not only to unemployment but also to our inadequate, unsystematic relief. There is suffering under this kind of relief not only during a depression but always, for unemployment is always with us. The working of American welfare practices in depression is merely an exaggerated example of the way in which they always work. But a depression is an opportune time to study them, for widespread unemployment brings out the evils in bold relief.

This book has been written as part of the records of these times; and it will be of practical use after the depression is over, because it will not be over for thousands of families. Family welfare societies in the large cities were still caring for victims of the depression of 1920 when the present one came on, and those broken by these years of unemployment will have to be provided for during the next generation. The findings of the book will therefore continue to be of value until we have so planned our economic order as to avoid depressions.

The extreme complexity of the present unemployment situation is only vaguely realized by most of us. People are in all sorts of predicaments; so are those who are trying to relieve need. We see, for instance, a family too proud to ask for aid, living on a mere pittance, children undernourished—the home breaking and the family being destroyed in the battle between pride and despair. In another case we see an apparently worthless man out of work—even his wife accuses him of not wanting a job. He is lazy, slouchy, indifferent. A physical examination shows anemia and incipient tuberculosis. Or there may be a real case of worthlessness—no physical defect explains the evident unwillingness to work. On investigation we find that habits of industry and thrift have been destroyed because they have repeatedly failed to bring any reward at all. Among the people trying to relieve need, there are those who realize the complexity of the problem and those who are rooted in the past and cannot understand the significance of what they see or deal with it effectively.

There is no civilized country in the world today which does not attempt to prevent extreme suffering in any portion of its population. In the United States, state laws provide various measures for taking care of the poverty-stricken old and infirm, the deaf, dumb, and blind, the hopelessly crippled, the feeble-minded and insane, and others unable to fend for themselves. The doctrine that these helpless classes should be protected is given clear statement in these laws, and no one would question their wisdom. But there is today a new type of helplessness affecting more than one-quarter of our population. Though the country has a vast store of food and other necessities, eleven million men are denied an opportunity to earn a living and are in want.

The essential cause of this situation (not to mention other causes, as the monetary aspect, speculation and others) is the unprecedented development in the technique of production during the past two decades within an economic system whose price system has remained antiquated. This has permitted the flow of a large proportion of the buying power into the possession of a few. The many have not had sufficient income to buy the goods produced and the result has been an inevitable excess production. The vast increase in production due to machinery can be appreciated from a few illustrations. When I worked as a boy in a brick and tile factory we produced less than a thousand bricks a day, per man. A modern straight-line continuous brick plant will produce 400,000 bricks a day per man. But for whom? Who possesses the buying power implied in that machine production? Near where I worked was a mill which produced not very many barrels of flour a day; a modern flour mill in Minneapolis produces 30,000 barrels a day per man. This is the story throughout industry and to some extent in agriculture as well. Because machinery has replaced men in such large numbers, and because those at work do not get enough income to buy what is produced, there is widespread unemployment, even in prosperity, and the periodic depression becomes a time of vast and long continued stoppage of industry, extreme poverty, deflation of all values, enormous losses to investors and failures of industrial and financial enterprises.

Experimentation has made possible our technological development and we may well believe that, through bold experiments in the economic and political fields, we shall eventually be able to bring our economic and political methods into adjustment to the new technology. Engineers already are suggesting experiments based on a clear cut analysis which goes to the very roots of our economic system.[3]

But while all this is being done we must insure the millions of innocent victims of this new industrial revolution against the appalling ravages of unemployment. The realization of this imperative need is dawning on many, even among those who do not realize the deep, underlying causes of this unprecedented depression. The purpose of this book is to show the need of a more comprehensive provision for the unemployed than has yet been made. What is required is a nationwide and coördinated system of social insurance and public works.

---

[3] For instance, read Dahlberg, *Jobs, Machines and Capitalism*.

PART I

SOCIAL EFFECTS OF UNEMPLOYMENT AND WELFARE PRACTICES

CHAPTER I

THE TWO CITIES

"ANY CITY, however small, is in fact divided into two, one the city of the poor, the other of the rich." This might be the opening sentence of any scientific study of a modern city. In fact it was written by Plato[1] in the first half of the fourth century B.C. It still is true,[2] though there are people living in the city of the rich and well-to-do whose sympathies and constructive planning envisage the whole city.

The city of the well-to-do, if reminded of the existence of the other, makes light of its poverty but talks much of ignorance. "The ill-nourished child is in our country not the product of poverty; it is largely the product of ill-instructed children and ignorant parents." This might be the complacent observation of any satisfied person in the city of the well-to-do. As a matter of fact, the words are those of President Hoover who gave the opening address at the White House Conference on Child Health and Protection in November, 1930.[3] While he was saying this, millions of industrious bread-winners were in poverty through no fault of their own and their children were in need. He chose to emphasize their ignorance and to belittle their poverty. Would it not have been truer to the facts

---

[1] *Republic*, book IV.

[2] "Although modern life is equalizing man, each new group which seizes advantage apes the exclusiveness of the 'superiors' it has dethroned." Burns, *Modern Civilization on Trial*, p. 40.

[3] "With the advance of science and advancement of knowledge we have learned a thousand things that the individual, both parent and child, must know in his own self-protection. And at once the relation of our educational system to the problem envisages itself, and it goes further. The ill-nourished child is in our country not the product of poverty; it is largely the product, of ill-instructed children and ignorant parents." *United States Daily*, Nov. 28, 1930. Supplement.

to have recognized both ignorance and poverty as two main causes of ill-nourished children?

Should a national conference on child health ignore the economic causes of ill-health? The sentiment of the conference was "No." Statements like the following were voiced. Eighty-seven per cent of the people of the United States own but ten per cent of the wealth and seventy-six per cent leave nothing when they die. This, it was said, throws some light on the extent of child dependence in normal times, for "when a father in this economic group dies he leaves nothing at all for the care of his children. An absence of thrift and industry or poor investment are the cause of this condition in some families but the wages of large numbers of hardworking fathers leave no margin for saving." On the other hand, "if our national income and national wealth had been evenly divided that year (1923) among the 24,000,000 families in the United States, the income of each family would have been approximately $3,000 and each would have had approximately $15,000 invested."[4] This voice must, then, have been that of a communist. No, it was the voice of Miss Grace Abbott, Chief of the United States Children's Bureau, speaking at the same conference. She reassures the city of the well-to-do: "I do not propose equality, but I do want to call attention to the degree of inequality which exists in the United States as a source of our social problems, and particularly the one we are discussing tonight, dependency among children."

Miss Abbott emphasizes the need of education as much as anybody but does not ignore the evil of poverty. Poverty isolates and the isolation makes education more difficult. Poverty and isolation condemn the poor to their usual mode of existence while material advantages raise the well-to-do to another manner of life. More than this, "the 13 percent of the people who own 90 percent of the total property in America may be said, roughly, to control 90 percent of America's in-

---

[4] Quoted from a manuscript copy of the address of Miss Abbott. By "leave nothing when they die," she means that 76 per cent leave estates so small that they are not probated, that is, not more than $258. She refers to the report of the Federal Trade Commission on "National Wealth and Income," pp. 3 and 58.

dustrial destiny."[5] Surpassing material enjoyments and the exercise of social control foster aloofness that unfits the well-to-do for the responsibility that goes with social control. The words of Plato, coming down through the ages, find us here in the United States still demoralized as a functional group by class aloofness, the vast latent energy and mental possibilities of the working masses undeveloped, the rich often indolent because of riches. Were it not for this ancient situation in which we find ourselves, this book would not be necessary.

Plato made his observations in a matter-of-fact way, much as they would be made today by any keen observer untrained in historical background. But to those who have grown up with an evolutionary point of view, what he said has a deep significance. Inequality among men, resulting in some form of domination of the weaker by the strong, is found as far back as we can go and the problems resulting from this inequality are the essential problems of social psychology.[6] But the differentiation of society into exclusive classes is comparatively late in social evolution. Among primitive peoples, if blight or disease struck the food supply of one section of a tribe, the rest knew about it, not complacently as a matter of gossip, but really knew, and the primitive custom of sharing was in operation.[7] Children were carefully instructed to share with the needy.[8] If the unfortunate tribe was a hostile one, other tribes became painfully aware of it from the forays of the afflicted one. In other cases the tribe might undertake a long migration out of its home country into a better land.

To those cognizant of this virile and wholesome restlessness and struggle for existence among primitive peoples the world over and throughout countless ages, and of the quick response of the more fortunate to the needy section of a tribe, it is thought-provoking to see the present desperate need among the unemployed, and to recollect that these conditions have

---

[5] Atkins and associates, *Economic Behavior*, II, p. 74.

[6] Williams, *Principles of Social Psychology;* Murchison, *Social Psychology.*

[7] Westermarck, *The Origin and Development of Moral Ideas*, I, pp. 540, 545, 556-59.

[8] Crashing Thunder; *The Autobiography of an American Indian*, edited by Paul Radin, pp. 56-59.

existed for three years while the rank and file in the city of the well-to-do have known little or nothing about it other than by hearsay. This brings home to us, with telling force, the completeness of the division between the manual workers and the well-to-do which began with the origin of private property. Even the children of the well-to-do, who mingle with the children of the poor in school daily, know nothing about their conditions of life. Wherever the classes appear together, as in church or the movies, the poor "dress up," and are expected to, and thus cover up their real condition. Lack of money to do this during the depression has prevented many of them from enjoying these recreations.

The separation between the two cities is such that in few of them has it occurred to the well-to-do to start a systematic inquiry into the living conditions among the unemployed during the depression. After two years of unemployment, certain influential people in Chicago arranged a public hearing in five different areas of the city. So many wanted to testify that two simultaneous hearings were carried on from 3:00 to 10:00 P.M. Those who testified included the unemployed, milkmen, teachers, landlords, public nurses, insurance men and others. It was made clear that anybody might testify. Those behind the enterprise undertook to prove nothing but simply to make conditions known and get information into the newspapers. One of the members of the committee notes some of the findings, in which the committee were in agreement, as follows:

"(1) The real burden of this crisis is being borne not by any relief agency, but by the poor sharing with the poor. Small merchants, landlords, milkmen, school teachers, who have little or nothing themselves, are straining their own resources to the breaking point to help their neighbors, relatives and friends.

"(2) The present system of relief reduces every applicant to pauperism before he is given consideration. This of course is not due to a policy of administration but to a limitation of funds. No one finds it more unpleasant than the relief workers themselves. Nevertheless it does mean that the applicant must have been absolutely broken in purse and spirit before he can expect relief. He sees his savings dwindle, borrows on his insurance, borrows from friends and relatives, exhausts his credit, loses his home and finally in desperation comes to a point where all his American training has taught him it is a disgrace to come,—to ask for charity."

The Chicago experiment is interesting in showing the extent to which unemployed families are dependent on one another for help. The requirement of entire destitution before relief can be given shows the aloofness and indifference of the city of the well-to-do. Of course a public hearing gives only a part of the picture, for many would fear to speak lest they should lose the relief they might be receiving and others would shrink from it because of sensitivity.

The separation of the well-to-do and the poor dates back thousands of years before Plato to the time when the institution of private property had profoundly changed the attitudes of people. It had divided them not only into those who have considerable or much and those who have nothing, but into classes living an entirely different manner of life, in different sections of the city, mentally untouchable, though they might live in the same urban area. Briffault, after noting that in primitive society everything is shared, writes: "Primitive equalitarianism precludes civilization. The rough distinction of phases of culture into savagery and civilization is not so arbitrary and superficial as might be supposed. It represents two forms of social organization which are contrasted not only in their outward appearance, but are even more sharply distinguished by the principles upon which they are founded. . . . Civilization literally means living in cities. The permanency, the resources, the wealth, the organization, the culture of cities are the outward signs of civilization. But those resources are the effect of the power of a ruling class . . . which is non-existent in lower phases of social development. It consists not only in power to control natural resources, but in power to control men and to dispose of their labor.

"Civilization, it is considered, is marked by wealth, power, prosperity. But it is just as true that civilization is marked by poverty, slavery, and misery. . . . The development of civilization is not, accordingly, a gradual transition out of lower forms of culture, but a revolution from a state of social equality to one of social inequality."[9]

Plato said that the two cities are "at war with one another." In this country except in certain limited areas we have not seen much extreme antagonism. The acquiescence of the unemployed, their pauperization under the conditions, is what impresses us. To be sure there are mutterings and bursts of sullen resentment and an occasional riot, but the prevailing attitude up to the present time has been submissive.

One of the wisest of those who read this manuscript, a man in the thick of emergency relief work, retorted, on reading the above paragraph: "I disagree with you. There is a war. It is a war of classes. The buffer is the dole and even the pitiful dole we are giving is keeping the war in abeyance. But there are mutterings and more than mutterings. Sentiment is being formed among these masses and I believe the result will be drastic and vicious legislation put through by politicians who have got the ear of the masses. It will not be to their advantage." It may prove to be so. If the ears of the city of the well-to-do remain closed to the city of the poor, they will find other leadership.

We are speaking of conditions at the moment. Many of the unemployed, who in prosperous times were becoming home owners, have lost their homes and drifted back into the poor section of the city, so loaded with debts that they never again can hope to emerge, and yet they acquiesce in the situation as a mere misfortune. This acquiescence is the fact that impresses the sociologist. It rests on that complex of social attitudes that expresses itself in the conventional acceptance of the social order. One cannot but be amazed at this conservatism, in view of the emphasis of some social psychologists on the importance of organic drives. Drives are not nearly as important as we have thought. What we see is authority and subservience. Conservatism in the United States is accentuated

---

[9] Briffault, *Rational Evolution,* pp. 31-32; Williams, *Principles of Social Psychology,* pp. 10-11; Williams, The Foundations of Social Science, Ch. III.

because of the unusually large number in the middle class, which has shared the conservatism of the upper class.[10] Very many of those in need of relief because of the depression have lately been in this middle class and still have its attitudes. This psychological condition is expressed in the common explanation of the submissiveness of the unemployed: "Their acquiescence only shows their confidence in the fundamental soundness of our economic order." But that is merely the verbiage of rationalization of the attitude of acquiescence. The attitude is prior to the rationalization and in most cases exists without any rationalization at all. The middle class in the United States has traditionally been the prominent class, and its sentiments have been very influential among the poor. Hence their conservatism.

The submissiveness of the unemployed is not only our own observation but appears constantly in records of cities outside New York. We find such statements as these from Philadelphia:

Mr. Piala is submissive in his attitude toward the unemployment situation. He says it is wrong but does not know what he can do about it. He takes the initiative in seeking work and is very courageous, not asking for help.

Mr. Pasquale has resigned himself to his fate. He does not know what he can do about it, particularly when so many other men are facing the same situation. He has not lost his self-reliance, however.

Mr. Zepone's attitude toward their predicament is more or less optimistic. When asked if conditions are better, he invariably answers, "Not yet, soon maybe." He has made every effort to get work, leaving the house early every morning to find a job. He looks tired and says that walking the streets all day in fruitless effort is wearing. The two working boys are restless and not as hopeful as their father, particularly the electrician, who had counted upon going ahead in his trade. They, too, have not ceased in their efforts to find work. Mrs. Zepone has tried to keep up the spirits of the family and only admits to the settlement workers how discouraged she gets at times.

This is from New Orleans:

Mr. Monterey has faced the family's predicament with a great deal of courage. He has made valiant efforts to meet some of his

---

[10] Murchison, *Social Psychology*, Chs. 23-24,

debts and tries diligently to secure work. He seems to be reaching the breaking point, however, and has begun to feel that his situation is almost hopeless and eventually he will be forced to break up his home and place the children in an asylum. Such thoughts greatly upset him and he states that he is almost afraid to think of the future.[11]

Students of crime in recent years have warned us that the social fabric is a thin crust over a volcano of impulses. But students of this new poverty of three years' duration are impressed with the thickness of the crust. The wonder is, not that law enforcement is so difficult but that it is so easy.

In speaking of acquiescence let us not forget those pious souls in the city of the well-to-do, with incomes not appreciably diminished, who avow, "I think the depression is a good thing for us. We were going too fast." Nothing shows more conclusively how completely the city of the unemployed is excluded from "us" than such remarks, made in all sincerity, for, though thousands are suffering hardships in the other end of town, these their fellow citizens know nothing about it.

Acquiescence is, of course, merely what appears on the surface. Go beneath and one finds what is described in the succeeding chapters. The reactions of the unemployed to their predicament vary with the temperament of the person, with the degree of destitution, with the provocation at the moment and with the previous condition of the family. As to temperament often the breadwinner seems to lack any spirited interest in his family:

In a certain New York city, before the Emergency Relief Administration was set up, the coroner reported that a child had died of starvation. An investigator of the welfare office went to the home and found one child dead, another in bed with the mother, both of them too weak to get up, and the father sitting with two other children in a cold room. They had exhausted their credit at the grocery store and since then had been living on what they could get from garbage cans. For heating they relied on the wood they could gather from the rears of stores and on coal picked up on the railroad track. Some months before, the father had applied at the welfare office for aid and had been put off. Humiliated, he did not apply again. He had been an industrious workman but was not

---

[11] Elderton, *Case Studies in Unemployment*, pp. 300, 334, 148, 51.

temperamentally one who would fight for his family.[11a]

More aggressive was James Warner. He did not wait for his children to starve to death. He broke into a grocery store and took codfish, coffee, Campbell's soup and macaroni. That was burglary. He was arrested, tried and convicted. The evidence was plain that he committed the crime to feed his wife and boys. He was put on probation as a first offender and heretofore an exemplary citizen.

Exemplary citizens let their children starve rather than steal. The majesty of the law so requires. Another law, the Public Welfare Law of New York, requires that families in need shall be given adequate relief.[12] However, the majesty of the law has not required that that law be enforced.

Sometimes the attitude of acquiescence is broken by some extreme provocation:

Joe Sullivan, out of work over a year, was getting the bare subsistence given the unemployed in his city but it was too little to satisfy his children's hunger. He met the chief of police and told him he must have a job or something would happen. The chief jeered at him. This got under Joe's skin. The jeer rang in his ears. He broke into a store, took some clothing, was arrested and indicted for burglary and grand larceny. As we talked with Joe it seemed to us that the provocation, acting on his weakened body and neurotic mind, was what caused the crime. Later he was put on probation inasmuch as up to that time he had been a law-abiding man.

What did arresting Joe and putting him in jail do for his children? Some men in desperation have thought that, if they were caught in a crime, it would call attention to the needs of the family and help them get relief.

The previous condition of the family has a good deal to do with its reaction to unemployment and poverty. Many families during prosperity passed from the city of the poor to the city of the well-to-do and then depression plunged them back where they were before. The quick change from affluence to poverty was more of a stress than many could stand. Some of these people quickly responded to treatment for nervous disorders,

---

[11a] All cases for which an authority is not cited are given out of my own experience.

[12] See Chapter X.

others drifted into a neurotic condition. Should we not improve somehow an economic system which permits these sudden and extreme changes in the life opportunities of the people?

Acquiescence is, then, largely a name for an impression the observer gets, not a description of the psychological condition of the unemployed. Though they may appear to acquiesce, that does not describe their state of mind. Essential in this is the desire to work, the habit of being given work by an employer and of submitting to his directions, the idea of a right to work, a contempt for laziness, a sense of injustice at not being able to get work when a man knows that he is not lazy, an aversion to asking for charity, which traditionally has been the recourse of the worthless, and finally, an uncertainty about the present unemployment situation. For, though a man desires work, he cannot get it. He believes he has a right to work but what shall he do about the denial of that right? He sees men who are apparently willing to ask for charity faring better than one who is too proud to ask. He realizes that he is no better off than the utterly worthless workman. This uncertainty has for the time being paralyzed action among the unemployed.

RECENT INSTITUTIONAL CHANGES AND ACQUIESCENCE

Two conditions have served to reinforce acquiescence. One of these is a change in economic organization which began forty years ago and has gone on apace since the World War, the other is an increase in contributions for philanthropy. As to the economic change, the growth of great corporations, bringing thousands of men under one autocratic management, has accustomed them to live without liberty and has profoundly modified their political attitudes. "Much more striking than the inequality in the distribution of income which makes one man's scale of life ample and another's meager, is the inequality in the distribution of power which makes most of the population subordinate in a system of industry directed by a minority of industrial oligarchs. The authority which industry's owners exercise comes to them by virtue of their legal power to do as they like with their own. This legal power in

turn, like all law, is supposed to originate in the decisions of
elected representatives of the people as a whole and the judges
appointed by those representatives. Thus the concentration
of power in a few hands seems, according to political theory,
to result from the sanction of the entire population and to depend upon continuance of that sanction. Yet if all properties
were to be confiscated outright by the government, only 6 per
cent of the population would have been expropriated. If free
services were to be offered to the public by means of taxes
levied upon all properties of more than $5,000, less than 9
per cent of the population would be taxed. It is a source of
wonder that property owners succeed in setting any limit to
public expense and taxation."[18]

The concentration of economic power and autocratic control has produced an industrial subservience which in turn
has caused a political submissiveness. The attitude of the mass
of voters is like that of workmen in a great factory—the
workman's little part in running the machinery seems as
trifling to him as the voter's part in running the vast machinery
of government seems to him. And as technicians take little interest in teaching workmen the significance of their performance but seek only to control and use them, so politicians seek
only to control and use this mass of voters. The voters know
it, they know that they are controlled. They know that they
have not the initiative even to vote a ticket of protest. Hence
the exasperation, the mutterings, the threat of "direct action,"
on the part of the more aggressive. But most workmen do not
seem to feel this autocratic control very keenly, as long as they
can get work. Some of them may become excited over the
thought of being "wage slaves," but generally they know that
under any form of industrial relationship they are compelled
to give their labor on the terms made by those in control. To
them the great question is: what determines which individuals
shall control and which shall be controlled?[14] Unless a political

---

[18] Atkins and associates, *Economic Behavior,* II, pp. 74-75. Read the entire
chapter on "Income and Wealth" in this remarkable textbook on economics.

[14] Murchison, *Social Psychology,* p. 21.

campaign involves this essential issue so clearly that masses
of men can see it, they will not be greatly interested in the
economic issues of politics.

Then too the masses cling to the social order to which they
have been accustomed. Men can be aroused to fever heat against
a foreign power encroaching on their social order, as in India
and China, but they cannot be so violently aroused against
their own order.[15] One hears some of the unemployed speak
warmly of communism, but the Russian system is a mere
symbol, in the minds of those who mention it, of a reversal of
the traditional social control and a planned order in which a
man is sure of a living at least. Most of the unemployed distrust a man who expresses sympathy with communism. On
the other hand they realize the separation between themselves
and the city of the well-to-do and the rich. Governments re-
flect the breach between the classes in the division between
progressive members of a legislative body and the conservatives
who represent especially those detached from the poignant
experiences of the masses.[16] One hears bitter criticisms of con-
servative governments for their failure to make relief effective.
However a considerable number of the unemployed, recently
well-to-do, would have shown the same opposition to a rise of
taxes for adequate relief.

Acquiescence has been encouraged by the increase in contributions for philanthropy. The distribution of these funds
has required an increasing number of social workers. During
the depression, when class war, if it is anything more than a
bogey, might be expected to break out, one sees the army of
social workers handling the vastly greater army of unemployed
with ease. This has commended social work to the city of the
well-to-do. Social workers recognize the gulf between the two
cities but the attitude of many of them is that it is inevitable,
that the interest of the well-to-do in the poor would not be other

---

[15] Read Whiting Williams' article, "You Can't Let Them Starve," in the
Survey, Feb. 1932, and note that he says: "'Surprisingly patient' is the
testimony given by those in closest contact with the most distressed sections
of the public." (p. 461.)

[16] Read the Testimony of Sidney Hillman before the United States Senate
Committee on Unemployment Relief, Dec., 1931, pp. 343-46.

than sentimental, and that "we must sell them our social work program." It is implied, then, that the gulf between the two cities does exist and is to be bridged by scientific social work. The questions are raised: What will be the effect of selling social work to the city of the well-to-do? Will it remove the gulf between the cities or only make it more enduring because now it is safely bridged?

THE INTERDEPENDENCE OF THE TWO CITIES

Increasing numbers of well-to-do are coming to see that the two cities are interdependent and this realization is expressed in recent reports on emergency relief work. Thus, a report of the New Jersey Emergency Relief Administration states, on the first page, that "the condition and welfare of every class of people in this state reacts upon the condition and welfare of every other class."[17] The realization of interdependence has followed, but very slowly, the fact of increasing interdependence.

Certain conditions in the modern city forbid us to overemphasize the resemblance between the division in the slaveholding state and that in the industrialized community. Among these are the following: The intelligent employer in the city of the well-to-do knows that he is dependent on the energy and goodwill of workmen in the other city. The store-keeper knows that his prosperity depends on their patronage. The professional men lose money when their clients from the other part of town are unemployed. All vendors of goods or services know that their income depends on the economic condition of the masses.[18] Infectious diseases among the children of these masses are caught by children of the well-to-do in the public school. The manufacturer goes to his office with a cold caught from his child who caught it from the child of one of his factory hands. Malnutrition starts epidemics in the city of the poor which spread to children of the well-to-do. The modern city differs from the ancient in this: that infectious diseases are

---

[17] State of New Jersey, "Emergency Relief Administration," January, 1932, p. 5.
[18] Hobson, "The World's Economic Crisis," *The Nation*, July 20, 1932.

now known to be infectious and this dependence, along the line of health, of the one city on the other is plain to any thoughtful person. Another line of dependence is that which results from modern amusements. The well-to-do are dependent for the kind of movies they may witness on the taste of the masses who patronize movies, and, for the wholesomeness of the atmosphere in which they enjoy the picture, on the masses' knowledge and practice of hygiene. They are dependent for the safety of the streets along which they drive, on the habits of drivers from the other city. The increase of crime is awakening the city of the well-to-do to a realization of its mistake in leaving the city of the poor, with the underworld that preys on rich and poor alike, too much out of its calculations. Municipal government has broken down because, among other reasons, it never has been built upon the basis of mutual understanding and coöperation that is required by the interdependence between the two cities. These facts of interdependence are, however, increasingly becoming thoughts in the minds of the well-to-do. But the thoughts are too apt to stir merely fear and self-defense. With an increase of intelligence the fear will give way to planning and the carrying out of projects for the elimination of evils that have thrived in an atmosphere of aloofness, ignorance and indifference.

THE ATTITUDE OF ALOOFNESS

The aloofness of the well-to-do involves certain well-defined patterns of behavior. It rests on a sense of financial security and a feeling of social superiority, as compared with the insecurity and inferiority of the other city. The well-to-do cannot understand the sense of insecurity of people living a precarious existence. They think that they are entirely contented, that they prefer that kind of a life. Thus do they project into the masses their own security and contentment. The separation rests also on their larger opportunities for social contacts and for mental activity. Mental activity depends to be sure on the nature of the individual as well as on his opportunities. But opportunities are vital. These are enjoyed especially by the well-to-do. Their thinking, however, is cramped by their attitude toward the problems of the social order. Many learned people share this attitude and it detaches their learning from vital problems. Even the most gifted personalities have been thus detached and evasive because of their subservience to privilege, as we see in the case of Goethe, and still are, as we see in outstanding personalities in our colleges and universities.[19] Culture as an experience of enlargement of personality has been circumscribed by an unthinking acceptance of the status quo, and has been used as a means of escape from disagreeable realities. Higher education often is essentially an escape from reality, not a penetration of reality. The control by privilege of higher, and of public education as well,[20] has accentuated this evasive aspect of culture. So a man may be cultured, actively interested in philanthropy, without a trace of snobbishness, on easy terms with the carpenter and milkman, while still entirely aloof and convinced that there never will be anything but a gulf between the two cities.

Among those of the well-to-do to whom culture means nothing and the material enjoyments everything, their sense of distinctness is accentuated by thinking that the masses, a large proportion of whom also are centered on their limited material enjoyments, are envious of those more advantageously situated. This makes them suspicious of the masses. As a matter of fact the poor are not generally envious. They are quite largely absorbed in their life with one another. They want jobs but not what belongs to anybody else, though, if jobs are not to be had, some of them may think of getting what they need by deceit or force. But generally they want only what belongs to them. And a time of widespread unemployment mellows them in their relations with one another and they share food and shelter in a wonderful generous way. A young man said to his boss, "I don't believe I ought to have all this work. Bill needs work. Can't he have three days a week"? He was honestly willing to give up work he needed in order to help Bill. This is typical of what we find everywhere among the

[19] Hobson, *Free Thought in the Social Sciences*, pp. 53-54.
[20] Counts, *The American Road to Culture*, pp. 23, 38, 189-92; Counts, *The Social Composition of Boards of Education;* Counts, "Education— For what?" *New Republic*, May 18, 1932, pp. 12-13.

unemployed. Men and women of the city of the well-to-do in their addresses and speeches would not express their false notions about the city of the poor if they stopped to think that thousands who read the papers will laugh at their absurd statements. The one city makes itself amusing by its misunderstanding of the other. On the other hand, when an understanding person tells the truth, there is interest, and people are set to listen and learn. How necessary this is in view of increasing interpendence between the two cities and at a time when conditions provoke antagonism!

THE STRUGGLE FOR SOCIAL CONTROL

Both the well-to-do and the poor sometimes belong to the same group, as an ecclesiastical group or a political party. When they do, the well-to-do control the group. There is a struggle for social control between groups composed of, or controlled by, the well-to-do. Propertied interests, social clubs, political cliques, ecclesiastical groups, rival one another for prestige and to win control for their ideas. Relief problems are regarded from the point of view of the groups with which men identify themselves in the rivalry for control. This is true in city, state and nation. The financier senses the financial significance of proposals for adequate relief; the politician looks at these with a view to the fortunes of his party; child welfare experts from the point of view of the needs of children. Is not the latter as important to get, for the future of America, as that of the financier or the politician?

MENTAL HYGIENE AND THE TWO CITIES

The interdependence of the two cities, in the face of the traditional aloofness, intensifies the strain between them. This takes us into the field of mental hygiene. Aside from the pronounced mental disorders that may result from isolation due to wealth or poverty,[21] the traditional antagonism itself is unwholesome, for an essential hygiene principle is that people require a reasonable sense of security in order to function

---

[21] Menninger, *The Human Mind*, pp. 62-63.

normally. As contrasted with this we find suffering and discontent in the city of the poor and solicitude about this among the well-to-do. Mental hygiene for the whole body politic, as contrasted with our American mental hygience for abnormals, cannot be achieved while the division noted by Plato, between those who are assured of the material requisites for a good life and those who have not such assurance, continues.[22] As Dr. Frankwood Williams says, mental hygienists in American have so centered on the victims of maladjustment that they have failed to think of mental hygiene as a program for all the people, rich and poor, for "keeping well people well, and so organizing life and the emotional development of the individual, that the anxieties and fears that lead to defensive reactions on his part and which end in inefficiency, unhappiness and often illness and anti-social conduct, may be minimized so that he may be in position to contribute of his best."[23]

With all our "rugged individualism" we never have learned what it means to be a wholesome, socialized individual. In the early days of America there was a profound faith in the potential man. The exemplary individual was one who would migrate with his family into the wilderness and hew a farm out of the primeval forest.[24] Then the conditions of life became easier and individualism ceased to be a type of action and began to run to emotion. At first the test of a man was that he could produce an astonishing physical result. Then making "big money" and splendid displays of wealth came to denote conspicuous success. Neither test shows insight into the potentialities of the individual. This failure to understand the potential man and to lay the foundations in childhood for a socialized adulthood is the main cause of the failure of democracy. Dr. Williams puts it in this way: "Our difficulties are said to be economic. This is a secondary matter. Our difficulties are psychological. . . . Democracy, with its 'freedom,' places a

---

[22] Leiserson, "Who Bears the Business Risks?" *Survey*, March 1, 1931, p. 596; Slichter, "Unemployment Relief by Business," *New Republic*, Dec. 30, 1931, p. 181.

[23] Read the article by Dr. Frankwood Williams, formerly Director of the National Committee for Mental Hygiene, in the *Survey*, Jan. 1, 1932.

[24] Williams, *Our Rural Heritage*, p. 50.

premium on the most primitive, infantile, aggressive impulses of the individual and heavy penalties upon socialized impulses. . . . A system is created in which . . . there is adequate outlet for only one part of men's impulses—only the impulses which serve personal ends—'ambition,' 'success,' and the like in terms of individual aggrandizement. Extreme as the statement may seem, the world is under the mastery of primitives; intelligence, high-sounding titles, dignity, do not make the masters less primitive."[25] This type "is adult in physical development, but . . . emotionally lives the life of a child. It may not be possible for us to be so specific as to say that a given individual is chronologically twenty-five years of age, has a physical and intellectual development in accordance with his age, but has the emotional development of a child of seven. What we shall recognize, however, is this: that this business man, this school teacher, this judge of an important court, this publisher, this reformer, is an adult in years, has an adult physical development and a keen intellect, but emotionally lives the life of an adolescent, or of a child, or even of an infant. As the possibility of this situation comes to be generally recognized and these individuals to be identified, I am inclined to think that we . . . shall come to say to them something like this: 'You have reached physical adulthood and you have an unusually keen intellect. . . . Your decisions in important matters, however, are made, not in accordance with the facts, but in the light of the unsolved emotional problems of your own personal childhood. . . . The fact that your high order of intellect has brought you to such prominence and position of power in the community does not alter the situation. . . . The world needs you, but the world can use you only after you have grown up.'

"The world is full of such and they are to be found not only in humble but in high places. They may not be so easily identified as the intellectually defective, but we shall come to identify them and to deal with them. We shall come to observe more closely our leaders, whether these leaders be in politics or socal science, law or medicine, religion, ethics, morals or reform. In the meantime, in our homes, schools, and

---

* Williams, "Psychology in Dictatorship," *Survey*, May 1, 1932, p. 135.

colleges, where our future leaders are being developed, we shall become as interested and as careful in the emotional progress of children and students, as in their physical and intellectual development."[26]

Because we are creatures of habit we continue to have the emotional attitudes we had when we were children. We do not seek to understand our own capabilities. We look for the approval of others instead of to realities. If we form convictions on the basis of reality we fear to stand alone, and we cannot accept defeat with the tranquillity of the undefeated. What is the test of socially-minded maturity? This question must be answered in the light of the struggle for social control. Life is essentially struggle. Ideas that are true appeal to the many only as those who hold them vie with the opposition for social control. Even Gandhi has constantly appealed to the people to make his gospel of non-resistance prevail against those who preach violence. There is no escape from struggle, even for the non-resistant. Therefore socially-minded maturity requires that we discern the realities of our situation, that we see what is unalterable in the situation and accept it without conflict, and lay hold of the alterable with a virile intelligence, reach well-thought-out convictions, advance them persistently with a mind open to new ideas, and with power to remain inwardly undefeated. It is not necessary to succeed, except in meeting this test of maturity.

Institutions are means through which individuals may be able to test higher in this maturity as the years go by. So institutions must be kept flexible and subordinate to individual needs. Are our institutions serving this end? Or are they augmenting the unsocialized, infantile impulses? "Aggression is not in itself a-social; it is inherent in a human being; it is the power by which he grows. The significance to others of a bundle of aggression emerging from a uterus will depend upon the handling of this bundle. The bundle goes first into the hands of women."[27] So we see the central importance of

---

[26] Lecture by Dr. Williams at Yale University, published in *Social Aspects of Mental Hygiene*, pp. 45-46.

childhood and of motherhood. The psychological significance of institutions depends on the degree in which they permit the mothers to become mature and socialized.

What is the significance of this conception of the socialized individual, for the division between the two cities? What we have everywhere are men and women who fail to meet the test. This is true at all times but especially in the testing time of depression. In the city of the well-to-do many of the privileged cling to their advantages like children. They will not face the facts of interdependence and the plight of the unemployed. They resist a necessary increase in taxes. They must have their usual luxuries. The thousand and one ways of enjoying a petty social superiority are clung to as obstinately as food habits. In the city of the poor, likewise, the unemployed want what they have been accustomed to. They resent having to accept a standard diet, even in cities where the diet is fairly adequate to preserve health. Yet here and there we see conspicuous examples of maturity. Who will say that the test of maturity is often better met than by the woman who, as she was leaving the welfare office, said in a quiet voice: "I wonder whether any of you social workers, with your everlasting questions, could do better than I do, feeding and clothing and trying to keep a family of five decently on nine dollars a week"! The social worker thus addressed, who had no one dependent on her but who was tied up socially with the city of the well-to-do, had just excitedly asserted, in conversation with an associate about a threatened cut in salary, that she could not live on less than $2,000 a year. Yet she had been trying to explain the realities of her situation to a client who must keep a family of five on nine dollars a week.

---

[27] Williams, "Psychology in Dictatorship," *Survey*, May 1, 1932, p. 135.

CHAPTER II

THE NEW POOR

THE EFFECTS OF a depression on children and youth are, it is said, merely the effects of poverty, seen also in prosperity, but more widely in depression because unemployment spreads poverty everywhere. This is true and yet the poverty of a depression differs from that of prosperity. It is the poverty of millions of heretofore independent families. To be sure, in the years of prosperity increasing unemployment had resulted in many capable men and women being without a livelihood. This number has vastly increased in depression. Thus we have "the new poor." Who are these new poor? In prosperity they include men thrown out of factory jobs by the invention of machinery; clerks displaced by calculating machines; musicians superfluous because of sound pictures; cigar-makers idle because of the cigarette habit; waiters out because of cafeterias; many other workmen at large because of changes in fashion; middle-aged men let go because many corporations do not hire men over thirty-five or forty years of age; many men not wanted because their places have been taken by women. When depression came, the ranks of the new poor were swelled by others: more factory workmen, craftsmen, clerks, salesmen, contractors, salaried men and people who had counted on their children to support them but whose children could not find work. Many seasonal workmen had always earned enough in the season to carry them through the slack period. Now the season was briefer or non-existent.

The depression, with its millions of new poor, did not come suddenly though it broke suddenly. Dr. Leo Wolman has estimated that in the most prosperous years of the past decade, 1,500,000 men were out of work in this country, this

figure rising to 2,315,000 in 1927. Mr. Linton B. Swift,
executive secretary of the Family Welfare Association of
America, has said that the relief given in a large cross-section
of American communities more than trebled from 1916 to 1925
and that the increase continued from 1925 to the depression.
During these years of increasing unemployment, social workers
were still working with the new poor caused by the depression
of 1921. There was, then, the wreckage of the receding wave
of 1921 and of the oncoming wave of unemployment which
broke in the present depression. Mr. Swift adds that this increasing unemployment throughout the period of supposedly
great prosperity "was an indication to most social workers that
somewhere, somehow there was an unhealthy condition in our
whole economic and industrial structure." Before the depression his Association got out a special report on industrial conditions entitled, "The Time to Plan is Now." Yet all this was
kept out of the press and no planning was done by our governments or industrialists, though this Association represents some
228 family agencies in practically every state in the Union,
serving approximately four million men, women and children,
and is affiliated with agencies serving one to three million
more.[1]

The vast increase in the number of industrious workers out
of work through no fault of their own has given the problem
of poverty a new aspect. Among those in contact with these
poor it has caused a new attitude to the poor and their children.
When school principals and visiting teachers speak of the misbehavior that is on the increase among children because of
poverty they say: "But he isn't a bad boy"; "She isn't a bad
girl"; though the boy or girl had done something that very
bad boys or girls do. They realize that children are so plainly
victims of conditions caused by unemployment that they are
not to be blamed. So we have "the new poor" among adults
and "the new misbehavior" among children and youth.

It is interesting to observe this change of sentiment in the
community toward the misbehavior of children. The old moral

---

[1] Testimony of Mr. Swift before United States Senate Committee on
Unemployment Relief, pp. 87-93.

indignation is weakening throughout large sections of the population, Catholic, Protestant and Jewish. Families are at sea as to what to do, schools and churches have scarcely begun to use the new methods of mental hygiene,[2] and child welfare societies reach only a fraction of these children and youth.

Unemployment inevitably weakens or destroys a wholesome pride in independence. The very idea of being dependent on a welfare office was unfamiliar to the new poor. At first they did not know what to do. At the office their attitudes varied from embarrassment or assumed indifference to resentment at the questions asked, and from gratitude for relief to dissatisfaction with what was received. Many parents said sincerely: "If it was not for the children we would not ask for help." Others pleaded a right to relief because for years previous to their unemployment they had been contributors to the community chest. The fortunate ones soon again secured other employment. Those who failed to do so began to develop an attitude of depending on relief. As a matter of fact, they were dependent. Work was not to be had.

In cities where no men and women without children were relieved at the public welfare office, those in dire need became desperate and sometimes would borrow children. Where only married people were relieved, a man in desperation got a wife, a woman got a husband. In one city an industrious fellow long out of work and with no resources at all was told that the office did not help any single man. He married the first woman he met, one likewise turned away. How will these marriages, born of desperation, affect the family of the future?

Children, as well as adults, have been pauperized. They are inevitably involved because the welfare office regularly gives the family a grocery order and children are sent to the store to bring home the food. This continues week after week, month after month, year after year of the depression. Hence some children become known to other children as living on charity. Many of these feel humiliated at first but later become indifferent. They meet other children in the store on the same

---

[2] See Chapters XIII–XIV.

errand. What other families are getting is a main topic of conversation in the homes and among children at play. Thus do welfare practices affect even as remote an aspect of the behavior of the people as the play of children. Will not these children too readily expect the city to support them when, in a few years, they are married and rearing a family?

The pauperization of youth is a matter of common comment among the unemployed themselves. "Why, it's making bums of these young fellows!" exclaimed an irate master carpenter, a father of sons out of work.

Children differ in their resistance to this pauperizing effect of relief. Even when parents acquiesce, for the sake of their children, the latter sometimes assert their pride. We find instances of this in New York cities and in other states. Here is a paragraph from a record of a depression-afflicted family of Pittsburgh:

> The younger children do not seem to realize what their father's not working has meant to the family. They know they cannot have a great many things that other children have but it has made them only wistful. Mary, however, seems to have felt the deprivation and it has made her assume a defensive attitude. She has lost the wistful air she had a couple of years ago. When Lucy was given overshoes and stockings by the teacher she was very much pleased, but Mary did not like it at all that people should be giving them clothing. She came home from school one day and said that the school children were saying that they were begging. Her mother told her it was better to have things given them than to steal. Another thing that has hurt Mary is that Adeline, who used to be her best friend, never comes near her now except to quarrel or make an unpleasant remark.[8]

This pauperization of the unemployed is not inevitable. It is due to our welfare practices. Two measures would diminish the evil somewhat: first, putting relief entirely in charge of those who have training and experience in relief work and, second, providing work relief as far as possible. As to the first measure, the effects of a hurried, thoughtless giving of

---

[8] Elderton, *Case Studies in Unemployment*, p. 99.

relief are described by Dr. Queen, Associate Secretary of the Detroit Community Union:

"Do we realize that the very processes of relief-giving may contribute to demoralization?

"When you search the house, demand documentary evidence, turn interviewing into inquisition, and refuse to give aid until every resource is exhausted, you invite deceit and trickery. When in addition you herd folks together in crowded offices you humiliate them beyond measure. When your newspapers carry headlines about 'welfare frauds' and 'dole cheaters' . . . they do not contribute noticeably to your clients' pride and self-respect. When you rush your people through hurried interviews in crowded rooms you inhibit free and frank discussion. . . . When you make 'loans' they cannot possibly repay, you break their sense of responsibility. . . .

"Now in times like these it may be necessary to make exceptionally careful 'investigations,' to hurry people along, to withhold relief from those who can possibly do without it. . . . If these things are inevitable, no condemnation is meant; but let us not deceive ourselves: such procedure plays havoc with human personality."[4] He goes on to say that, while the need of expert staffs is greater than ever, in many places there is a reaction against them because they are thought to be expensive.

Work relief should be given where possible, though it may be more expensive than direct relief, and it should provide for a fairly adequate family budget, with instruction by the welfare office or a nutrition committee in a wise use of funds. Work relief is still relief. Men and women may come to depend on the work furnished and may show a lack of interest in searching for better work. But the weakening of independence is not so pronounced as that which results from outright charity. Furthermore work gets the father into action and out of the home during the day, gives the mother a chance to carry forward her family duties unworried and heartens both of them. Work relief also seems to make the money received go further,

[4] Queen, "What is Unemployment Doing to Family Social Work?" *The Family*, Feb., 1932, p. 300.

for the assurance of an income stimulates the planning of expenditures.

The duration of a depression is a vital factor in the loss of independence. At first pride may delay seeking relief, even after the children are suffering.[5] However, after months or years of unemployment pride may seem lost, especially when a large number of families in the neighborhood are getting relief. The effect of family and neighborhood attitudes on the children should be emphasized. In a pauperized neighborhood children get what social workers call the "gimmes" and is it difficult to see that training ahead will materially change this. We must not overemphasize this point. Children in all classes want what attracts them and sometimes social workers call this natural childish impulse the "gimmes." But there is also the more pronounced parasitic attitude. Still these children are no more dependent than spoiled children of the rich, but they are more numerous. This dependence continues, as do the other effects mentioned in the succeeding chapters, long after the depression is over, and it is this deterioration, accelerated as one depression follows another, that disturbs the far-sighted social worker.[6]

Thrift also is weakened by depression. People who have saved and then have seen it all go think: "What is the use of saving!" They find themselves no better off than the family that saved nothing. They merely were able to "keep off the town" longer but finally came "on the town" just like the worthless family. Therefore many families, when they get work again, spend wastefully. Then, too, the personality gets a peculiar twist from the anxiety of a depression. When people get into an emotional, anxious condition, if they earn money they "blow it in," as a momentary compensation for their anxiety. The reckless spending of money for a drink, or for a radio or an auto, at a time when one could wish for more sensible behavior, doubtless often has its explanation in this tendency of the personality to react recklessly after a period of anxiety and stress.

---

[5] Calkins, *Some Folks Won't Work*, p. 140.
[6] Testimony of Mr. Swift before United States Senate Committee on Unemployment Relief, pp. 92-93.

Here is one of many cases we have seen of the effect of the depression on thrift and enterprise:

Axel Cramer was an expert tool-maker who earned good wages working for an automobile company. He and his wife were industrious and frugal and enjoyed planning for little Axel and Isabel and Edith. He built a home and put into it much careful work. All his spare time was given to the building and beautifying of this home. Then came the depression and he could not get work. He used up his savings and eventually had to sell the house that meant so much to them all. He was forced to sell at a great sacrifice because of the drop in real estate values. Finally he had spent everything and came to the welfare office broken in spirit. He said to the woman in charge: "What was the use of my working and saving? My home is gone. I have nothing. I am no better off than the pauper who never saved a cent. I am too old ever again to get a decent job." He was only forty-two but many corporations do not hire men over forty. How is he to support and educate his children? With sullen resentment, alternating with hopeless despair, he feels that industry and thrift are not the virtues he was brought up to think them. What about the effect of this on the children he is bringing up?

Some men have been affected in a different way, especially young men. They are saying: "We are going after the money, no matter how we get it. This talk about loyalty to an employer is all sentimental nonsense. He will fire you without a thought." The lot of the workman means to them extreme uncertainty and they are out for "big money" that will lift them above this. Just how they plan to win it is not stated.

The new poor cannot be understood without recollecting that the previous period of prosperity raised many to a higher standard of living than ever before. As compared with that the sudden drop to destitution and the dole is an appalling change. In isolated parts of Canada and in the Southern mountains I have known families whose poverty was as extreme as that of many unemployed families receiving relief and yet they were in good spirits and the home was fairly happy. They had had no sudden reverses. Members of the family of an unemployed man in the modern city compare their present with their past. They may also compare their condition with that of families in better circumstances. The sense of loss and of social inferiority rankles and sets up a mental conflict. Another reason for greater suffering than that of isolated peoples is their economic dependence. The isolated farmer and the mountaineer feel themselves masters of their fate, while the workman in a great corporation feels entirely dependent on a job.

This sense of insecurity saps the joyousness of life even in prosperity, and in depression not only is the job, the economic prop, knocked from under, but a central feature of our traditional relief policy is to make the unemployed uncertain about relief. We seem to think that a sense of insecurity is the essential incentive to well ordered living. This is the mistaken assumption of an economic order that is based on the primitive struggle for existence, resulting in the emergence of a privileged few to whom the masses are to be kept submissive. This order is to be contrasted with the ideal of those who would have a program of mental hygiene for all the people and base this on an economic order planned to make possible for all a reasonably secure livelihood. Such an order is the first step in our plans for the wholesome childhood to which every American has a right.

CHAPTER III

HOMES DESTROYED

WE SAY THAT the family is the foundation of our social order. What kind of a family are we speaking of? Let us look at what unemployment is doing to these foundations of the social order. The earnings in prosperity of many heads of families now unemployed had enabled them to begin payments on homes and to lay aside money for the education of their children and for emergencies and old age. These savings have been used up. Houses have been mortgaged to the limit and many families have lost their homes. Life insurance policies have lapsed. Thousands of children will have to go without their education and try to get work instead. The parents will have to give up their dream of independence in old age and fit into whatever kind of home the child can provide, if any. Temporarily mothers have secured employment where possible, families have crowded in with relatives and friends, they have gone into debt to the limit for food, rent, fuel, medical attention and other necessities. For years after the breadwinner secures work again, his wages will have to be divided between the purchase of the necessaries of life and the payment of debts. The so-called pessimism of a period of depression is, therefore, not merely an emotional state of investors who contemplate their paper losses. It has a solid basis in the blasted hopes and the plight of the unemployed masses, and their children are heirs to these blighted expectations.

One enters homes where destitution has gone the limit. Furniture has been sold or taken away by the installment dealer. Utensils and bedding have not been replaced. Sometimes one finds a family living in unheated rooms in the winter, no food or fuel in the house, gas and electricity turned off, little bedding and scanty clothing. We find this extreme destitution not only in New York cities but in other states also. The suffering of children under these conditions is graphically described by a youth of nineteen whose home is in Philadelphia. This description was written at the request of settlement workers in Philadelphia and they vouch for its entire accuracy:

It is only with the severest economy that we are able to exist comfortably without luxury. But when any member is without work we cannot meet expenses. We are compelled by necessity to resort to evil, shady or underhand methods to secure necessities. Our moral principles are discarded in the effort to secure a livelihood. We beg, borrow with no intention of repayment, appropriate illegally, food, clothing and money. We become corrupt during the long interval of unemployment. But this is trivial to what ensues.

We are met by another catastrophe; another member of the family is "laid off." Our rations of food and clothing are continually less. The lack of food causes us to become weak in body. We are merely able to drag ourselves about. Our clothes in rags, we become slovenly, never caring to shave or wash ourselves. Our mental condition becomes degraded and dull. . . . Our only desire is for food and more food. Our bodies become weaker and weaker and our minds drag into the mud. This leads to something worse. We come to look upon life as drudgery and the people in it as our bosses who beat us whenever they can. We become fanatics who believe life owes us a living. We feel that people are treating us meanly by not giving us food and clothing. We think that human beings are not human but beasts and brutes who tantalize us at every opportunity. Our faith in human beings decreases tremendously. No one is our friend but everyone is our enemy. This brings about another loss of faith.

We begin to lose faith in ourselves. Family life becomes a chaotic mess. We do not trust each other. We quarrel and argue about insignificant matters. We detest each other's presence. We worry about bills such as rent, electric, gas, etc. We become so heated in our arguments that we begin to have fist fights, throwing chairs and utensils about during the fights. This finally ends in something tragic.

Every family tries to keep its furniture, kitchen utensils and sleeping quarters intact. If any of these articles go, that is the last straw. The family is destitute. So, when no more money is obtainable, we are forced to sell the contents of our home. Within a short time the home is turned into a house, empty of all furnishings, rugless floors, tableless kitchen, chairless and bedless rooms.

This is sufficient to take all the life out of our bodies. We become a down-hearted, brooding group of famished bodies, too ill to care what becomes of us, too tired and fatigued to keep on living. What a life![1]

This family situation is only part of the picture of the child's intolerable situation. It is merely the picture of the home. Boys and girls remain in such a home as little as possible. They prefer to roam the streets.

One who comes suddenly into a destitute, nerve-racked home has an experience he never will forget—the wife hysterical, the husband not knowing which way to turn, despondent after a long day's tramp in search of work, the children listening with scared eyes. Differences that never before broke out into open antagonism now become acute. For instance here is a family in which the father is a Polish Catholic and the wife a Russian Jewess. This had caused some disagreement before but never intense hostility. Now they throw their differences in each other's faces and actually come to blows and the relatives on each side take it up. When people are in an ugly mood it finds vent along the lines of these deep-seated antagonisms.

Let us not think, however, that such scenes are confined to the city of the poor. Among the well-to-do when the necessity to economize arose, wives had tantrums, would not listen to the husband's explanation of affairs, passionately rejected the idea of cutting out this and that expense, and accused him of incompetence, or, what is harder to bear, sneered at him. The children stood by, innocent victims of the emotional scene, and in some cases no doubt permanently affected by it. We would not accuse the women unduly but we have seen poignant cases of utterly selfish refusal to look at the changed circumstances of the family, sometimes resulting in wild scenes, at other times in habitual nagging and sneering which produced a home atmosphere that slowly undermined the husband's health, and the wife's too for that matter. Sometimes the husband, instead of the wife, is the perverse one and sometimes both are uncontrolled. Here is an utter disregard of child welfare in the very citadel of childhood, the home. Some people

---

[1] Elderton, *Case Studies of Unemployment*, pp. 385-87.

3

may think that children will learn from these spectacles the folly of such behavior, but child psychologists tell us that the contrary is more apt to be true, that children tend to be made emotionally unstable by these family scenes.

Back of these thousands of unhappy homes is the competitive economic system which in prosperity seduces an unsuspecting public into extravagant buying and then requires a sudden and extreme retrenchment. This system puts too great a strain on human nature as we have it, as yet untrained in self-control and the rational choice of the material means of a satisfying life. Here our principle of interdependence comes in. The economic system affects the home and the home affects the system. If the system does not permit homes to exist in which character can be developed, then workmen will lack character and industry will suffer. Industry has drawn some of its best workmen from the farm home because the farm makes for industry, self-control and thrift.[2] Our economic system must be planned with a view to making possible character-building homes, instead of being, as it is, primarily a profit-seeking mechanism. As such its effect on the physical and mental health and character of workmen and on the homes in which their children are reared is not considered by those who manage industry.

There has been a general reduction in the income and standard of living of wage-earning, and of salaried families as well. This has thrust the thousands of families that were living at a subsistence level in prosperous times into abject poverty, while those always in chronic poverty are now sharing in the standard of relief meted out to these erstwhile independent groups. Above this level are the families which were enjoying a comfortable income, many of them maintaining a standard of living beyond their income. A good percentage of these for a considerable time after the depression held tenaciously to standards that were too high, even in prosperous times. They went deeply into debt when they could have economized, and eventually found themselves with no resources at all. Will the

---

[2] Williams, *Our Rural Heritage*, pp. 88-92.

depression, by forcing the standard of living of these families down, teach them not to be extravagant when prosperity comes again? Surrounded by all the inducements to spend of a profit-seeking economic order, will they thrust these temptations aside and save money to tide them over the next depression? The suggestions to spend emanated not only from every form of business advertising and from the suggestions of the spending community but also from high officials and economists who exhorted the public to spend and so keep prosperity with us. The public spent but did not keep prosperity. Of course no economic order that depends for its smooth running on the whimsical spending of 24,000,000 families and on the conjectural production of several hundred thousand business firms can run efficiently. Must not the economic order be controlled and planned for the public welfare? Controlled and planned by whom? So we come again to the problem of social control.[3]

Most families, even in prosperous times, have an income only sufficient to meet their present needs. We must start with a true conception of family life, which is this: The 24,000,000 families in the United States are going concerns just as truly as the 268,783 corporations reporting net income in 1928. While a family runs along on a regular income, things go fairly well in most cases, though the income may be small. But when income stops or is greatly decreased, the margin of many families is wiped out. What actually will happen depends in a measure on the attitudes that have been fostered during prosperity. Where the father and mother have developed loyalty to each other and have built up loyalty in the children, this may be intensified in depression. The experience may bring the family closer together, at least for a time. They talk over and agree on one sacrifice after another. But long continued unemployment becomes very disturbing in all families. Loyalty merely increases the anxiety, for the loyal one feels the suffering of the others. In families not so loyal the relations become still more strained. Prolonged hunger and worry, loss

---

[3] Read the discussion of this problem by Ralph E. Flanders, vice president of the American Society of Mechanical Engineers, and Professor Wesley C. Mitchell in *Mechanical Engineering*, Feb., 1931, pp. 99-110.

of sleep and daily disappointments wear them down into a neurotic condition. Men in the habit of going to work regularly are not contented at home and become irritable and morose. The children bother them. They treat the children harshly and the latter develop an attitude of resentment toward their father. One little girls told her friends: "Father doesn't like us any more." The man's sitting around the house may irritate his wife. Husband and wife may nag and reproach each other for past mistakes. She may lose confidence in him and accuse him of not trying to find work. She may even express the wish that he might die so that she might be eligible for the widow's allowance. He may, after many attempts, suddenly give up trying to find work and even appear indifferent to it when it comes. If he chances to earn fifty cents he may get drunk. A man of formerly high character may get a police record. This family tension has a profound effect on children.

Against this picture of married life in depression single blessedness may seem blessed indeed. But a study of those living unmarried does not justify this conclusion. As unemployment continues single women begin to brood and become mentally unfit for work. Single men who perhaps formerly earned high salaries drift into the life of the down-and-outer.

One of the outstanding attitudes in the present unemployment is the harsh disapproval of the unemployed man just because he is out of work. Wives who have been loyal heretofore develop a futile, nagging attitude. Says Miss Addams: "An astonishing number of these women, ridden by fear lest their children starve, continually harass a disheartened husband who comes home from a futile search for work by the assertion that any one can find work who really wants it."[4] This attitude passes to the children and this general antagonism toward the father often results in permanent alienation.

Miss Kahn, executive director of the Jewish Welfare Society of Philadelphia, gives a case in point: "The other day a man came to our office, as hundreds do day after day, applying for a job, in order not to have to apply for relief. I think we have

---

[4] Addams "Social Consequences of Depression," *Survey*, Jan. 1, 1932, p. 370.

already stressed the reluctance of individuals to accept relief, regardless of the source from which it comes. This man said to our worker: 'I know you haven't any money to give us . . . but I want . . . a job.' Now, we have so many applications of that kind during the day that it has gotten to the point where we can scarcely take their names as they come in. . . . This individual interested me because when he heard that we had no jobs . . . he said: 'Have you anybody you can send around to my family to tell my wife you have no job? She doesn't believe that a man who walks the streets from morning till night, day after day, actually cannot find a job. She thinks I don't want to work.'[5]

The business and professional classes have taken the same attitude toward the unemployed man, though, as the depression has continued, this has gradually changed. There are still those, however, who feel that men do not wish to work. This assumption "is based upon a mistaken idea of what leisure means to the poorest. The well-to-do man has plenty of pleasant ways to spend his leisure time. The poor man has only his crowded home, where a busy wife does not want him around, or the street, where he tramps weary hours looking for work."[6]

The experienced social worker realizes that in most cases men do not want charity, though they may ask for charity out of dire need. What they want is work. Often we wonder that they do. If the reader could have seen men employed in the curing pit of one of the rubber corporations in the summer of 1932, working twenty-four hours at a stretch in the blistering heat of the pit, some of them carried out on stretchers in the early morning, the rest staggering to their beds, and always others eager to take their places, he would realize that men are willing to work, and would wonder at it. The twenty-four hour shift was an exceptional rush of work to enable the corporation to escape paying certain taxes, but the point is that men are willing to work under any conditions bearable or unbearable, as the profit-seeking impulses of employers dictate.

---

[5] Testimony of Miss Kahn before U. S. Senate Committee on Unemployment Relief, Dec., 1931, p. 75.

[6] Adams, *op. cit.*, 370.

The depression has in certain instances encouraged a brutal disregard of workmen in factory and mine,[7] because the multitudes of unemployed make resistance of exploitation difficult. Men rush in to take these jobs. Is it not time to consider the effect of this on the children? Their parents seem powerless to do anything about it.

BROKEN HOMES

Various conditions of the depression have caused broken homes. These result from the death of a parent under hardships; from family desertion by father or mother; from the inclination of parents to give up their children to an institution when they are powerless to care for them; from well meaning attempts to meet the unemployment situation by separation of husband and wife for the time being. Let us look at each of these causes of broken homes.

Fathers and mothers have died from the hardships of the depression:

Isaac Melvin had been industrious and independent up to the depression when he lost his job. He did his best to get work and the family used up their savings. Then they sold the home and used that money. Then he got $6 a week in relief. This meant slow starvation. The mother was confined and died from sheer weakness a few months after the baby was born. The children were scattered in foster homes. Isaac is over forty-five and too old ever again to hold a good job. The county must support them all now as a broken family, why not before as a united family?

When a mother dies the father often struggles to keep his family together. Usually a housekeeper cannot be secured and he may try to do the housework with the help of the children before and after the day's work. During the day the neighbors may come in and help, but the children run wild and he finally gives up. He can board with his family in another home if one can be found. But in most cases the children must be placed

---

[7] The commissioners appointed by Governor Sampson of Kentucky to investigate conditions among the miners of Harlan County reported "conditions almost too horrible for belief." This report was never published but a summary of it was printed by the American Civil Liberties Union in "The Kentucky Miners' Struggle."

in foster homes or in an institution unless there is a daughter or relative capable of taking the responsibility.

The hardships of the depression have driven fathers and mothers to suicide.[8] The suicide rate in New York has risen since 1929 but we do not know how far this was due to the depression. In only a small fraction of the cases do we have any definite knowledge of the causes of the suicide or of the personality of the unfortunate person. Furthermore we have no statistics of unsuccessful attempts at suicide, which are as important as the successful. The failure of the attempt often is purely accidental. The person really belongs to the suicide class so far as his personality is concerned.

Another cause of broken homes is that a father or a mother suffers a mental breakdown because of the stresses and strains resulting from the depression and is committed to a hospital. It is difficult to make certain just what part the depression has played in these cases.

Families are broken because the unemployed father in desperation commits a crime. There are instances of this in New York and in other states. Here is a Philadelphia family of father, mother, and six children, the oldest twenty-three, the youngest eight years of age:

> The family at its best had good standards. The children were going to school and were well clothed and fed. . . . It was a happy and united family until unemployment came. Eventually their savings were exhausted, and the wife took boarders because the family needed the money. As soon as this happened the oldest boys left home and have not been heard from since. Overwork and nervousness wrecked the health of the mother, and a tumor developed in her breast. . . . Illness due to lack of proper clothing . . . affected the health of the two younger boys. . . . At the beginning of the unemployment period, the father's attitude was that of a stoic. . . . One day when things looked very black and life in the family was becoming unbearable, he brought home quite a sum of money. He had met some seamen who smuggled drugs. He was persuaded to dispose of them, and being inexperienced, was trapped, arrested and sentenced to ten years of hard labor at the Federal prison in Atlanta.[9]

---

[8] Chapter IX.
[9] Elderton, *Case Studies of Unemployment*, pp. 130-32.

Boot-legging is more common than selling dope and has occasionally been winked at by public welfare officials. In two cities at least, if the commissioner found that the unemployed man who had applied for relief had been selling liquor to support his family, he said, in effect: "You don't need relief," the implication being that, as long as the man kept off the books of the office he would not be informed on. The man was encouraged by the official to go on committing a crime, in fact was driven to continue because apparently he could keep his family going in no other way. Poverty drives a mother into illicit relations to help her family and then, because of her immorality, the welfare office will not help her.

Another cause of broken homes is family desertion. We do not know whether family desertion has increased or decreased during the depression. Certain conditions of prosperity are favorable to desertion; certain other conditions of depression are favorable to it. In prosperity, a man who wants to escape his family has a reasonable expectation of getting a job in another city. In depression he is not apt to get a job, and if he deserts to another city and applies for relief, he is apt to be sent back to his home city. Men know this and so hesitate to desert during a depression. On the other hand, they may find the family tension too much of a strain to be borne. To avoid the reproaches of his wife and the annoyance of his children a man may form the habit of staying away from home from morning till night. He walks the streets or visits speakeasies or pool-rooms, not because he wants to but because he has nowhere else to go. Some night he may not come home at all. His wife may hale him into court on a charge of non-support and desertion may follow. For some men the suffering of their children becomes too poignant. They desert and then come back after a time. When asked why he deserted one man said, "Because I could not give the kids anything to eat." Many of these men have up to this time been exemplary fathers and good providers, never before dependent. Some of them leave home to avoid losing their minds in the dread monotony of distress, others with the idea that, if they are gone, the family can make a stronger appeal to a welfare agency. Women sometimes desert. A mother with three children took a boarder because her husband was out of work. Later she took the children to live with the boarder. Then he lost his job. Now she is looking for another boarder.

Homes are broken by parents committing their children to institutions to save them from worse distress.[10] In some cities the institutions are so full that commitment for other reasons is difficult. Children of families heretofore independent are thus thrown into institutions for homeless children and suffer all the evil effects of such an experience.

Homes are broken up as a result of temporary separations to meet financial stress. The family may be evicted and the wife's family may come and take her and the children to her former home while the husband remains and shifts for himself or goes to his former home. The family may never get together again:

James Fryer, twenty-three years of age, has a wife and three children. James married young because he wanted a home. His father and mother separated when he was a baby and he was brought up by his grandmother, who died when he was seven years old. After that he lived in a foster home and shifted for himself. So James naturally wanted a home, married young and had one up to the time of the depression when he was thrown out of work. His wife finally went with the children to live with her brother. James was passionately fond of the children and felt utterly lost without them. Finally he pawned a watch in order to raise money to visit them. Now he is resolved to raise himself above the level of an unskilled laborer and is taking a course in a vocational school to learn aviation. But it is doubtful if he will succeed. His wife has foolishly reproached him for not supporting them. His children see him rarely and no longer know him. James is heart-broken and the family may never be reunited.

The break-up of the home may be only temporary but its effect on the family may be lasting:

John Stewart was an industrious young man. He and his wife were still in their twenties. He lost his job and could get no work and finally their savings were used up. Their landlady shut off

---

[10] Testimony of Mr. Billikopf before United States Senate Committee on Unemployment Relief, Dec., 1931, p. 122.

their lights because they could not pay the rent and told them to move. They could not get a house. John applied at the public welfare office for money to pay rent and was put off. His wife and baby were sick at the time and finally her brother came and took them to his home, already crowded, in a near-by city. John left home to search for work and, when he returned, the landlady had moved their furniture out into the yard. It was in the dead of winter. John went to the police station for lodging but they allowed no lodgers. The chief gave him money for a night's lodging. The next night he sat up in the watchman's shanty at the railroad crossing. The public welfare commissioner had got him a job for the next morning but toward morning he fell asleep and he did not appear at the job on time. The commissioner "bawled him out." John's wife and baby had come back and, having no home to go to, they sat in the waiting room of the welfare office from ten to three before the commissioner would see them. Before night a place for the family to stay in had been found. Why was not this done without causing the family all this distress? But this was just the beginning of their troubles. When these experiences have gone on for months or years of a depression, do we wonder that the romance has been taken out of married life?

Where young couples have not actually separated, depression may destroy their faith in the possibilities of family life and weaken their confidence in each other. Young people have not acquired the capacity for adjustment that comes only with mature years. They have not the resignation of an older couple who realize that they have not much longer to go on. Time only will tell whether these breaches will widen to the point of separation.

The depression has caused much estrangement between relatives. A married sister is incensed because her married brother will not help her. A mother-in-law finds her opinion of her son-in-law justified. Indulgent parents finally have to "shut down on" spoiled married children. Continual borrowing from relatives and the necessity of making loans or gifts result in disputes and estrangement. Where families crowd in together there are disagreements.

The behavior of people during a depression depends of course on two factors, the poverty and dire need on the one hand and the kind of personalities that react to these conditions on the other. One sees a great range of behavior, from that of the utterly childish man or woman to a maturity that compels admiration. Here is a mother of a family which has been dependent on public relief for a year, who showed us a dress she had made for her eight-year-old girl and then began to cry about the child's not having new shoes to go with the new dress. To avoid her childish emotion her husband has formed the habit of keeping disagreeable truths from her, though later she overflows the more in self-pity because he has deceived her. In the very next family visited, the mother surprised us with her mature patience and good judgment under hardship. The same differences are seen among the well-to-do. One wealthy man admits the necessity of high income taxes to meet the situation and another, far richer, fumes like a spoiled boy against the "extravagance" of the government in voting an appropriation for unemployment relief.

The family situations we have described reveal certain processes which must be kept in mind if we are to consider wisely the various remedies suggested for unemployment. First, we see everywhere the force of habit asserting itself where intelligence is required. In depression we are asking millions of families suddenly to alter their habits of consumption with good grace because of a reversal of fortune. It may not be a question of need but merely of giving up what people have been in the habit of thinking they need—much that they would be freer and more comfortable without. But strength of habit has been fostered throughout the course of social evolution,[11] and only the unusual person has the intelligence to make any considerable alteration of habits without demoralization of personality. This is as true when sudden affluence pours the good things of life into the lap as when deprived of what one has habitually enjoyed. Unusual prosperity or depression causes families to lose their poise, and either emotional condition of people, as buyers of goods, affects the working of the economic system. Because of this force of habit, one who considers human nature in its relation to the economic system finds the question arising in his mind whether the welfare of the people would not be enhanced by some regulation of their

---

[11] Williams, *Principles of Social Psychology*, pp. 10-11.

consumption, both indirectly through stabilization of income and directly by some limit on the production of goods which provoke only a conventionalized wasteful spending of money.[12]

Suggestions that income is too unequally divided are almost always advanced for the benefit of those with small incomes. We should emphasize as much the advantage to those having large incomes, especially the advantages to their children. The children of the rich acquire habits which may make life disappointing. Many of them when they grow up are unable to maintain the standard of living which they had as children. They seldom can start married life with that standard. Girls are condemned to life-long unhappiness by an economic system that builds up habits of enjoying luxuries in childhood and youth and then requires them to forego this manner of life in order to live with the man of their choice. For if the girl is one of several children she will not usually inherit enough income to live as formerly and for many years may inherit nothing. This is not mere theory. We see unhappy wives who grew up in rich homes and cannot adjust themselves to the standard of living provided by their husbands, some of whom have become psychopathic for that reason. We see husbands who are discontented and sometimes psychopathic because they cannot have the standard of living they had in youth. These men and women would be better off if their parents had not had large incomes; and their families and associates who have to endure them would be better off. Thus the habit-bound aspect of human nature has to be reckoned with in the building of an economic system for human welfare. Some of us who have been intimately among the people during the last two years are quite convinced that people, high and low, lack the intelligence to adapt themselves, without serious stress and strain, to the changes that are inevitable under our system. This lack of intelligence is nothing new. It is as old as human nature itself. Philosophers have been accustomed to hold up for admiration a man who had such intelligence. So rare are such people today that modern writers point to Marcus Aurelius, as Aurelius pointed to Socrates, four hundred years before: "He knew

---

[12] Atkins and associates, *Economic Behavior*, II, Chs. XXXI-XXXIII.

how to lack, and how to enjoy those things in the lack whereof
most men show themselves weak; and in the fruition,
intemperate."

Another essential fact to bear in mind is the dependence of
the family on the economic order. Our individualistic economic
system dates from the agricultural era of free farmers that
followed feudalism. In this era "freedom of enterprise" and
"rugged individualism" were born. The egocentric economic
attitude[13] accentuated the family-centered family, which has
survived today.[14] The attitude of every family for itself, which
rests on an individualistic economic order, was justified by
Adam Smith with the explanation that an invisible hand would
guide this individualistic order for the welfare of the whole.
In times like the present the invisible hand is quite invisible,
and as we have said, it has been necessary to rely on the neigh-
borliness of the poor to ease the stress of unemployment. The
self-centered family is an inevitable product of a self-centered
economic order,[15] and we do not see how it can become socially
minded until certain changes in that order are made.

Difficult as many members of a family find it to face their
own family situations, it is far more difficult to face this problem of the relation of the economic order to other institutions.
It is this hesitancy that makes our political activity futile. Mr.
Soule quotes a distinguished economist who avers that our
ineffective political activity makes inevitable a long decline in
western civilization similar to that by which the Roman Empire
slid into the Dark Ages. But he believes that men will stand
up and fight against this fate.[16] That would be a mature attitude. Will our home training and education produce fighters
in numbers? Is not the average home in the city of the well-
to-do more or less a nursery in ways of evading the realities
of our economic and political life? Does not public and higher
education involve a good deal of training in escaping real
problems, which to be sure, the average student rejects for
his own ways of escape? The exasperated teacher fails to

---

[13] Atkins and associates, *Economic Behavior*, I, Preface, Ch. I.
[14] Williams, *The Expansion of Rural Life*, p. 89.
[15] Williams, *Principles of Social Psychology*, Ch. XX.
[16] Soule, *A Planned Society*, pp. 277-78.

realize that the elusive student is doing just what he is doing. The teacher is trying to escape the real world and the student is trying to escape the teacher. The school or college teacher withdraws within his intellectual self where he can shut out the follies of the campus and wander in the green pastures and by the still waters of his specialty. How many fighters is this kind of education producing?

CHAPTER IV

HEALTH IMPAIRED

THAT UNEMPLOYMENT and relief practices have impaired the health of children is evident to anyone who knows the city of the poor. But data suited to an inquiry of this kind never to my knowledge have been collected so as to afford a pre-depression background. This makes it possible for those who desire, relying on their prestige, and pointing their statements with a citation of certain statistics, to assert that the depression has not impaired health. Thus Secretary Wilbur declared at the National Conference of Social Work in May, 1932: "I think that unless we descend to a level far beyond anything that we at present have known, our children are apt to profit rather than to suffer from what is going on."[1] "Our children" —yes, the children of Mr. Wilbur and other complacent residents in the city of the well-to-do have not been affected, may even have profited; but physicians, social workers and nurses among the great army of the unemployed know that the health of many children has been injured.

We naturally think first of the effects on the unborn child. Some half-starved mothers have died before the child was born, some have died of sheer weakness after the birth of the child, and infants have died from weakness and defects due to the condition of the mother. Still it is true that statistics of infant mortality in New York cities have continued to show a slight decline during the first years of the depression though it by no means follows that this will continue. The effect of malnutrition usually is not death of mother or child but a weakened mother and an unhealthy child.

To understand the effect of the poverty and malnutrition of

[1] *New York Times,* May 17, 1932.

the mother on the unborn child, we must consider that the child has its own circulatory and nervous system, but there is an exchange of nutrient and waste materials between mother and child. The maternal blood supplies oxygen and nutrient materials to the child and the child may absorb toxic substances from the blood of the mother.[2] The effects of the depression on mothers and through them on unborn children are, therefore, probably as follows: First, if the mother is undernourished the child does not get the necessary nutrient materials from the mother; second, if the mother is over-worked or worried the toxic substances in the maternal blood may pass into the body of the child; third, the difficulty of birth may be increased and this may cause a birth trauma in the child, with its later effects which might contribute to behavior difficulties.[3]

During the early growth of the unborn child occurs the formation of units of tissue out of which develop the nervous system and other organs. The health and vigor of these organs depends on the normal functioning of the heart, kidneys, and digestive organs of the mother and on the embryo getting from the maternal blood the necessary nutrient materials.[4] The functioning of the maternal organs may be impaired by hardships and the blood may be impoverished. Our attention was recently called to a case of a child born in 1932 with a defective organ which the attending physician asserted was probably due to malnutrition of the mother, especially a lack of food containing calcium—a mineral found plentifully in digestible form in orange and tomato juice, cod liver oil, milk and certain vegetables. In such a case of course we know only what the physician says. We know that the baby is defective and that the mother lacked foods containing calcium because she had no money with which to buy them and could not get them through the public welfare office. How many more cases of this kind

[2] Dodds, *Essentials of Human Embryology*, pp. 71-73, 235; Kenworthy, "The Pre-Natal and Early Post-Natal Phenomena of Consciousness," in Dummer, *The Unconscious*, p. 185.

[3] Rank, *The Trauma of Birth*, pp. 46-73; Murchison, *Handbook of Child Psychology*, p. 29; Watson, *Parents and Their Children*, p. 67; Healy, *The Structure and Meaning of Psychoanalysis*, p. 173-76.

[4] Kenworthy, *op. cit.*, p. 181.

there are in depression than in prosperity of course never will
be known. In the case we are writing of, the mother was not
only half-starved but worried because, as she said, "I'm afraid
Dan (her husband) is going to lose his mind. He paces the
floor and says queer things and flies off the handle at any
little thing." He was worried because he could not get work
and the family, especially his wife, were suffering severe
hardships.

The unborn child is protected against malnutrition of the
mother by various devices of nature, among these the fact that
the embryo will take calcium from the mother's bones and teeth
if her blood does not supply it. The old saying was, "A tooth
for each child," but many women these days are giving more
than one tooth. It is to be regretted that physicians who know
of these cases have no time to trace out and write up the relation of unemployment and poverty to the mother's condition.
Possibly reports of these cases will later get into the medical
journals.

In many cities expectant mothers cannot get enough nourish-
ing food to keep them in health. Here is a statement from a
letter received from a state department of health in answer
to inquiries made in the winter of 1931-32 as to the effect of
the depression on the health of expectant mothers: "It has been
apparent for some months past that women coming to the pre-
natal consultations conducted by this Division (Division of
Maternity, Infancy and Child Hygiene) are showing definitely
the effects of insufficient or improper diet. In some cases it
was reported that families had been living for weeks on potatoes, in which case they would not have fallen particularly
low in weight but showed other evidences of improper nourishment. They all report husbands and other members of the
family out of work and are depressed and hopeless." An agency
of public health nurses in one city reported in the fall of 1931:
"Many of the mothers are unable to provide themselves with
even one glass of milk a day. Our calls for free milk have increased forty-one per cent since 1929, and these from much
higher types of families than we have ever had before."

Public welfare officers should center on providing nourish-

4

ing food and necessary medical care for expectant mothers and on relieving them as far as possible from the anxieties incident to the depression. This is not generally done. One public welfare official, when asked for relief on the ground that the woman was an expectant mother, would reply, "But I am not responsible for your having a baby." It is to be expected that, among the thousand and more public welfare officials in New York, such vulgarity will occasionally be encountered. The more usual attitude toward the expectant mother is indifference so far as action by the office on her behalf is concerned. One who knows about the work of a good many public welfare officials writes: "A small proportion of those I know best would, I imagine, be careful to see that an expectant mother had extra nourishment, though I would not expect many of these to consult the family doctor first, as would be good case work procedure, to be sure that the mother should have extra milk. In certain cases, as you know, the doctor would definitely advise against extra milk at this time. However, as a rule I should be rather surprised to find a public welfare official making a practice of special milk or other nourishment for expectant or nursing mothers." Accurate information about the practice of welfare officials cannot be gained by sending out questionnaires or, at the present time, from any other source. Not only welfare officials but also health officers often fail to realize the importance of proper nourishment and their attitude is an obstacle in any movement to improve conditions.

BIRTH CONTROL

Birth control information is denied to mothers, under the laws of New York and other states, unless the situation is more acute than the stress of a depression. Furthermore, to many the hardships of the depression came very suddenly and the need of birth control had not before been apparent. Finally there are couples who attempted to practice birth control but were forced to give it up by relatives and the Church:

John Bukowski, twenty-three, and his wife, Mary, nineteen, had no children. They dared not for John had had no work for a year. John's father and mother lived near by and also were in poverty. The mother-in-law did not like Mary. She wanted to come to Mary whenever she felt like it to talk out all her troubles, but Mary did not want to hear them. She was incensed that John and Mary had no children though they had been married almost a year. So she and old John went to the priest and told him about it. The priest came to the home of young John and Mary and told them that they must do nothing to prevent conception for that was a mortal sin. This scared John and Mary. It did something else. As the social worker could see in Mary's blue eyes, restless now that her sense of social responsibility had been dissipated by the ecclesiastical warning, it released all the old longings. And there was John, idle, insistent and drifting into a more irresponsible attitude as month followed month of unemployment. So, regardless of their impossible economic situation, Mary had a girl baby within a year, which died soon after birth because, as social workers who had charge of this case aver, the mother was half starved during the whole period of her pregnancy and the infant was under-nourished during its brief life and was too weak to live.

Here we have an illustration, and more might be given, of the church's ignoring its social responsibility for wholesome childhood and driving a young couple into the same irresponsibility. "What about the responsibility of the economic order for providing the worker with work to support his family?" may be the Church's rejoinder. But how many children is the economic order responsible for? Not for as many as John and Mary would naturally have. The birth control issue cannot be evaded in that way. Church, family and community all are interdependent in this matter and the Church cannot ignore this interdependence. Social workers believe that, as a result of the attitude and practice of the Church, thousands of children who should not have been born are born into homes of poverty and social deficiency, and this is true in prosperity as well as in depression. In many cases doubtless the ecclesiastical pressure is sufficient to overcome the common-sense scruples of husband and wife. The result is an added expense for poor relief and delinquency which is borne by the community.

THE EFFECT OF THE MOTHER'S MENTAL STATES ON THE CHILD

While the unborn child may suffer from malnutrition of the mother, so far as we know it is fortunately beyond the reach of harm from her mental states except as these may affect the chemistry of the nutrient materials provided by the maternal blood. There seems to be no truth in the superstition that the fears of a mother may pass to the child. Some mothers are afraid that their worry or their insomnia caused by the depression may influence their baby and that the child may thus be a prey to worry, or may suffer from insomnia, or may have some particular dislike or hatred that has obsessed her. All solicitude about the transmittence of these fears seems to be groundless.

That fears are not transmitted to unborn babes is very important for mothers to know at this time when so many are passing through deep waters. For instance, in one case a husband went insane from worry because of lack of work and was taken to a state hospital. During these months the wife was an expectant mother. She was threatened with eviction and could not pay for gas or electricity. The gas and electric service was shut off. This refusal of a welfare department to pay for light and fuel is difficult to understand, except on the assumption that they have no funds. Apparently they expect their clients to go back to the use of candles. As to gas, if the unemployed are so civilized as to want to cook their food, evidently that is their hard luck. When the mother under these conditions was about to give birth to her child she was not sent to a hospital for that would have been too expensive. However, some cities provide free pre-natal care, hospital care during confinement and post-natal care for all women unable to pay.

LACK OF FOOD

Bread-winners sometimes are so under-fed that they become physically unable to take a job when it is offered. A certain man who worked part time in a factory had only potato peelings for his lunch, having left the potatoes at home for his wife and children. He sat off in a corner eating, that the other men might not see him. Such extreme destitution is unusual but thousands of working men are weak for lack of food. This is true also of boys and girls.

Several large cities report a decrease in the garbage collected in unemployed sections of the city. In a ward of one city there was a decrease of seventy-five per cent. This is due to buying less vegetables and fruits which yield much waste and also to eating what is ordinarily thrown away.

During a depression the unemployed must go on a diet which has been "forced below reasonable standards to bare essentials." Professor Sherman of Columbia University describes what must be done as the family is forced lower and lower: "Thus if forced below reasonable standards to bare essentials, we may . . . most wisely meet the emergency by concentrating . . . upon . . . these three essential groups of foods: (1) milk and its products, (2) fruit or vegetables, (3) bread and other cheap sources of calories." He then goes on to say—and we do not like to think of this, though it has been true of thousands of families during the depression years—that, when the family is forced below the level of the bare necessities, they must be advised how to spend in order to make the permanent physical injury as little as possible: "If there are times and places of such dire destitution that sacrifices must be made even among the bare essentials of bread, milk and some fruit or vegetable, each in the cheapest available form, what then? Shall obvious hunger and a starved appearance lead to the crowding out of milk by bread because a penny spent for bread goes farther to still the pangs of hunger? To go too far in this direction is to incur the even greater tragedy of the lifelong injuries which result from the 'hidden hunger' of the mineral and vitamin deficiencies. 'Milk builds bone and muscle better than any other food.' And more than this, milk is both the cheapest and the surest protection from nutritional deficiencies which open the way to diseases and life-long injuries to health, happiness, and working efficiency. 'The dietary should be built up around bread and milk.' The lower the level of expenditure, the more one must forego other foods and concentrate effort upon providing these two, supplemented by a little of some inexpensive fruit or vegetable. . . . One must guide the expenditure of inadequate funds for food in such ways that the children affected may be brought through without life-long injuries." Even if body weights are subnormal for a time, the diet must be such as to provide a "basis of sound bone and lean tissue."[5]

Has this advice been followed? In one New York city where the per capita consumption of fluid milk was less than a pint a day, before the depression, the consumption has been reduced one-fourth to two-fifths during the depression. This reduction is for the city as a whole. Where the unemployed live, the reduction would be more. As contrasted with this actual consumption of milk, the nutritional standard is one and one-half pints to one quart daily for every child and every expectant or nursing mother and half this amount for each other adult.[6] The State Department of Health wrote in 1932 that "the children coming to the state clinics have not shown the effect of the depression in loss of weight. . . . Their color, however, is often very poor and they are listless and depressed." An examination of some of these listless children shows that they have sacrificed the vitamin and mineral foods for the starchy ones. The diet of many children is almost entirely sugar and starch. The National Organization for Public Health Nursing in 1931 reported an increase in malnutrition from 18 per cent in 1928 to 60 per cent during the depression in one health center in New York City where statistics had been carefully kept over a period of years. Children are paying for the depression literally with their health.

Says Dr. T. B. Appel, State Secretary of Health of Pennsylvania: "A census of undernourished children in a normal year (1929-30) showed 18 per cent undernourished or approximately 140,000 in the state out of a school population in these districts of 768,000. Incomplete reports so far received this year from a sufficient number of schools to give a fair estimate

---

[5] Sherman, "Emergency Nutrition," Reprinted from *Child Health Bulletin*, Nov., 1931, and copyrighted by the American Child Health Association.

[6] The United States Childen's Bureau, *Emergency Food Relief and Child Health*, p. 2.

show that the percentage of undernourished children has increased to 27 per cent. . . .

"As these data cover only children in the public schools, and as it is a recognized fact that when undernourishment is present in a family it is more marked among children of preschool age, it would be safe to assume that the percentage of undernourished pre-school children is definitely greater than the figures given. Added to this it is easily appreciated that in the average family sacrifices will be made by the other members in order that the children may receive proper food; and with these two points in view it would be safe to assume that there are from 25 per cent to 50 per cent more persons suffering from malnutrition in the state at the present time than in years before."[7]

Because malnutrition has not yet markedly affected statistics of morbidity, many welfare officials and others have taken the attitude, why worry? If in the future slowly developing diseases like tuberculosis begin to show an increase, shall we then be as complacent about the situation as we are now?

Malnutrition has caused various diseases among children. Physicians produce case after case to prove it. These cases ought to be worked out and published in medical journals. We should like to know if there has been any increase in the rare disease called keratomalacia which is due to a deficiency of fat soluble vitamin A. This vitamin is found especially in milk and butter, egg yolk, cod liver oil and spinach. None of the cases of the disease during this depression have, so far as I know, been reported in medical journals but there is an excellent report of one that, as the author tells me, resulted from poverty in the last depression.[8]

A diet poor in vitamin A may stunt growth and lower resistance to infectious diseases of eyes, ears, sinuses and lungs. So many of our staple foods are poor in vitamin A that it is important to provide children with the foods that contain it in abundance.

---

[7] *Bulletin of the Pennsylvania Tuberculosis Society*, January, 1932.

[8] Wilson, "Report of a Fatal Case of Keratomalacia in an Infant, with Postmortem Examination," *American Journal of Diseases of Children*, Nov., 1923.

A deficiency of vitamin B may result in disturbances of the digestive tract and constipation and may stunt the growth of children and cause nervousness. In some sections of the South there has been a decided increase in pellagra during the depression which may be due to a deficiency in vitamin B. This vitamin is abundant in whole grain cereals, tomatoes, spinach, raw cabbage, milk. Vitamin B is made up of two factors, vitamin F which is the anti-neuritic factor, and vitamin G which is a curative for pellagra.

There are cases of scurvy in children of six or seven months to two years of age in families of the unemployed. This disease is caused by a deficiency of vitamin C. This vitamin is found in milk but not in sufficient quantity and milk must be supplemented by foods rich in vitamin C, as orange juice, spinach, peas, tomatoes. The amount of vitamin C which children must have to protect them from scurvy is only a fraction of the amount needed for full health and vigor and maximum growth. A lack of this vitamin may cause sore mouth, stiff joints, defective teeth, irritability and a general lack of stamina. In order to insure enough of it, instead of relying on only one food element containing it, several such foods should be eaten each day. The body is limited in capacity to store vitamin C, so that the diet, especially of children, should contain it in abundance. We may add that the body is incapable of storing enough of any vitamin to permit a person to continue in health on food deficient in vitamins through a prolonged period of unemployment.

Rickets have developed in children whose parents are unemployed and in poverty. Rickets are caused by a deficiency of vitamin D which is necessary for the assimilation of calcium and phosphorus. This vitamin is found in abundance in the milk of properly fed cows and in cod liver oil. Lack of this vitamin also causes decay of teeth which is a symptom of probable malnutrition elsewhere in the system, makes a child's bones soft and impairs the lungs. Certain experts have recently announced arrest of decay of teeth through a diet rich in vitamin D, this arrested condition indicating improvement elsewhere in the body.

Among families unemployed and in poverty we have found cases of nutritional anemia, that is, anemia due to a lack of food containing iron. Milk contains iron but not enough of it and children need whole wheat and other cereals, green vegetables and egg yolk.

In general we may say that we have found among the unemployed diseases due to lack of proper food, and physicians believe that these diseases are due to unemployment and poverty. The tendency in a time of unemployment is to give up all but the cheapest foods, those that quiet the pangs of hunger at least cost, which are the carbohydrates. Children do not die of starvation but they have nutritional diseases; some states also showed an increase of communicable disease in 1931.[9] Some cities that have attempted to provide a balanced diet at very low cost have not guarded against malnutrition. For instance, Toledo is said to have fed fifty thousand persons on an average of six cents a day per person.[10] The public welfare office of Syracuse, after a study of the Toledo diet in the spring of 1932, found it inadequate and decided that the lowest per capita cost of a diet that would barely nourish the unemployed averaged eleven to fourteen cents a day per person.[10a]

The New York State Department of Health does not regularly collect statistics of nutritional diseases and no special studies of these diseases have been made in recent years. If there were statistics, these might not show any increase in nutritional diseases during the depression and yet the depression might be causing these diseases. The reason is that families with sufficient income are constantly learning to provide the proper food for their children so that there is normally a decrease in diseases due to malnutrition, wherefore the increase during a depression among those in poverty might be concealed by the decrease elsewhere due to education.

The main difficulties in the way of adequate food for the children of the unemployed are insufficient relief funds, lack

[9] See the testimony of Governor Pinchot before the U. S. Senate Committee on Unemployment Relief, Dec., 1931, p. 215.
[10] Taylor, "Decent Standards of Relief," *Survey*, May 15, 1932, p. 181.
[10a] Public Welfare Department of Syracuse, *The Syracuse Plan.*

of an effective plan like that adopted in Syracuse, and lack of arrangements for instructing families in the best use of the funds they have. Then there is the political control over welfare officials, some of whom are compelled to give grocery orders on stores where the proper food for children cannot be bought. Finally there is the prejudice of many families against the best foods. It is fully as important to educate people about what food is best for their children as to provide money for food.

Good work has been done by local nutrition committees organized by the American Red Cross and the International Institute of the Y. W. C. A.[11] Such a committee is made up of teachers of home economics, of representatives of the public welfare office and the private family society and volunteer nutrition workers. These volunteers are trained by the teachers to go into the families of the unemployed and teach them what food to buy and how to cook it for the best nutrition of their children. They have used Bertha Wood's book on *Foods of the Foreign Born in Relation to Health* and, with this knowledge, have been able to work out adapted menus that have not repelled the tastes of the families and have enabled them to get maximum nutritional value for a minimum expenditure. In some cases these nutrition committees have brought about a very marked improvement in the physical condition of children of the community. Welfare offices sometimes are willing to increase a family's food budget a bit when they believe that it will really benefit the family.

OVERCROWDING

The depression has affected the housing of the unemployed. Three effects stand out. First, families that could not pay their rent have had to crowd in with other families. Second, families have had to move into low-rent sections of the city and this has demoralized the children. Third, evictions have had a harmful effect on children. As to the first effect, families

---

[11] American Red Cross, Organization of a Nutrition Service, National Board of the Young Women's Christian Associations, The International Institute an Important Resource in the General Relief Plan of the City.

in all the cities have had to double up. Instances of two families living in one apartment are common and sometimes three families crowd in together. Three, four, five and even six persons are found living in one small room. Other families are living in the cellar where the landlord has allowed them to move from the apartment above, others in garages. Dr. Elliott, headworker of Hudson Guild, said recently of conditions in New York, "I have never seen people living in such inhuman surroundings."[12] We know of no city that has made a systematic study of the overcrowding due to unemployment. Says Miss Dorothy Kahn, executive director of the Jewish Welfare Society of Philadelphia: "We have no measure in Philadelphia to-day of the overcrowding that is a direct or indirect result of our inability to pay rents for families. Only the other day a case came to my attention in which a family of ten had just moved in with a family of five in a three room apartment. However shocking that may be to the members of this committee, it is almost an every-day occurrence in our midst. Neighbors do take people in. They sleep on chairs, on the floor. . . . There is scarcely a day that calls do not come to all of our offices to find somehow a bed or a chair. The demand for boxes on which people can sit or stretch themselves is hardly to be believed."[13] Overcrowding is found not only in large but in small cities, and there are the usual results of congestion: improper sleeping arrangements, slovenly housekeeping, disorder, uncleanliness, friction, frayed nerves. Overcrowding is one of the causes of the decadence in sex morality discussed in a succeeding chapter.[14] Children are among those most seriously affected by these conditions.

MOVING SLUMWARD

There has been more moving than in prosperity and more frequent movings by many families, and always to poorer neighborhoods and often to unfit apartments. Says the inter-

---

[12] *New York Times*, Jan. 13, 1932.
[13] Testimony of Miss Kahn before the U. S. Senate Committee on Unemployment Relief, Dec., 1932, p. 75.
[14] Chapter VII.

viewer at the welfare office: "How much rent are you paying?"
"Thirty-five dollars a month."

"What! Your budget won't stand that. You'll have to move."

So the family starts slumward. Landlords who have maintained good tenements are injured, while one who has a firetrap or an unsanitary relic of the past is subsidized by the city—a poor use for city funds. Children heretofore living in a good section pay for the depression by being turned loose on the streets of the slum, unprepared to cope with its dangers and temptations. We have seen some tragic results of this forcing of industrious unemployed into the slums.

Not only inability to pay rents but also loss of ownership is a cause of moving slumward. The use of the real estate tax to meet the expenses of emergency relief forces the unemployed who own homes to pay the taxes for relief. "A mine is closed, a factory about which a village centers is shut down, and the burden of relief falls upon the very men themselves in need of public help. The situation is less obvious in cities, but exists there on a large scale." "During sixty days last year in Detroit and its immediate vicinity, 50,000 small home owners were obliged to give up all equity in their property and to see the loss of their entire savings, because they could not earn the money either to meet the payments on their mortgages or to defray their taxes."[15]

Probation officers cite case after case of families driven into the slums by the depression, and of boys and girls demoralized and finally brought into the court. I go with them to see these families, and the facts are incontrovertible. Here is a boy who has been sentenced to a reform school because unemployment sentenced his family to the slums. His mother had to go to work by the day, the boy was unsupervised and got into one difficulty after another until the reform school seemed to be the only solution. Here is a girl who ran away from home because she would not live in the slum neighborhood. Her strong, wholesome impulses rebelled against the surroundings

---

[15] Addams, "Social Consequences of Depression," *Survey*, Jan. 1, 1932, p. 371.

and she went to work elsewhere as a domestic. The court does not feel justified in compelling her to go home, though she is technically an ungovernable minor. A child clinic is sorely puzzled to know how to advise a court in such cases.

EVICTIONS

The extent of evictions may be inferred from such figures as these: In Baltimore in October, 1931, 650 eviction notices were being served by the People's Court each week. In Buffalo 268 petitions for evictions were filed in November, 1930, and 190 final orders were issued by the judge; 306 petitions were filed in November, 1931, and 282 final orders were issued. In Cleveland evictions increased from 1,959 in 1927 to 5,777 in 1931. In New York City, says Dr. Elliott, one judge had 425 eviction cases before him in one day. Twenty-six per cent more warrants were issued in New York City in November, 1931, than in November, 1930, and 59 per cent more than in November, 1929.[16]

The unemployed live in constant fear of eviction. Families served with notices sometimes live with their goods packed up for a month until a cheap tenement can be found. Evictions get little publicity. The newspaper reporter passes by the family put out on the street and then gives the oldest boy half a column after he has joined a pilfering gang and done something worthy of note. Evictions often are carried out in a way that gives children a shock they never will forget. In some cities an old flop-house or a church is kept open for families and they lie down on the bare floor without blankets. Sometimes the welfare office moves the household goods into a van, and the family, with no home to go to, lives in the van over night until a tenement can be found, the children stowed away among the furniture. In other cases they do not even have a van. Think of the effect on a sensitive child of an eviction where the household goods of an industrious and deserving family were moved out into the back yard, there drenched with rain, while the mother had to go to the school

---

[16] Wead, "When the Rent Comes 'Round," *The Family*, February, 1932, p. 315.

and tell the children they had no dinner and no home. This family finally got shelter, but the fear of another eviction still hung over it. Occasionally an eviction is brutal, as in the case where a city marshal attempted to dispossess a family in which a child, under a doctor's care, was sick abed with a fever. The refusal of the family to let the child be taken out of bed so that the furniture might be moved on to the street started a riot participated in by other tenants about to be evicted and their sympathizers and there was a pitched battle with the police. The wonder is that such episodes happen so seldom, when one considers the strain these families are under.

Families are not only evicted but their household goods are sometimes sold. Says Miss Kahn: "Evictions in Philadelphia are frequently accompanied not only by the ghastly placing of a family's furniture on the street, but the actual sale of the family's household goods by the constable. These families are in common Philadelphia parlance, 'sold out'."[17]

In some cities many landlords have accepted the fact that rents cannot be paid and have been willing to let the tenants remain, unless there was a prospect of securing one that could pay the rent. Many landlords need the rent in order to pay taxes. They have opposed a rise in taxes for relief funds because they were giving relief in the form of rent. Certain cities have tried to bring some order out of this chaos by organizing committees to meet with landlords and work out a temporary adjustment.[18] Welfare offices have followed the policy that no family can be without shelter, but aside from that families have been left to wrestle with their rent problems. In one city the policy of the public welfare commissioner was not to pay rent until eviction papers were served; then to move the family into another house and pay one month's rent; then no more until they were again evicted; then one month's rent in another place. It has been well said that the "generally evasive attitude which some agencies have felt forced to adopt regarding rent is probably communicating itself to clients and may,

---

[17] Testimony of Miss Kahn before U. S. Senate Committee on Unemployment Relief, p. 74.

[18] Wead, "When the Rent Comes 'Round," *The Family*, Feb., 1932, p. 316.

if not safeguarded, seem to suggest that this is the only way the client also can meet the situation. The attitudes of both client and agency are of course dictated by the exigencies of the emergency situation, but probably we need to give more thought to the consequences of these attitudes."[19]

LACK OF HEAT AND CLOTHING

In most cities in New York destitute families cannot get more than one-half a ton of coal a month and on days in the coldest weather they may have little or no coal. One goes into homes where there is no fire at all and the temperature outside is below freezing. The people have colds and are miserably undernourished but may not at the moment appear to be any worse off.

One of the most common needs of children is for clothing and shoes. In the cities, in the cold months, children have had to wait days and sometimes weeks for shoes. Frequently children are found wearing misfit second-hand shoes, which injure their feet, forced on them by the public welfare office. Older children are prevented from working for lack of shoes. Scanty clothing is still more common. Poorly clad children are ashamed of their appearance and sometimes go and hide as one enters the house.

Suitable clothing obviously is necessary if boys and girls are to get a job and hold it and if they are to enjoy any social life.

LACK OF CARE OF HEALTH

Incipient illnesses of children and adults have been neglected. Dental care has been postponed. Even where there is a free clinic many people cannot pay carfare to the clinic or pay the clinic fee. Those who bring their children have no money to follow the instructions given. School nurses have found it difficult to get parents to improve the nutrition of their children or to attend to their illnesses because the parents are submerged in the struggle to provide food and shelter. People accustomed to a private physician have been reluctant to go

---

[19] *Ibid.*, p. 315.

as charity patients to a hospital or clinic or have not known that patients are treated without pay. Clinics and hospitals have been crowded. Children have been discharged from hospitals sooner than they should be. Children with abscessed ears or tonsils have been refused admission because of more serious cases. In some cities the public welfare offices have cancelled all free tonsillectomies; in other cities operations have been dated months ahead. Tuberculous patients have had to wait weeks or months for admission to a sanatorium.

In cases of actute illness families who could not pay a physician or go to a hospital have had to rely on doctors who would visit them without charge. Visting nurses have attended acute cases longer than usual because of the slow progress but often not as long as they should be carried, while chronic cases have been more or less left to the family to give what care they could.

The generally prevalent effects of the depression on the health of children in the cities are, then, low vitality and malnutrition, an increase of diseases due to malnutrition, increased susceptibility to the common diseases, a longer convalescence, delayed care of diseased conditions. In how far growth will be stunted and permanent organic troubles will result we do not know and never will know.

As to the effect on specific ailments, much disease is not recorded in vital statistics, such as infections of the respiratory tract, disorders of the digestive organs and nutritional diseases. These are the diseases that public health workers especially notice among the unemployed. But people do not call a doctor for these troubles unless they become acute, though they may lead to more serious sicknesses later on. There will probably be a lag in the effects of the depression on health and some effects will manifest themselves in the indices later. This is possibly true of tuberculosis.

There has been a marked increase in the use of public facilities for tuberculous patients, and an increase of cases in some states, for instance in Pennsylvania.[20] There the waiting list of applicants for sanatorium treatment was much greater

---

[20] *Bulletin of the Pennsylvania Tuberculosis Society*, January, 1932.

than before the depression and the patients admitted were often in a worse condition. "Indications point to the conclusion that there will be an increase in the death-rate from this disease."[21] Tuberculosis is a disease which develops slowly and the full increase in the number of cases would not appear in several years.

The question arises as to the responsibility for the impairment of the health of children during the depression. The Public Welfare Law of New York State expressly provides for the care of the health of children through the welfare office.[22] If the law were well enforced, children would not be paying for the depression with their health. Its enforcement is primarily the obligation of the local communities. If these cannot raise sufficient funds their sense of social responsibility should impel them to appeal to the state and, if the state government will not give adequate aid, to the federal government. Unless backed by a responsible community the welfare office has not the funds nor the incentive to attempt effective health work.

No matter how heavily the well-to-do might be taxed to support the unemployed, the latter would continue to be the chief sufferers because of the depression. The amount spent for relief is but a small fraction of the wage loss during the depression. "I have seen the estimate (of the amount given for relief in the United States) as $100,000,000 (a year). I am going to be conservative and put it at $200,000,000, but for each of the last two years, 1930 and 1931, the average in lost wages and salaries from unemployment, not including, as far as I could ascertain, wage cuts, but from unemployment, was over $10,000,000,000 a year."[23] This loss has been borne by doctors in unpaid services, by landlords in unpaid rents, by merchants in the extension of credit to families who never will pay. But the large part of it has been borne by the families of the unemployed themselves in their loss of homes and of savings, in the piling up of indebtedness, in health impaired, nerves shaken, and moral deterioration. "We must not forget that the heavy

---

[21] *Ibid.*
[22] Sections 105, 106.
[23] Testimony of Benjamin C. Marsh before United States Senate Committee on Unemployment Relief, Dec., 1931, p. 290.

end of the burden of industrial unemployment comes down on the families of wage earners. . . . No matter if the federal government, the states, the counties and private charitable agencies help them, they are bearing the main burden."[24]

The city of the well-to-do has various ways of closing its eyes to these grim realities. One of these ways is an escape into statistics. "Figures don't lie," they say, and "statistics show no significant general increase in infant or adult mortality." But there are significant increases in certain sections. Even if this were not so, still, as Mr. J. Prentice Murphy, executive director of the Children's Bureau of Philadelphia, says, "you can starve for a long while without dying."[25] And as Mr. Walter West, executive director of the American Association of Social Workers, has pointed out: "It has been difficult for us to deal with the situation on a statistical basis because . . . we are very likely to be dealing with amounts spent or money raised, much more than we are with amounts needed."[26] Will not inadequate relief be more expensive in the long run than adequate? Consider not only the ill-health, the pauperization, the family disintergration already described but also the nervous disorders and moral deterioration dealt with in succeeding chapters. The effect of all this on the America of the future cannot be stated statistically. Is not the citation of scattered statistics and the refusal to think of the situation in the long run merely an attempt to evade responsibility?

Social workers need to be trained in social psychology and in statistics in order to discern the defensive and evading attitudes of which statistics are used as rationalizations. Those moved by these attitudes often are not conscious of them. They merely repeat the rationalizations they have heard from others. The discernment of these attitudes puts the social worker on her guard against a too ready acceptance of "sta-

---

[24] Testimony of Paul U. Kellogg before U. S. Senate Committee on Unemployment Relief, Dec., 1921, p. 86.

[25] Testimony of Mr. Murphy before the U. S. Senate Committee on Unemployment Relief, Dec., 1931, p. 55.

[26] Testimony of Mr. West before the U. S. Senate Committee on Unemployment Relief, Dec., 1931, p. 71.

tistical proof" which her experience belies. Her experience is valuable for the interpretation of social statistics,[27] but only when she is so trained in social psychology as to be capable of some insight.

Another way of escape from disagreeable realities is to assert that "no one must starve." This implies that people must have relief though it may not be entirely adequate. But to quote Mr. Murphy again: "Where relief is inadequate you often have clients starving while they are helped. There are situations where you might as well do nothing as to give half a reasonable budget, as in the case of a tubercular mother, or a mother with a bad heart, or a man recovering from tuberculosis or an industrial accident."[28]

Facts about the effect of unemployment on health convince only those open to conviction. This depends on whether an individual is sympathetic enough to inform himself on conditions and sincere enough to face the facts. It has been shown elsewhere that this sympathetic attitude is contrary to the common egocentric attitude which we derive even in childhood from our money getting economy and that our attitudes determine the course of our thought.[29] Two equally intelligent men may be confronted with the same facts and draw opposite conclusions because their attitudes are contrary. Read the descriptions of need in the Report of the United States Senate Committee on Unemployment Relief and in the same volume the arguments of some people for relying on private contributions. The facts of need were the same for all, if they saw the facts. If they did not, what right had they to appear before the committee? Assuming that they saw the facts, they still differed radically in their conclusions. How many of those taking the attitude for private contributions applied to themselves the good old adage: "Show by what you do that you mean what you say?" The testimony before Congress proved that the unemployed were in dire need throughout the country

---

[27] Abbott, *Social Welfare and Professional Education*, p. 173.

[28] Testimony of Mr. Murphy before the United States Senate Committee for Unemployment Relief, Dec., 1931, p. 53.

[29] Williams, *The Foundations of Social Science*, Ch. XIV.

in spite of the private contributions. Was not reliance on these
a rationalization of the egocentric attitude, of an inclination
not to sympathize with need, to evade responsibility, which
could not be escaped under an adequate taxation policy?

CHAPTER V

NERVES SHAKEN

THE HOME IS to the child the place of security whither he retreats when sick or afraid or disappointed or anxious or just tired and ready to rest. A sense of security is essential to emotional stability. If the home does not give the child security, where can he find it? Children in the homes of the unemployed lose their sense of security. They cease to feel that they can depend on their parents.

The parents themselves have lost their security. Men and women are bewildered by what has happened. Nothing shows the separation between the well-to-do and the poor more conclusively than the inability of the former to understand this state of mind of the unemployed when one tries to explain it. A certain man who could not understand and who held a well-paid position was told that probably the firm would have to let him go. Then there came over him a realization of what a sense of insecurity means. Finally he got so wrought up that he went to his superior with the exclamation: "For God's sake end my suspense and tell me whether or not I'm going to be fired. I haven't the least idea what I'll do." He told this later to the social worker who had tried to explain to him the sense of insecurity of the unemployed and added that now he understood what she had meant.

Even in prosperity workmen feel some insecurity. It is customary among employers to discharge men without giving them much time before they must leave, often without more than a day's notice. Where skill is required employers do not lightly discard a skillful man but workmen realize the uncertainly of their tenure. Furthermore, with so much technological unemployment, even in prosperous times, workmen are conscious that others are ready to take their places. Insecurity is bad enough at any time, but in depression millions have lost their jobs and do not know where to turn.

Children in these families feel the anxiety of their parents and it affects their behavior. Older children suffer also because they must go to work to help support the family when they are not old enough for that responsibility. Perhaps most children are not trained as they should be to take responsibility. They may have been indulged too much and may feel resentful when they have to give up clothes and pleasures to contribute to the family necessities. But there is a difference between this plain selfishness of children and the natural shrinking from responsibility before a child is old enough for it.

The younger children of a family suffer from their contacts with their nervous elders, though many of them are not visibly affected by it. We have seen children who apparently were not affected and other records agree with ours on this point. Thus we find such statements as this: "There is no apparent change in the attitude of the children, although they are keenly alive to the feeling of discontent that prevails in the home." However, we are not to conclude that a child is not affected merely because he or she does not show the effects at the time. Any psychopathic hospital will have records of psychoneurotic cases that date back to childish experiences which, at the time, did not betray even to parents the slightest evidence of any such effect on the child. On the other hand we know children who have been obviously affected by the emotional instability of their parents. Other records give similar cases. For instance we find this statement about a family in Cambridge, Massachusetts:

The bitterness engendered by the experience [unemployment], especially in the father, will probably be a lasting impression. A definitely anti-social attitude is evident in one of the little boys. This is possibly an echo of the father's repeated bitter statement that the country should provide work for the man who is willing to work and does not want charity. It is hard to say what attitude may develop in later life in this child's adjustment to society.[1]

---

[1] Elderton, *Case Studies in Unemployment*, p. 130.

So this little boy is paying for the depression. It is costing him a normal personality, as it is thousands of other children. The child may get his father's resentment or he may develop an attitude of fear and shrinking because his father has changed from a kind parent into an ugly animal. So we find in the records such statements as this: The children "cling to her (their mother) and are afraid of their father."[2]

The solicitude of children on account of family situations comes out in curious little ways. For instance, a little girl of eleven went as a "fresh air" child from New York to an upstate town for a two weeks stay. Her father was a laborer and the family had suffered from unemployment for two years. He was then working every other week for $25 a week. There were several children. Ann was pale and thin and evidently had been undernourished for a long time. After a few days of enjoyment in her fresh air home by the lake, bathing with other little girls and learning to paddle a canoe and having her first ride in a motor boat and her first sail, she sat down to write a letter home. This is all she wrote:

"Dear Mother:
Did father bring home all his pay"?

Either because solicitude for her family was still uppermost in her mind, in spite of all the new joys, or because she did not like to tell her mother of her enjoyment because of her consciousness of how the family were suffering, she made no mention of the fun she was having. It seemed to us that the family cloud hung over her during the entire two weeks.

Where a home is temporarily broken up because the father is unable to get work and the parents have to commit their children to an institution, the experience seems to have a lasting effect on some children. After the family is reunited they show a nervous anxiety in certain situations, which seems to be a result of the experience. Records from cities outside New York, as well as our own, support this conclusion. For instance: "The effect of breaking up the home has caused the children

---
[2] *Ibid.*, p. 134.

to be very suspicious and the oldest boy is distrustful of his parents. It is also difficult to get these children into clinics to have their defects corrected. They fear they are going to be sent away."[3]

In the case of older children, to the disturbing influence of anxious parents is added the strain of an unsuccessful search for work. The situation was well described by Miss Kahn before the United States Senate Committee on Unemployment Relief: "I think it has not been brought out that in the early period of this so-called depression, one of the out-standing features was the fact that young people could get jobs when old people of forty years and over could not, and it has become quite customary for families to expect that their young members who are just coming of working age can replace . . . the father. It is easy to forget about these young boys and girls 14, 15, 16, 17, 18 years of age. . . . These young people are having their first work experience, an experience not with employment but with unemployment . . . they are looked to as potential breadwinners in the family, they are under the same strain, the same onus that the father of the family is under, suspected of malingering, suspected of not wanting to work—all of these things which the average individual sees not as clearly as we see them in terms of millions of unemployed."[4]

Many of these boys and girls develop mild forms and sometimes more severe forms of neuroses. We find neurasthenia. Because of nervous exhaustion little difficulties are magnified and look like great obstacles. Boys and girls lose courage and want to give up entirely. We find psychasthenia. Boys and girls sometimes are so obsessed with the necessity of finding work and the fear of not finding it that they can think of nothing else. I have just talked with a boy who is the sole support of his mother. He has been out of work for seven months and can think of nothing but the necessity of finding some kind of a job. He has lost fifteen pounds from worry

---

[3] *Ibid.*

[4] Testimony of Miss Kahn before the U. S. Senate Committee on Unemployment Relief, pp. 75-76.

and has a severe case of psychasthenia. Those who stand against adequate relief and make the children pay are getting not only their pound of flesh but many pounds. When they are again employed some children suffer from a constant fear of losing the job. Their psychasthenia continues. It is woven into their mental processes and will afflict them for years, perhaps for life. We find hysteria, a tendency to explode over little things. Potentially explosive situations in family relations, in neighborhood relations, in relations with employers become actually explosive. Youths become so "sensitive" that antagonisms develop over little slights and snubs.

In addition to these well-defined types of neuroses there is a great variety of emotional disturbance caused by the depression. We find bewilderment and mental confusion, a loss of assurance and a sense of futility and inferiority. Other youths have an emotional sense of superiority, as they feel that they are a part of a much talked about problem. We find, on the one hand, a fatalistic feeling of helplessness against too great odds, on the other hand aggressive resentment and bitterness against "capitalists" or against certain employers or corporations in the neighborhood. Again, there are on the one hand, cases of an extreme restlessness and a craving for excitement leading to gambling, drinking and sex escapades, and on the other a loss of pride and self-respect, an avoidance of social contacts and a retreat within the lonely and depressed self.

We have found these nervous disorders among the youth of New York cities and, according to our records, they are found in other states. Different mental troubles are sometimes seen in boys of the same family. For instance it is said of a family in New York City: "The rather severe behavior problems of the younger boy, which consisted of truancy, staying away from home, quarreling with the older brother, disobeying the mother . . . were all greatly increased by the tense atmosphere in the home. . . .

"The older boy, always quiet and responsible, took a great deal of the worry upon his own shoulders and withdrew more and more from activities with boys his own age. He was torn between the desire to go on with his schooling and the feeling that his help was needed."[5]

To what extent are these nervous troubles temporary? May we expect that those afflicted will entirely recover when prosperity comes again? We cannot say. We know that the emotional attitudes acquired in childhood persist with extraordinary tenacity. Doubtless we shall reap what we are now sowing because of the inadequate protection we are giving these children.

Nervous disorders are devastating to family life. One has to study the records of a psychopathic hospital fully to realize this. The therapy of the hospital involves a study of the family life of patients and the removal of conditions that have caused the disorder, if possible. The cause is often found to be unemployment, which has strained the relations between parents and children to the breaking point. Here is a typical case. A father and son had been out of work for many months. They stayed around the house a good deal because they had nowhere to go. Each developed a grouch against the other and one day they had a fight. The father had the boy arrested and he was turned over to the psychopathic hospital. His case was diagnosed as one of emotional instability caused by the depression. His father was found to be suffering in the same way. The boy was sent to live with his grandfather, where he got along all right. The relations between this boy and his father probably never will be the same again. They were alienated by the depression.

Human frailty requires no apology. It is a cold fact that must be accepted. The nervous system is the most delicate of mechanisms and our economic institutions have not been developed with any consideration of the requirements for mental health of the workers, but with a view to winning profits for the owners. However, those with mental disorders have to be cared for and that responsibility rests on the whole community. Therefore the community must deal with the economic causes of mental disorders.

Mental disorders alienate husband and wife. The records of

---

[5] Elderton, *Case Studies in Unemployment*, p. 84.

a psychopathic hospital yield a volume of stories, no two just alike, about the ways in which husband and wife have been alienated, temporarily or permanently, during the depression. Even where the alienation is only temporary their relations may never be the same again. The memory remains, the lack of assurance continues and the sense of insecurity as to the future saps the joyousness of life. For instance a certain young woman was brought to a psychopathic hospital suffering from neurotic fainting spells. She would have them on the street or anywhere, and would be taken to a general hospital and transferred from there to the psychopathic hospital. At first she was merely treated and returned home the same day. But she continued to be sent to the hospital and finally was kept there for observation. It was learned that her young husband had been out of work for a long time and finally had taken to drinking when he could earn the price of a drink. He never before had touched liquor. She saw him going to pieces for lack of work and the extreme worry developed this neurotic condition. The hospital insisted that the city provide this man work. He was given work, stopped drinking and her fainting spells ceased. But who will say that the relation of this husband and wife ever again will be as happy as it was before? Such an experience instills a dreadful sense of insecurity. If his work is regular, the years will dispel this anxiety more or less. But will work be regular, after this depression, for the millions now out of work? What reason have families for thinking that it will be?

Another kind of case that has been appearing in psychopathic hospitals is that of the unmarried young woman who has lost her job, has no relatives or friends to whom she feels free to turn, broods over her predicament and suffers physical privations until the combined effect of forced inactivity, loneliness, hopelessness as to the future and privations starts a mental disorder. We have just had a case brought to our attention of a young woman who, in addition to all these distresses, lost all she had saved because of a bank failure. This was the last straw and she had to be taken to a hospital.

The psychopathic hospitals that were visited could not furnish statistics of the increase of cases due to the depression. Before the depression began, the increase of mental cases had become an outstanding social problem, and it is to be assumed that this increase would have continued during 1930-1932 if there had been no depression. How much of the increase during these years can be assigned to the effects of unemployment and our inadequate welfare practices is, therefore, impossible to determine.

The increase in institutional cases is going on in spite of the effort of psychiatric social workers and others to keep mental cases out of institutions and in their normal social relations, as far as possible. The wisdom of this policy is, in many cases, doubtful. It is due to the mounting public expense of mental disorders, to the crowded conditions of institutions and the lack of proper facilities for treatment.

It is sometimes asserted that the mental disorders caused by the depression would have come sooner or later if there had been no depression. If this stress had not arisen some other would. This opinion gains plausibility from cases of well-to-do and rich people who suffered financial losses and became psychoneurotic but were not by any means in need. Well organized business men began appearing at the psychopathic hospitals soon after the depression started. Wives of well-to-do and wealthy men began having break-downs. Physicians point to the fact that many of these people showed some trace of emotional instability earlier in their lives. For instance, here is a woman who began having psychoneurotic spells as a child. Her father was a wealthy and prominent man, punctilious and somewhat of a martinet in his home. She married a man of a similar type, wealthy, well-organized himself and expecting the members of his family to show the same traits. This family was hit by the depression, had to discharge two servants, though they still kept two, and had to cut down contributions to charitable organizations. Shortly after the woman had cut their church contribution, which had been some two thousand dollars a year, to five hundred, she had a break-down. She had been very devoted to her church. Such cases are offered as supporting the contention that people afflicted mentally, as a result of the depression, were unstable emotionally before, sometimes from childhood, and sooner or later would have broken under some stress. But why were they unstable in the first place? In the case cited, the instability was said to be due to the family life of the woman when she was a girl. But we have just shown that the depression is causing these home conditions for many children. That is, the depression is laying the foundations in children of the emotional instability which will predispose them to breakdowns. Therefore, though it may be true that in the case of grown people, the stress of a depression is just one of many situations that may precipitate a break-down, it may be fairly argued that in many children it marks the beginning of the emotionally unstable personality that will predispose the individual to be undone by some stress later on.

No doubt many people who have temporarily broken under the depression and who have had "a mental cathartic," as one expert terms it, will be stronger ever after. They will not again have hysteria over what the Joneses might say when they heard that they had lost their money. They have learned to rid the system of other foolish emotional attitudes, to get and keep a sane view of their own capabilities, to preserve equanimity in time of stress. While church attendance is diminishing, for lack of church clothes, the spiritual background of many people is strengthening. Nevertheless, with all due allowance for these fortunate outcomes of many breaks and near breaks, the fact remains that children and youth are too young to react in this way. They are more apt to be shaken by an emotional experience which will predispose them to one or another type of psychoneurotic reaction later on.

The question arises as to the final responsibility for these mental injuries of children and youth. In New York the Public Welfare Law provides: "A public welfare district shall be responsible for the welfare of children who are in need of public care, support and protection." The office is to act in a way to prevent mental troubles, and if the commissioner has reason to suspect the beginning of a mental trouble, he is to provide an expert mental and physical examination.[6] How-

---

[6] Sections 103, 106.

ever, most offices provide little or no mental hygiene treatment. The obligation to prevent mental disorders obviously requires a public welfare official to make such provision for a family as will relieve it of the intense anxiety that will cause disorders. This is not done. In the last analysis, it is due to the attitude of the community. The people are generally ignorant about the provisions of the law. They know nothing about the effects of unemployment on the mental life of the unemployed. If these are brought to their attention some are indifferent, others show shocked interest but this does not lead to constructive action. On this ineffective community sentiment must the responsibility for conditions finally rest.

There are two main groups of mental sufferers: the unemployed who are up against dire need, and the well-to-do who have taken a fall, who needed only a turn of the market to put them back where they were, and to encourage whom "rosy promises" were long made. To the latter Mr. Lippmann, after noting the failure of the professional optimists, addresses his own preachment: "The prevailing nervousness is the result, not of what the people at large have suffered but of their disappointment. The very great majority of us are still in a material sense far better supplied than any people in all history. The nervousness comes from the fact that we have lost so much of what we imagined we had that we do not at the moment see an end to our losses. We are magnifying our losses because we had inflated our gains. The memory of those phantom profits haunts us and has established in our minds a wholly false standard of what we have a right to expect; it has been the false standard of what is normal that has, during the disappointments of this year, exaggerated out of all proportion our real losses and our real perils."[7] Into this series of ideas distressed souls among the well-to-do are invited to escape. But what about the unemployed? Are their sufferings largely imaginary? Would it not help those who are wrought up over their paper losses if they would face the real suffering of others and try to do something about it? The

[7] *New York Herald Tribune*, Jan. 1, 1932, quoted in report of U. S. Senate Committee on Unemployment Relief, pp. 375-76.

real situation is hunger, cold, some people living in tents through the winter months, some children barefooted in the snow,[8] many more people without proper shelter and many children with bare feet sticking through their shoes. People with imaginary woes would do well to get interested in those with real troubles.

---

[8] U. S. Senate Committee on Unemployment Relief, p. 347.

CHAPTER VI

MORALE TOTTERING

MORALE MEANS an integration of personality that makes the individual effective in social adjustment. Children as well as adults are dependent for integration on the opportunities afforded by the environment. The school carries on the integration begun in the home. It may prepare the child for adequate adjustment to life or may become a monotonous routine, curbing wholesome desires. When we have come to appreciate this social function of the school, we shall realize that it is primarily a character building enterprise. As such it is closely related to other child welfare institutions.[1] We may, therefore, begin our study of the effects of unemployment on the morale of children in the school. Begin there with the visiting teacher who is the central figure in character development and work back into the homes. What visiting teachers see in the school furnishes the clues which they follow out in their efforts to improve deteriorating morale.[2]

It is a common observation in the large cities that many children come to school hungry. This, teachers say, has various effects. Hunger makes some children irritable, others sleepy. Either condition interferes with study. Compulsory education becomes merely compulsory school attendance. The undernourished condition also makes children irritable, quarrelsome with one another and quick to feel resentment against the teacher. A school principal in a large city remarked: "I said to the teachers last fall: 'Whenever you have a discipline case,

---

[1] Seman, "The Place of Character Development Agencies in our Jewish Social Program," *Jewish Social Service Quarterly*, Sept., 1931, p. 17.
[2] On the training and work of the visiting teacher read Abbott, *Social Welfare and Professional Education*, Ch. V; Benedict, *Children at the Cross Roads*.

ask this question: What has he had for breakfast?' Which usually brings out the fact that he has had nothing at all."

Low vitality may cause children to care less than before about their general appearance. Then, too, poverty makes it more difficult to buy the materials with which to keep clean. One principal of a large school writes: "There is every evidence that clothing has to be worn longer and handed down to a greater extent to younger children. And clothing has to be worn longer between washings. Mothers must economize on soap and hot water." Also the mother feels too tired to be as particular as she once was. So her attitude and their own feeling combine to make them careless about how they look.

Teachers find that family quarrels are more frequent than formerly. Children get into a quarrel and cannot drop it even after it is settled. Home quarrels are more frequently brought to teachers by mothers and children than before. One common complaint of mothers is that a child is irritable or sulky and will not speak to her.

Parents also bring other problems to the school principals and visiting teachers. The latter become "trouble shooters," on whom the community comes to rely, and no economy could be more foolish than to diminish the number of these experts at the time when they are most needed. The number should be increased. Fathers and mothers appreciate more than ever before what a school can do for them and their children, and this sentiment should be fostered at this time when other institutions are inadequate.

Children often are foolishly allowed by their parents to try to find work, when the labor market is crowded with children out of work. These children are sometimes taken advantage of by employers, who pay them very low wages. The public welfare office sometimes pieces out these insufficient wages paid children with relief, instead of challenging the justice of the wage, and thus the public is really helping the employer pay his wages. Still employers feel not only justified but rather virtuous in paying these low wages because the children "need the money." However, the exploitation of children is not as widespread as might be supposed, because of the ease with which employers get adults to do the child's work at the child's pay.

Children bring to the visiting teacher, whom they learned to know while in school, accounts of the way in which they are being exploited as laborers. They say: "Why, Miss......, I cannot pay my carfare and get my lunch for that." It takes wise child guidance to point out convincingly that the child must not lose his or her faith in all people just because some employers are taking advantage in this time of dire need.

Children are on the streets selling this and that, trying to make a few pennies for the family, and incidentally falling a prey to the temptations involved in this semi-begging. We have met these children in all the cities investigated and we find similar cases in records from other cities. For instance: "Sam, who is fifteen, peddles nuts of various kinds around the neighborhood and spends much of his time out of school in the so-called 'soft drink' places,—in reality bootlegger's places. He goes from one to another, wherever there are men gathered in the pool rooms and cigar stores to sell his nuts. Sam is becoming difficult to manage."

UNEMPLOYED CHILDREN

The loss of morale among older children is still more evident than among younger for they have finished school and are old enough to work but can find no work. From the meagre reports at hand, more working children have been unemployed than for any other age classification of workers under sixty. What this means in terms of welfare is stated in a pamphlet issued by the Division of Junior Placement of the New York State Department of Labor, which has supervision of the seventeen junior employment offices in New York State: "Experience has shown that a period of business depression means to the interviewer in a junior employment office a seemingly endless stream of boys and girls applying for work. Day after day these children come, thousands of them each month, many without breakfast, insufficiently clothed or without carfare to get to a job even if one were offered. On every hand too, from

parents, teachers, and social agencies, comes an almost un-
varying story of dire need at home, of serious unemployment
among older members of the family, and of children leaving
school only to join the already hopelessly large number of unemployed boys and girls.

"To meet this incessant demand for work, the number of
jobs available is wholly inadequate. During the period from
November 1, 1930, to June 1, 1931, for example, for every
job available for seventeen year old boys and girls, there were
approximately three applicants, for every job open to sixteen
year olds there were four applicants and for every job open
to children under sixteen years of age there were approximately
five applicants."

Remedial measures for youths out of work differ, in the
nature of the case, from those for adult unemployed. Work
relief cannot be provided for children because they cannot be
employed on public works. If employers are urged to make
emergency jobs, this merely displaces adult workers.

The most valuable relief is that which gives these boys and
girls further training. The adult workers who first lose their
jobs in a period of unemployment are those who have had no
special training and who began their working life very young.
These child laborers drift into occupations that are blind
alleys and they become our drifters and misfits. They are not
only the first to be laid off but the last to be hired when conditions improve. In a time of unemployment the emphasis
should be on training the young rather than on trying to find
them employment. Schools should adapt their vocational classes
to the emergency situation.

The mental attitude of working children makes this new
school adjustment difficult. Merely to be thrown out of work
does not put a child into a mood to go back to school. He is
apt to feel humiliated that others of his age are so far ahead
of him. Nevertheless, the right kind of a school will benefit
these children. And it will encourage children who have not
yet left school to keep on in order to start life in a vocation
in which they will not be so hard hit by a depression as is the
untrained boy or girl.

WANDERING CHILDREN

Thousands of boys[3] (one estimate places the number at two hundred thousand[4]), with a scattering of girls, are wandering over the United States, some of whom have no homes, but most of whom have left homes which unemployment had made unbearable. The majority probably are between sixteen and twenty-one, though many are younger. In the centers established to care for these boys in some cities there are boys from almost every state in the Union.[5] Some of them ran away from home, others were told by their parents to go and find a job. Some of these boys have been on the road a year and a half, have been unable to find any work at all and have not been allowed to stay anywhere more than twenty-four hours. Some boys have been back and forth across the continent several times; nothing is done to settle these boys anywhere, they are just kept moving. They hitch-hike and ride freight cars. I have seen freight trains pass with a hundred or more riding between and under the cars, and no telling how many more inside. Railroad officials rule that transients shall be put off and each town plans to protect itself from an avalanche of hungry boys by setting a twenty-four or forty-eight hour limit on their stay. So the boys have to be endlessly on the move. One day a boy was found reading this letter from home: "The mine is closed and is going to stay closed. Dad is unable to find work. I am trying to find a job in the shirt-waist factory and so is Margaret. Stay where you are. Love. Mother."

"Stay where I am," he cried. "Little they know about it. I've been back and forth between San Francisco and New Orleans seven times, 'cause I had to. Every town I got to, the police came around and said I had to move on in twenty-four hours."[6] Many of the hitch-hikers are killed walking along the highways. In 1931 over eight hundred transients were killed

---

[3] McMillen, "An Army of Boys on the Loose," *Survey*, Sept. 1, 1932, pp. 389-91.

[4] Davis, "200,000 Vagabond Children," *Ladies Home Journal*, Sept., 1932, p. 9.

[5] McMillen, *op. cit.*, p. 391.

[6] Davis, *op. cit.*, p. 9.

on the highways of California. Many are killed also on the railroads. Some of the roads have put on empty cars to lessen the casualties and to prevent breaking into cars. Some boys are given jail terms by the magistrate of the city where they get off or are thrown off. The fact that he is giving a boy a jail record merely for leaving a poverty-stricken home and wandering about does not seem to bother him. On the contrary he feels rather self-righteous about it—"If every town gave you thirty days as I am going to do, you'd soon stay at home where you belong." In some cities boys are prevented from getting off trains by police who meet every train and are ordered to shoot at any boy who gets off—shoot into the air— in order to intimidate them. The boys are, of course, half starved, often sick from eating bad food, exhausted, hunted and demoralized. It is with difficulty that sick boys get medical help. Those suffering from chronic ailments, as tuberculosis, can find no medical aid at all. Some cities keep flop houses for these boys where they are given the poorest kind of food and sleep on the cement floor, but outside of these cities their dwelling places are the "jungles" along the railroad track— spots under trees where often hundreds of boys congregate, cook what food they have been able to get, and sleep. "Railroad officers are practically unanimous in attesting the honesty of the present migrant throng. Thefts have increased little if any on most of the lines."[7] But in the "jungles" they meet hobos and criminals and learn lessons in crime. Miss Davis tells of one boy who went out to find work because his father, ill with diabetes and smitten by the depression, could not support the family and who, unable to get work, had been persuaded by two men to help them rob a bank. A man was killed and, according to the law of that state, all were equally liable for the killing, and the boy along with the other, was sentenced to death for murder.[8]

These thousands of boys, most of whom are wandering through no fault of their own, victims of unemployment, are bound to suffer permanent injury and general demoralization.

---

[7] McMillen, *op. cit.*, p. 390.
[8] Davis, *op. cit.*, p. 46.

Nothing is being done for them except casually in some cities. They are merely forced to move on. Naturally every locality is concerned with conserving its resources for its own needy and so gives these rovers the cold shoulder. Miss Grace Abbott offers some suggestions as to what should be done: "Unless there is some constructive planning, thousands of young people who graduated this year into unemployment and dependency will seek escape from intolerable home conditions in the irresponsibility, adventure and quasi-outlawry of a transient life on the road." She urges adequate relief for the families of these young people, an effort through publicity about the hardships of wandering to keep youths from taking to the road, the provision of further schooling for those who are coming out of school this year, and new types of recreation. "These are of fundamental importance in maintaining the morale of young people at a very critical period. . . . Repressive measures to stem the rising tide of transients are wholly impractical, but there are steps which the federal government might take in aiding the states. Assistance should be given preferably to the state agency charged with responsibility for the relief of unemployment, but in the absence of such to local communities in which it is shown that the local transient burden exceeds the load which any community can reasonably be expected to bear and which set up a program for care in which the Federal Government can participate." "If Federal aid were given, attention could be concentrated on stopping the army of transients where it now is." "Each application for a Federal grant would be expected to outline a plan for a local training program of some description for those who cannot be sent home." "We may expect, unless something is done, that the army will be recruited by large numbers who are coming out of school this year."[9]

SCHOLARSHIPS FOR BRIGHT CHILDREN

Many of the children who have to leave school because of financial stress are very bright and their families are so loaded with debts that these children never again will go back to

---

[9] Davis, *op. cit.*, p. 50; McMillen, *op. cit.*, p. 393.

school unless helped. The amount of the scholarship need not be large. In many cases five dollars a week during the school year or even less is sufficient. This is an enterprise for Rotary and Kiwanis clubs, churches and lodges.

These bright boys and girls often develop a very pronounced attitude of resentment against society because of having to give up school. The injustice rankles. They cannot forget it:

Oliver Gorham had to leave shcool at fifteen and go to work. He developed a keen resentment because of his lost opportunity. Then he happened to get the attention of the children's bureau of that city, which was able to place him in a vocational school. There he took high rank and his resentment was disappearing. But just when his progress was most promising he became sixteen and the bureau could no longer help him. He had not yet learned enough to get a fair start in life and went out, possibly to use his brains against society instead of constructively.

The poignancy of the disappointment at having to leave school is brought out in this story of a Chicago boy, [10] taken from the records of Hull House:

"What the teacher say, Jimmie, when she talks to you?"

Jimmie Capasso blushed, and in response to his father's question shrugged his shoulders and mumbled, "Oh, nothing."

His brother Louis, eleven years of age, in whose eyes Jimmie was some important fellow, piped up, "The teacher said that Jimmie was a bright boy and he ought to go on to high school."

A smile which threatened to spread over Mr. Capasso's face at the beginning of this speech changed to a frown. The mother bending over the stove looked up with interest. . . .

"What's the matter you, Jimmie, you want to go to school? Sixteen year I work pick and shovel . . . you big now, you fifteen . . . no more school; you get him job." . . .

There were a dozen boys in the waiting room of the first place he went to—a candy factory on Harrison Street. Jimmie sat in the corner of the room feeling very much out of place. After an hour's waiting a man came out and said, "Not hiring any boys this morning." . . . It was nearly noon when he slunk up the alley, like one who has committed a crime, and slipped into the smelly shelter of his poor home. . . . Jimmie was at home alone. He lay face down on a bed, tired, disappointed and discouraged. The thing he had looked forward to for years was not to be his. All but two of his

---

[10] Elderton, *Case Studies in Unemployment*, pp. 194-201.

graduating class had gone on to high school and he, brightest of the boys, couldn't go.

Walking over to the cupboard he took from a shelf the picture of his graduating class. He had "come good" in that picture, his high forehead, eyes far apart, and his hair carefully parted in the middle. His blue serge suit had cost eleven dollars and was the best suit he ever wore. . . . As he put the picture back he saw his father's revolver. Taking it down he handled it nervously. Stories of hold-ups came to him—that boy they called "Casey," who had held up the man on the north side and got away with it. Casey had tied a cloth over his face so the man couldn't tell who he was. Taking one of the cloths from the line drying over the stove, Jimmie tied it about his face and went through the antics of a hold-up man. . . . "Stick 'em up"! he whispered, brandishing the gun. "Hand over that wad! Gee if I only had the guts to hold up some guy, I could tell them I found it, and then I could go to high school. Stick 'em up!" he commanded, this time feeling a bit more confident. Crash went the gun! The explosion in the small closed room was deafening. The revolver fell clattering to the floor. The bold hold-up man of a minute before was now a trembling and much-frightened boy. Tearing the cloth from his face, he opened the cellar door and flung the gun down into the darkness, and later hid it.

Jimmie's attempts to get work were fruitless. He would start out every morning, go to one or two places asking for work, then sneak back to his home and in a warm corner behind the stove step out of the world of reality through the portals of a story book. He had gone three times to the candy factory on Harrison Street, and felt that it was useless going there again. One of the boys suggested trying the Loop Stores. The first one he went to got him all excited. They gave him an application blank to fill out and he was sure he had a job at last. . . . At the next store, he was given another blank and had to go through the same routine again. He realized then that filling out an application blank didn't always mean a job. It was often just a convenient way of saying, "We don't want you."

As the days passed and he found no work his father became more severe. Jimmie looked forward with dread to his parent's return from work each evening. His mother would warn him at the approach and he would drop the book he was reading and slip out a side door. One day Mr. Capasso came home earlier than usual and caught Jimmie reading. He was convinced by this time that his son was lazy and that he didn't want to work. "What's the matter you, Jimmie"? he raved, "Your mother all the time cry. Antoinnette no got shoes. You eat, sleep, no can find work. All the time read book. You good-for-nothin' bum." Silently Jimmie took the rebuke. His father had called him a bum. That night he slept little. He was conscious of every toss and groaning of his two brothers sleeping in the bed with him. He resolved to get a job in the morning or not to come back home.

It was dark when he got out of bed and put his shoes on—he had slept in his clothes. He left the house before his father was awake. The temperature was down near zero and a strong wind was sweeping in from the lake. Jimmie got as far as Canal Street. His determination to get a job began to waver. He knew he couldn't face those employers again and ask for work. And he was cold. He'd go back and get warm and start out a little later. As he approached the house he saw his father dimly through the ice-coated windows of the kitchen. He hadn't the courage to go in and face him. He stumbled down the steps into the dark cellar out of the biting cold.

He couldn't get a job and he didn't even have the "guts" to be a bandit. God, if he could only have gone to high school! In a corner he found the gun where he had hidden it under some old boards. As he picked it up, the door leading to the kitchen opened and his mother came down the stairs. He crouched, hardly daring to breathe. He could hear his father cursing in Italian because he didn't get a job. His mother returned to the kitchen with an armful of wood and closed the door.

The boys had said that a bullet in the heart just took you off like nothing. You never felt it. What was the use of living? He could picture himself lying in a casket near the kitchen window with flowers and candles and all the people from the street coming in to look at him. His father would be sorry, then, that he wouldn't let him go to high school. And he wouldn't have to look for a job. Placing the muzzle of the gun against the place on his sweater where he could feel his heart beating, he pulled the trigger. There was a jarring sound which seemed a long way off. His side felt numb. He threw the gun from him and the effort sent a stinging pain through his chest. It felt as though someone was holding a red-hot poker against his bare flesh. The pain increased with every breath. He crawled on his hands and knees carefully up the stone steps and out into the cold air. His head was dizzy and things seemed blurred. He must get a job or his father would hit him now. If the pain would only give him a break. He rested for a minute, in the narrow passage between the two buildings, and then with a burst of courage started down Bunker Street toward the Loop for the second time that morning.

A trolley passed as he neared Canal Street. It seemed to be floating in air. Dimly he saw the outline of the clock tower on the freight station. He tried to tell the time, but the spots of light which took the place of figures danced before his straining eyes. He reached out and held on to a lamp post. "If I could only get a job," he sobbed, and slid down on the cold pavement, unconscious.

At the county hospital, the doctor who extracted the bullet said that Jimmie had a good chance to recover. But Jimmie didn't want to get well. Recovery for him meant looking for a job which he couldn't find. He lay there listless, not caring. There was a scene when his parents came in to see him. "You, Jimmie, why you kill yourself"? reproached his father. . . . His mother wrung her hands and moaned. Going over to Jimmie, she kissed him and kept repeating in Italian, "My big boy, why you kill yourself"? The nurse, fearing the effects of the excitement, ushered them out.

The papers, ever alert for the spectacular, wrote up the shooting, "Boy of Fifteen Can't Get Job: Shoots Self." Every day for weeks Jimmie had fought against odds. That battle was not mentioned. They had written up his defeat. The nurse showed Jimmie the newspaper clipping. Above the write-up was his picture taken from the graduation group. His class ribbons hung from the lapel of his coat, and in his right hand was the rolled diploma. He was glad he had on the blue serge suit. He never could figure out where his mother had gotten the money for it. He smiled feebly as he read his name in print, and turned his face to the wall to hide the tears.

A year later the father showed me Jimmie's picture, and while the tears streamed down his face told me of the bad luck that was following his family. . . . "My girl, fifteen, she died, sick a de chest. Jimmie, fifteen, he die. . . . Mother she all time cry. Children no got shoes, no clothes, sometimes go to bed hungry. Who going to help me? Next boy, Ralph, he still too young. Wait 'nother year before he get through school, go get job."

The outcome of this case is unusual but it is typical of many deserving boys and girls who have lost the opportunity for an education and are well nigh as hopeless, though they may not be so goaded to desperation.

DETERIORATION THROUGH UNEMPLOYMENT

The integration of personality involves the satisfaction of two main organic desires, the desire for action and the desire for rest and sympathy. The desire for action is satisfied by wholesome work and the desire for rest and sympathy by real recreation. Children and adults are dependent on their environment for work and recreation. They have to take whatever is offered, whether it satisfies or not. Our social order does not very successfully meet the need for character building work and recreation. In a period of unemployment people are deprived of both and there is a deterioration of personality.

Essential in morale is the attitude to work. It is the nature of the organism to function, to be active in the satisfaction of its needs. The whole animal creation is active in getting subsistence. The human organism is not different from any other in this respect. The glands pour their hormones into the blood stream, the cortical and other nerve reserves are in unstable equilibrium. There is, then, an organic desire for action, just as there is an organic desire for food. The desire for action cannot be denied satisfaction, any more than can the desire for food, without weakening the organism. During unemployment men have not the proper nourishment, they are forced to be inactive, they lose muscular tonicity, vitality runs low. They become submissive, apathetic, incapable of exertion on their own behalf. This is the physiological basis for the acquiescence described in Chapter I.

Again, this country was originally settled by workers and since then the majority of men have had to work for their living. Men want to work because they have acquired this attitude from our rural heritage. Furthermore, the worker is socially approved as contrasted with one who will not work. Workers condemn lazy people who are willing to live on charity. From the beginning there have been two main social classes, the independent workers and the dependent. Men have aspired to be in the independent class and still do. Wherefore men's sense of a right to relief, even when involuntarily thrown out of work, is much weaker than their feeling of a right to work. So the proudest suffer in silence. Men have even attempted suicide rather than ask for relief. This humiliation is due to the old belief that any man who deserves a job can have one. The belief persists, even under modern conditions that belie it. Because of our social heritage, then, as well as because of the physiological drive toward action, men want to work and this desire is essential in morale. The whole series of moral ideas involved is merely habits and attitudes built up by a certain kind of environment. This was the environment of the independent farmer and the artisan who always had gainful

work to do. The ideas were handed down from father to son
and preached from the pulpit. But take away the environmental
incentive and the teaching and preaching become mere talk.
Let a man be inactive long enough and there comes a time when
he loses the habit of action. His habit then is to be inactive.
He no longer has the pride of the worker. He no longer condemns lazy people. He no longer feels that he has a right to
work. He no longer is averse to asking for charity. The right
he feels most keenly is a right to relief. This fundamental
change in the morality of a people comes slowly but surely.
We already are beginning to see evidences of it. Social workers
can see that men's bodies are becoming soft, that their minds
are losing their objectivity and dwelling on emotional states,
that men are becoming emotionally unstable. Instead of the
initiative which they once had as workers, men show an aversion to making any effort at all. One sees this in the work
relief where men who once bounded into their work move
hesitatingly. They are dependent on the stimulus of their
working comrades to keep them going. The sneering remarks
about the lack of industry of the unemployed show an ignorance
of the deterioration that results from idleness. Men are victims
of unemployment and are not to be sneered at because of
deterioration.

The principles of the moral code which grew out of the
economy of the past are thus given the lie by the conditions
of the present. Men were taught as children that industrious
work is rewarded but the industrious man finds himself denied
an opportunity to work. They were taught that thrift enables
a man to achieve economic security, but the thrifty see their
savings vanish and find themselves in the same waiting room
with the thriftless. As Rabbi Silver said in an address before
the National Conference of Social Work in May, 1932: "The
reward of years of faithful labor are the breadline and the
eviction order. The thrifty are compelled to consume their
savings in idleness and they ultimately find themselves in the
same wretched plight as the spendthrift and the wastrel.
Our system teaches the dignity of labor and surrounds it with
all forms of indignity. Youth is taught to eschew idleness, to

work hard and to accept gladly the high discipline of labor. Yet thousands of boys and girls who have become of working age since 1929 have not been able to find a day's work since and have been consigned to idleness, which is the seed-bed of mischief, crime and delinquency."[11] The point is that our moral code developed out of the habits associated with the daily work, by which alone the settlers of this country were able to survive in their never-ending struggle for existence.[12] With no work to do men are not held up to the moral code. Neither law nor preaching nor mere force of custom will preserve morality. It is essentially a type of behavior, which will continue only where economic conditions require, encourage, and reward wholesome work.

The significance of unemployment for adult workmen is, then, that it weakens the habits that constitute the morality of the worker. Its significance for children and youth is that they never acquire these habits at all. The class whom unemployment has especially injured are the boys and girls who have become of working age during the depression and cannot get work. Just at the critical time when they would begin to make the group attitudes toward work and independence, their own personal attitudes, they are denied the opportunity to do so. So demoralization is especially in evidence among the youth.

Field workers of the New York State Department of Mental Hygiene, as they travel from city to city, find many children who do not learn readily in school and so do not develop work habits in school. These mental hygienists say that society has depended on the jobs these children might get to give them work habits and stabilize them but that, during the depression, they are not getting the jobs. The result is that they are deteriorating in morale.

Boys out of work get the same bad habits that men do. The father and older boys and sometimes girls may take to drinking. They get liquor by referring men who are looking for it to a speakeasy. They are paid for this service in drinks.

[11] *New York Times*, May 18, 1932.
[12] Williams, *Our Rural Heritage*, Chs. V-XVIII.

Many boys and girls who never have drunk before have taken to it because of hunger and misery and because they can get liquor. This makes family conditions much worse.

These demoralizing effects of unemployment escape complacent members of the city of the well-to-do. They are more apt to be mindful of the deteriorating effect of prosperity, its ease and indulgence—"we have been going too fast,"—while depression means to them a momentary seriousness as they contemplate their depleted coupons and curtailed extravagances. So Secretary Wilbur, in an address to the National Conference of Social Work in May, 1932, declared that the depression is not so serious as many suppose, that "civilization is broken out with hives which irritate and bother us."[13] Those who have read the preceding pages realize that many people have been more than merely bothered.

DETERIORATION THROUGH LACK OF RECREATION

In the same address Secretary Wilbur expressed "real concern" about "the emphasis on amusement rather than recreation, the apparent decrease in substantial reading." Isolated from the city of the poor, pre-occupied with the problems of his own class, their lack of a serious interest in reading, he proceeded to tell social workers from all over the country, who were immersed in the problems of the unemployed, that one should be concerned about the poor's wanting to be amused. As a matter of fact one of the outstanding effects of the depression is that it has taken from the unemployed the usual means of recreation. Poor as these are—mainly movies—they give the members of the family an opportunity to get away from the vexations of a poverty-stricken home. Old and young alike need a change, but just when they need it most they have no money for any kind of recreation. Boys and girls who have nowhere to go and have not suitable clothing to enjoy social life naturally drift into questionable places which are the only refuge for those down and out. One city in New York, at least, has come to an appreciation of this

---

[13] *New York Times*, May 18, 1932.

situation during the depression and has formed boys' and girls' clubs that meet evenings in the public school buildings.[14] To furnish children wholesome recreation is well nigh as important as to give them food and clothing.

The mere statement of the loss of opportunity for recreation means nothing to the reader without concrete cases. The point is that a family may get public or private relief of bare needs but is allowed nothing for recreation and so cannot get away from the tension which unemployment inevitably brings into every home. So a family may go to pieces even though it is getting relief enough to satisfy bare needs. Here is a husband twenty-eight years of age, a wife twenty-seven and one boy, who are being given necessary food by the public welfare office but no recreation:

Edward and Eunice Taylor are well-educated and industrious and had a model home up to the time of the depression. They had no relatives who could help them and eventually had to give up their house and move into the home of another family with whom they had had a pleasant acquaintance. The house was crowded, trouble developed, and Eunice became so nervous that she could not sit still. She cried and wanted to end it all. She had no money to go out for diversion. Before her marriage she had been a nurse but now she could get no work because so many nurses were registered ahead of her. She accused Edward of not wanting to get work though, as she told the social worker, she did not mean it. But he thought she had lost all confidence in him. Finally Eunice disappeared. After a week she came back. She had had her diversion. Questionable? Yes, but she was not quite so near the breaking point as when she went away. This was her first lapse and those on the case believed that it would not have happened, but for the long unemployment. The continued anxiety month after month, year after year, is what wrecks morale. Probably Eunice will be going again. This family is almost on the rocks and there is the child, a fine boy of seven. As we have already said, family loyalty may make the suffering too poignant to be borne.

Joseph Winn is a skilled workman of thirty-two, his wife, Bertha, is twenty-seven and they have one boy of five and another of three. This family first came on the records of the public welfare office in April, 1931, when they had spent all their savings and

---

[14] Geneva, N. Y. under the leadership of Chief of Police R. W. Morris.

sold all their property and spent the money. Later Bertha went with her boys to live with her parents and Joseph to live with his parents, until they could no longer keep them. Then they started to live together again. In their destitution, worn with long anxiety, with no escape from it, no recreation, Bertha worried Joseph with her reproaches, which she really did not mean, and by little flirtations with young fellows who happened to come in, which gave her a momentary escape from the strain. Joseph, unstrung with worry at not getting work, got very emotional over the fear of losing her when, as he said, he saw her "let a fellow kiss her." Between June, 1931, and February, 1932, he was three times in the psychopathic hospital. The doctor declared that his condition was entirely due to anxiety because he could not support his family and because he was in debt one hundred and three dollars and was worried about his wife's behavior and about what would happen to the boys. The boys are beginning to show the results of the family tension. This family, then, is getting the bare relief given the destitute, but the anxiety for the future has broken their morale, and they are just about to go to pieces. They have no diversion, no way of escaping their plight, even for an hour, except in questionable ways. Bertha visits Joseph daily at the hospital. If, to keep out of there herself and to keep well enough to look after her boys, she indulges in the only kind of diversion within her reach, can we blame her? We could fill a volume with these stories of human frailty under unemployment and the welfare practices. Recreation sometimes seems to be even more important than food.

Psychopathic hospitals are at loss as to what to do with patients who have recovered and are well enough to go out. If they go back to the same home conditions that caused the disorder, they are apt to lapse and be returned to the hospital. And the hospital often cannot improve the home conditions.

We have discussed the tottering morale of the unemployed living in families. Still worse often is the condition of the unemployed living alone. Misery likes company even though it be miserable company. Many unemployed young people living alone get into a condition in which it is unsafe to be alone. Here is a letter from a young woman, hardly more than a girl, who proved to be perfectly normal when she finally found help. Her condition was entirely due to unemployment. She was too uncompromising in her morality, even when crushed to the earth, to make a living as thousands of young women are driven to do. She wrote:

I am making an appeal to you for advice and aid, since both my attempts to take my life have failed. I feel now that after all, there may be another lease on life.

Last August I was taken ill and went to the hospital for a serious operation. During the time that I was in the hospital I lost my position, which I had had for four years and exhausted my savings and friends forgot me.

When I came out of the hospital I was forced to give up my home, and dispense with my clothes and little valuable things in order to live. From time to time I grew more despondent, not being very strong and unable to work. I could think of no way out and I decided to end my life. I can't give any definite details of how I did this or why, but I shot myself through the stomach. It all seemed as tho' it didn't happen; I can't say that I even felt any pain—I was unconscious and then semi-conscious for two weeks. During that time friends moved me to a room in a different part of the city. When I regained health, I tried to get my nerve together. Altho' I had the best of care I was in a very critical state of mind and body.

I tried all over the city to find work and was refused in every place. The first job I was able to get my health wouldn't permit, those I could do were impossible to find. Even maids work was refused me; often was I told I was too refined and educated to fill the position offered. Finally I was put out of my room and, having grown despondent again, and feeling there was no other way out, I turned on the gas in the home where I was living and prayed to die. But again I failed and went thru' the agony and suffered untold torture—after which I came to my senses and realized that I surely should forget pride and exert my energies in finding something to keep my mind busy.

I am therefore appealing to you to help me find a position which will help to keep my mind employed and help me to forget the past and so start a new life on an upward trend. May I have an interview with you at your earliest possible convenience.

Young men also are driven to attempt suicide. A manager in the public welfare office of a large city recently went over the case of a young man who came there for assistance and was told that he would be given work relief. The man remarked that he had an injured side and could not do that work. An investigation disclosed that he had shot himself and was only recently out of the hospital. Walking about had opened up the wound again. The manager reproached him for being so lacking in back-bone as to try to take his life and the young man replied: "I determined to kill myself rather than come to this." So it appeared that he had too much back-bone to permit him to ask for charity.

Not all who attempt suicide are destitute. Here is a man who tried to take his life because he was worth only about a hundred thousand dollars. He had been worth on toward a million but had lost most of it and the comparison of his present with his past condition gave him a sense of failure and a contempt for himself that he could not stand, so he tried to end it all. Nothing is more destructive to morale than this sense of futility. Wherefore should not one's thoughts and ideals be identified with projects the worth of which is not determined merely by whether one happens to make or lose money? This is difficult because, under our economic system, the worth of any idea of a man employed by a corporation, not only of managers but of research men and engineers, is judged by one standard: Will it pay? Will it increase the profits of the company? If not, it is not considered, though it might be important for the safety of small investors, for the comfort of workmen, or the welfare of the consuming public.[15] The worth of articles submitted to most magazines and of books submitted to publishing houses is considered from the same point of view. Thus ideas have to run the money gauntlet before they get before the public. Wherefore there is an inevitable conflict between the spirit of business enterprise and interest in ideas and projects for their own sake or for the public welfare. Most men accept the money standard and feel that they have failed unless they have achieved financial success. This standard is imposed on children and little by little discourages the pursuit of projects for their own sake that is so conspicuous in children. Active little boys become inactive, cynical youths uninterested in anything that does not promise some personal gain. The economic system must be altered in a

---

[15] Williams, *Principles of Social Psychology*, Chs. V-VI.

way to stimulate achievement rather than money getting. One has only to think of the services of a Lincoln to realize that the money standard does not represent real achievement. Nothing is more essential to morale than to put money in the same category as coal or oil, that is, as a mere means for the satisfaction of needs. That being its function let income be distributed in a way to satisfy real needs and improve the morale of the people.

CHAPTER VII

SEX ATTITUDES AND PRACTICES

PROSPERITY, AS WELL as depression, has certain effects on the morale of children. There is hardly a phase of morale that is not affected by prosperity as well as by depression. Take gambling. The idleness and restlessness of depression causes boys to gamble. They can forget their worries in the thrill of the moment. But prosperity also stimulates it. Boys have more money for gambling than in depression, wagering devices multiply, and betting manias spread among boys and girls. On the other hand there are many competing pastimes in prosperity while in depression this may be the only one left. One can gamble with a penny. Thus certain conditions of prosperity lead to gambling as do certain different conditions of depression. If one could prove that there is less gambling in a period of depression than in prosperity, this would not prove that the hardships of depression do not lead to gambling. One sees boys gambling who never before did so and would not now if they were not idle and eager to make a penny, as well as ready for any diversion suggested.

Again, take stealing. In the prosperous days of easy money and under the pressure of business interests to buy and so keep prosperity with us, thrift flew out of the window in many homes and boys and girls became used to having things. Their poorer companions saw what they had, coveted what they saw, and there was an increase of stealing among these less fortunate ones. Then came the depression, stealing from cupidity diminished, but the conditions incited to stealing from other causes.

Again, take the relation between the sexes. Our prosperity was an epoch of joy rides and road-houses for many boys and girls. There is less joy riding today and the road-house business is "quiet." This phase of sex behavior is on the wane. On the other hand various conditions of a depression incite to other sex practices. In describing the effects of depression on sex practices and delinquency therefore, we are not implying that prosperity has not its own effects. But we are now concerned with depression.

Sex Practices and Personality

One of the essential forces in the integration of personality is power of concentration and persistent effort in the solving of problems and the doing of tasks. One of the main causes of impairment of this power is an emotional upset in the past experience of the child.[1] Such an upset, in older children, often is related to some sex experience. Sex attractions, unrequited sex advances, an unwise mutual attraction, uncontrolled passion, sex reveries weaken the capacity of boys and girls to attend to their school or other work. Attention to the other sex should not interfere with work but should be a means of wholesome relaxation after work is done. The main purpose of child training is to assist a boy or girl to such an integration of personality as will develop the potential rhythm from concentrated effort to pleasant relaxation. When this integration becomes an ideal it regulates behavior toward the other sex in a very wholesome way. All sex behavior that interferes with the realization of this ideal is unwholesome.

This rhythm of behavior is intimately connected with the functioning of the glands. Absorbing work tends to stimulate thyroid and pituitary secretions and to diminish gonad secretions, while idleness may result in an increase of sex hormones. This action of the organism is entirely physical and beyond rational control except as the individual may maintain his ideal and program of daily, absorbing work and to that extent control the organic processes. Unfortunately this is impossible under our economic system.

---

[1] Brown, "Continuous Reaction as a Measure of Attention," *Child Development*, Vol. I, No. 4, Dec., 1930, p. 286.

SEX PRACTICES IN DEPRESSION

Two conditions of a depression conduce to immorality. First, men and boys are no longer held fast by the discipline of regular work; so there is a letting down and youths as well as adults lapse into subservience to impulse. Second, family tension and emotional instability result in unwholesome sex practices. Sexuality is a vent for pent-up emotion and even children are affected in this way. A young lawyer whose practice included "wayward minor" cases told us of a certain section of a city where the sexuality of children was open and unabashed— "a bad situation" was all he understood about it. We found that those children were members of families under stress of unemployment. This is not saying that unemployment directly caused it. Unemployment increases family tension and that causes emotional instability in children which finds expression in sexuality.

These sex practices are, in the first instance, an impulsive, thoughtless reaction to emotional tension but they come to be more or less consciously cultivated as a compensation for family troubles and other miseries. Modern life makes this compensation all too easy. There is the idle youth with a car. Those who have lost their job and their car use the machine of a more fortunate friend. Then too girls are socially older than they were a few years ago. The auto has banished the wholesome slow maturity of the past and spread everywhere a premature sex sophistication. And the conditions under which girls live in depression enhance their interest in things sexual. School teachers say that as girls' clothes become more shabby, as they begin to wear made over clothes of other people, they go more to an extreme in the use of cosmetics and "make-up." As a girl's sense of inferiority increases because of poor clothes and the drop in the social position of the family, her impulse for recovery inclines her to an extreme use of the means of sex attraction within her reach. Girls become more extreme in their sex abandon with boys. One evidence of superiority coveted by girls is popularity with the boys and many of them are willing to pay a heavy price. Teachers say that they observe more indifference to conventions than before, more "lawlessness" as some teachers phrase it.

Another situation conductive to sex irregularities results from mothers who are employed keeping their daughters at home from school to do the house work. Fathers and brothers, though they have nothing to do, will not do women's work, so it is thrown on the girls. Often the mother is at work, the father is looking for work, a boy friend drops in and this leads to sex irregularities; or the girl spends part of her time on the streets and gets into trouble.

The increased sex interest of boys and girls leads to more reading of pornographic magazines than formerly. Reading takes the place of joy rides and is less expensive than movies. Children who cannot afford to buy these magazines rent them. In a certain city the school teachers recently uncovered a "magazine racket." A boy would rent a magazine to another boy over night for one cent and over the week-end for five cents. A boy who is "too good" to read such a magazine may be sneered at, so the renting has something of the semblance of a genuine racket.

The depression has caused a decadence of morality, not only among the immature but also among those old enough to marry. Many engaged couples feel obliged to postpone marriage in depression and this sometimes leads to irregularities. Girls are much more apt to marry just for support during hard times, and many of these marriages prove to be unfortunate. If the girl finds that she is not supported, she is not apt to be an agreeable companion. In many cases the two are so unsuited to each other that separation sooner or later is inevitable.

Another cause of increasing sex delinquencies among older girls is that mentally defective girls who were, up to the time of the depression, cared for in their own homes, because their families did not want to have the stigma of having a daughter in an institution for defectives, were forced to go out and help support the family. Many of these girls have been working as domestics and, not being mentally able to cope with men who prey on girls, some of them have been getting into sex difficulties. Some are diseased, others are turning up in psychopathic hospitals. For their own protection these girls should be placed by their relatives in institutions for the feebleminded. But in some states the institutions are overcrowded and there is no room for them.

Statistics of unmarried mothers have not shown any significant increase in our cities thus far during the depression. These statistics are very imperfect because not all illegitimate births are registered. If the statistics were complete what would a decrease in such births show? We do not know. It would not prove any decrease in illicit relations. It might be due to the fact that young people were learning birth control; or it might be due to an increase of abortions. Statistics of unmarried mothers mean nothing unless interpreted on the basis of all the contributing factors, which cannot be shown statistically for we have no statistics on the extent of birth control or on abortions.

Girls sometimes drift into immorality as a sacrifice for the needy family. Let us be specific and state a family situation in a city of New York State:

Mr. Gordon had a good wife, one daughter of seventeen, another of fifteen, and three other young children. He was an intelligent, hard-working man and had never before been in straits. The family were devoted to their church and highly respected in the community. Then came the depression, no work, tension. Evelyn, the oldest daughter, and her father walked the pavements seeking work week after week, month after month. When their resources were exhausted the public welfare department allowed the family $5 a week of relief and the man got one day's public work at $3. This must pay for their food, clothing, rent, light, and fuel. Hungry, exhausted, nerves frayed, father and daughter returned home at night, and often there were sharp words. Finally one night Evelyn disappeared. She had gone to work in a "closed dance hall," that is, a place where men do not bring their girls. Girls are furnished. She got five cents a dance and danced from eight p.m. to three a.m. She was not allowed to sit during this time. She must solicit any man who entered. A "ballyhoo man" shouted from the center of the hall to pep them up. She earned about $4.85 a week from the dancing and what she could get from the sale of her tired body after three. She had to live with the trap drummer for the privilege of working there. After awhile she contracted a venereal disease and was thrown out. Meanwhile her family had lost its place in the community. Father, mother and children ceased going to church. Their clothes were unfit.

The relevant facts in this case are: a family of seven were allowed only eight dollars a week for their support in spite of the fact that the Public Welfare Law of New York provides that relief shall be adequate. A careful check of this case shows that the family had no other income and that the girl had no previous record of delinquency. She had done well in school and was a thoroughly fine girl. The family was degraded and a girl was broken and diseased. This girl and her sister and brothers belong to the next generation of American mothers and fathers. What are we doing to the next generation?

Mary Haley was more fortunate. One of a family of six, she finally got a job at ten dollars a week. Mary's family could not get any relief at all. They must live on her ten dollars. They were half starved and threatened with eviction. She was tempted to earn more but is a girl of strong moral character and has withstood every temptation. The public welfare commissioner knew the situation. He knew the family had no other resources but became irritated at an occurrence due really to his own inefficiency. He did not care what happened to the girl. What he saw was only a girl, not one of the mothers of the next generation.

In the questionable resorts of a large city are found girls who, up to the depression, were known as strictly moral girls but who have lost their positions and are found drinking with men and making a precarious living. Thus are girls paying for the depression by sacrificing what we are accustomed to value most highly in womanhood.

Conditions that cause sexual immorality also cause venereal diseases. A disease may be just one in a long series of troubles for a boy or girl and may be due to troubles that preceded and may add to the troubles that follow. Girls who go to questionable resorts to make a living get venereal diseases. One who finds that she has a disease becomes the more desperate because she has no money for medical treatment. Boys get into the same predicament. A certain boy of nineteen who had faithfully helped to support a family of smaller children since he was fourteen was thrown out of work for months (at the same time his father had been out of work for a long period). He stole something and was put on probation, then obtained employment at five dollars a week doing a man's work for ten hours a day; then lost this job and became demoralized by the unemployment. Then he got a venereal disease, became hysterical because he had no money to pay a doctor for curing him and in this emotional state stole again and was regarded as a confirmed criminal. Troubles seldom come singly for unemployed boys and girls. It is the constant succession of troubles in the home and outside that is the undoing of many of them.

In the large cities the underworld has taken advantage of the needs of girls to exploit them. On December 20, 1931, the Committee of Fourteen of New York City, which for thirty years has combatted vice conditions in that city, reported that "the desperation of young women who cannot find work in this time of protracted depression is forcing many of them either directly into prostitution or at least into border-line occupations from which the ranks of prostitution are most generally recruited." The report stated further that "the underworld is showing increasing activity in taking advantage of this situation and of a temporary disorganization of official protective measures." The Committee pointed out that it was the first to expose a certain type of employment agency which recruits unsuspecting girls for vice resorts not only in New York and vicinity but also for Central and South America. It quoted Mr. Medalie, Federal District Attorney, as saying that local agencies were distributing as many as eight hundred girls a month to such places. It is also stated that conditions are not as bad in New York as in other metropolitan cities. When one considers the various ways in which girls get started in illicit relations in a period of depression—the idle young men driving around to pick up girls, the employers who take advantage of the need of a girl to hold a job, the family needs that drive her on to the street to earn what she can, the demoralizing crowding of two or three families into one house—one realizes how inevitably many of them finally drift into a life of vice.

Through these dark waters of demoralization and despair, so unrealized in the city of the well-to-do, and unheeded when thrust before the attention except for a passing sense of their poignancy or a shrug of incredulous shoulders, one finds certain currents which we shall do well to consider. Not only are those involved who have been swept off their feet by economic pressure but thousands of others who, knowing the conditions, think more and more lightly of moral standards and despise the self-righteous. These young men and women who are not financially in need but whose standards are beginning to waver raise queries that take direction according to their theories of morality. While many give themselves to self-indulgence without much thought, some profess to see certain good effects of the ferment—minds disabused of narrow moral ideas and of subservience to a false economic system which has betrayed these thousands of unemployed girls and boys. As we contemplate the sex practices in the light of mental hygiene, we are led to ask: what is being put in place of the vanishing standards? Is nothing arising out of the chaos more promising for personality than this girl's assertion of a right to satisfy impulses as she pleases, this boy's wish that people would mind their own business and leave him free to disagree with them in these matters, this girl's sense of rebellion against the secrecy that a self-righteous society makes necessary, this man's belief that unemployed girls are his legitimate prey? What the depression has done is to accelerate this sexual individualism, a revolt that was coming anyway but more slowly and in a fashion that could more readily have been handled constructively than now, forced on us as it is by this harsh, resistless pressure of economic need, despair, cynicism.

Social conventions are still holding outwardly and there are sincere and earnest efforts to reach in and do something about the real situation, with some beautiful and touching results. Such efforts require the utmost patience and considerateness. These boys and girls are not happy. Merely to reproach them and do nothing else only accentuates the emotional atmosphere that has driven them to mistaken behavior. The children and youth are hard hit. They need wise counsel and guidance.

Especially does every such boy and girl need to feel that some large-hearted and wise person is particularly interested in him or her. For example:

Rosalie Harris, fifteen years of age, was one of four children in a home where the depression had demoralized the father and pro-voked antagonism between father and mother. To escape this ten-sion Rosalie had slipped into questionable behavior outside and the social worker induced a woman of the city of the well-to-do to act as a Big Sister to Rosalie. Mrs. Jenkins, who had no children, invited Rosalie to her home, learned of her troubles, advised her, taught her good housekeeping, neatness in dress and gave her necessary clothing. They had tea together "just like real folks." Rosalie became devoted to her big sister and began to feel a sense of security and to have a purpose in life, that is, to please this woman whom she had come to love. Mrs. Jenkins suggested one day that she would like to know Rosalie's mother and was per-plexed when Rosalie seemed confused and noncommittal. Not until a month later did Rosalie say: "I would like to have you know my mother." A child of the poor shrinks from letting a friend in the city of the well-to-do see how her family lives. Not until her trust is very genuine does she feel that the friend will still love her after having seen her home. Mrs. Jenkins learned from Rosalie's mother that she had given up her bad companions. She also learned some-thing else very interesting. Rosalie had been regarded as dull in school but in four months her marks had improved seventy-five per cent. Mrs. Jenkins asked her how this happened. She replied: "Oh, I don't know. Everything is easier now." The libido side of Rosalie's life, that is, the desire to be loved, now being satisfied by Mrs. Jenkins' love for her, her attention to her school work was not weakened by the emotional stresses of an unhappy home or by reveries about sex experiences and she could do it with ease.

Rosalie's aim was to realize the ideals of behavior that Mrs. Jenkins and she had worked out together, and she refrained from doing what was contrary to this ideal. Girls get into sex difficulties often merely from their desire for affection. If they have the affection they crave, they will escape those dif-ficulties. The desire is not merely to be petted, but to be under-stood. To win a girl's affection a woman must have a discern-ing mind and infinite patience. The girl must believe that her big sister is not narrow but knows what is for her happiness. A woman of the well-to-do classes often is thought to know what is best merely because she is well-to-do and socially influential. But, on the whole, she must also be genuinely attached to her little sister, must make the girl feel her affection and realize that she knows what is best for her. She should have the good judgment not to build up a merely dependent attachment but to help the other to grow into the ideal that they have worked out together. This is not mere theory. It is being done. The new social work includes not merely professional but voluntary workers who, in doing this constructive work for others, have themselves learned how to live.

CHAPTER VIII

DELINQUENCY

THE LARGE MAJORITY of boys and girls brought into the juvenile court in prosperity or depression are arrested for stealing. Another delinquency is "wilful trespass," which includes entering forbidden premises, as yards or unoccupied buildings, walking on railroad tracks and picking up coal, entering cars, roaming water-fronts and entering boathouses. Another is "malicious mischief," as smashing windows and other destruction of property. Then there are the "ungovernable children" and the runaways.

STEALING

The effects of the depression on stealing are best explained in connection with the various causes of stealing. One main problem of the social worker is to determine what causes a boy or girl to steal. First, children steal because they have not the spending money that they had when their parents were at work. In the modern city, amusements are advertised and goods are displayed to attract children. They naturally want the things that our profit-seeking enterprises want them to want. They have these things in prosperity and get into the habit of enjoying them. When suddenly deprived of the means to buy these things they may steal the means if opportunity offers. Boys who steal because of this deprivation vary all the way from those who take something they think they need and, in the course of doing that, take also what they do not need, to those who are just selfishly intent on having what they do not need at all. This latter type of boy would be apt to get into trouble of some sort any time he was deprived of what he had habitually enjoyed. We have seen many examples of these two types:

Ernest Hill is a very bright fellow with no record of delinquency until the depression. During the long unemployment he could not have the clothing he used to have, wanted a sweater, broke into the Y. M. C. A. to steal one and while in there took some money also. He was not a selfish type and would not have stolen had he not thought he needed a sweater. He did not really need it.

Ralph Emmons is very selfish. His attitude is that, if his family need to get along without what they have had, at least he will not. He will have as good things as he has had in the past. So he stole various articles of clothing he did not need.

The psychopathic hospitals are getting more of these stealing cases than before the depression.

There are boys who had the use of an auto up to the time of the depression and then, deprived of it, took one to use for a ride; others took one with the intent to keep it. One of the main reasons for stealing an auto is a boy's desire to take his girl for a ride.

A second reason for stealing is some real family need. Many children feel a desperate desire to help out at home. The need is the excuse in their minds. In some family situations before us, is would appear as a valid excuse to any reasonable person. In others the stealing is not excusable to a reasonable person, but from the point of view of the child with his childish reasoning and in his situation, the stealing was inevitable.

Stealing from need is more common among boys over sixteen than among children:

John Norton is a criminal of eighteen. He is the eldest of six children. "I wasn't to blame for their having so many" he said "but I've had to work to help support them since I was fourteen." For four years before this crime he had given his parents his earnings. Then he was thrown out of work. He had not had a job for six months. His father had not worked for many months. One day in a public place he saw a coat hanging on a wall. Under a sudden impulse he searched the pockets and took $10. He was arrested and jailed. With help he paid back the money and was put on probation and later got a temporary job. What he needed was a job, not a jail.

A third reason for stealing is that children are taught to do so by parents or older brothers or sisters. They go to the market in the early morning hours to steal for the family. This instigation of stealing increases in depression.

Fourth, children steal because they never have been taught not to. A boy of thirteen made the remark that he thought every boy was a natural thief, though this boy never had stolen. He went on to explain that children naturally want things that attract them and may take them thoughtlessly unless taught better. Probably very few people can say that they never took anything that belonged to another. In the old days when boys went into the woods to build a hut they helped themselves to old fence boards. The owner did not like it but usually excused them. Children have to be taught, in their zest to carry out the plans of their imaginations, not to take what belongs to others. But in teaching them we must center not on the wrong act but on the process of which it is a result. The imaginative child lives in his own world, not in the real world, and has to be taught the difference between the two. Otherwise he will use his imagination to justify his stealing to himself and others. Now the miserable home and neighborhood conditions of a depression drive children within themselves. The imagination is stirred and strained to compensate for what is lacking in the real world. Pilfering gangs are active. Here is one record:

Edward has been detained for robbery at the House of Detention. He had left school and his mother urged him to get work. Not being able to find any he took to running about the streets with the gang,—commonly known as "The Forty Thieves." It is unlikely that he would ever have joined this gang had he found a good steady place to work, for the family influence has been very good.

Florentino, the oldest child, is now confined in an industrial school for driving away an auto—his excuse being that he wanted to see the world. Bernie, a boy of nine, a truant from school and given to pilfering, is now on probation to the Juvenile Court. No trouble of this sort occurred in this family up to two and a half years ago. . . . An echo comes from the industrial school at Manchester,—the boy writes his mother, "Be brave, mother, and tell the kids to be brave. I am to be taught a trade—something I always wanted to do—and then I'll come out and help support the family." Since this letter the following information has been secured. The family is to be evicted within the week and the children placed by order of Juvenile Court in the hands of St. Vincent de Paul Society. The mother is to go to an infirmary. In August there will emerge from Manchester a boy seventeen years old who will find the home gone, his mother away and his sisters and brothers scattered.[1]

Fifth, mothers have to go out to work to help support the family, so the children have no supervision and are on the street and follow their own devices:

Joseph Marino was brought into court for stealing two oranges and a cabbage from in front of a fruit and vegetable store. His family consists of father and mother and four children. The public welfare office allows them $5 a week and the father gets two days' work. He has not enough to eat to keep him in condition for work, nor have the children enough. The mother works when she can. One day when she was at work, the boy left home for the day and took the oranges and cabbage for his lunch. He chose food high in vitamins, anyway.

Secretary Wilbur, in the address already referred to, maintained that the depression has improved home conditions. He said: "We must set up the neglect of prosperity against the care of adversity. With prosperity many parents unload the responsibilities for their children on to others. In adversity the home takes its normal place. There is no substitute for intelligent parental care exercised throughout the day, at meal times and in controlling proper sleeping conditions at night." One who knows conditions among the unemployed groans over this description of their home life. The Secretary is thinking of the mother in his own class, with a maid in prosperity but forced to discharge her in depression and to do her own work, not of the maidless mothers of wage-earners' families who in depression are driven out to earn a dollar, leaving the children to get along as best they can. The Secretary's whole address is a good illustration of how completely a man of the city of the well-to-do may be separated from the other city and complacently interpret it in the light of his own. If there is ever any accounting for the present depression and its terrible

---

[1] Elderton, *Case Studies in Unemployment*, pp. 69-70.

effects, such ignorance and complacency in high places will undoubtedly bear a large share of the blame.

The children of the poor roam the streets and sometimes steal for adventure. Boys wander through five and ten cent stores to steal, just as country boys wander through the fields and woods to collect stones, bugs, butterflies and whatever else attracts their attention. One will see boys hurrying from school toward the five and ten cent stores, as country boys in spring hurry away to the fields and woods to hunt treasures. And as we used to display what we found to other boys and sometimes sell those things—slippery elm, spruce gum, frogs legs—so city boys display to their school mates what they got in this and that store, quite an amazing collection sometimes, and sell these things. They have their own "five and ten," only their prices are reduced.

Some store-keepers have the little thieves arrested and put on probation, but others make light of it when an adult returns things stolen by a boy. Store-keepers will not put netting around goods piled on counters and tables because it is thought that people will buy more if they are allowed freely to handle things. Thus boys are subjected to the temptations laid before those whom the merchant wishes to inveigle into buying. Furthermore, the number of clerks employed by stores is cut down in depression and children are not so carefully watched. Stores calculate on a certain percentage of loss from thefts and consider this more profitable than to take measures that would lessen the temptations before children.

Sixth, various personal situations and attitudes cause boys to steal. A boy who has not yet been thoroughly accepted by a gang will steal in order to prove his worth and so become a full-fledged member. A boy will steal because he will not take a dare or because he is the dupe of an older boy or of one more daring or clever. Boys who have some personal defect or weakness which makes them feel inferior steal to prove that they are not inferior. Boys whose parents have laid on them the burden of proving themselves superior to other boys and who have failed may steal to escape this disagreeable sense of inferiority. A boy may steal from another because the latter has better things than he has and feels superior because of it. So the stealing is to take the superior boy down a peg. These various personal situations and attitudes play a larger part in child behavior whenever corresponding situations and attitudes are predominant in the adult world. This is true in depression. It is a time of an exasperating sense of inferiority. Men and women are being humiliated by rebuffs from those to whom they apply for work and from the welfare office when they apply for relief. Boys catch this sense of inferiority in the atmosphere of the home. They are infected with it when they escape on to the street.

Seventh, a stealing episode is often tied up with a sex experience. Sex misbehavior is called sinful. The excited state of mind involved in sinning may incline a boy to go from one kind of delinquency to another. He wants to be a "divil." We have shown that depression incites to sexuality; so it does to stealing.

As one drives through the city of the poor and sees the groups of boys standing on the corners or roaming the streets with nothing to do, from four o'clock till bed-time, thousands of them in the aggregate, one wonders that there is not more stealing. Families have lost control over their boys especially during the depression and the community will have to find some occupation for them.

OTHER DELINQUENCIES

Boys out of work roam the streets and water-fronts looking for adventure. They enter old buildings thoughtlessly, just out of curiosity. This is technically known as wilful trespass. They may batter their way in and then the offence becomes malicious mischief or burglary. They trespass on the railroad track to pick up coal, jump on coal trains and take coal and then the offence becomes stealing. Depression has aggravated wilful trespass and malicious mischief.

A typical case of malicious mischief is that of Reddy Whitman: Reddy was going by an unoccupied building and suddenly let go at the windows with stones. He was nabbed by a policeman. The report of the social worker laid before the judge at the trial affirmed that "Reddy Whitman has been a good boy until this offense. He is a victim of a family situation in which tension has been aggravated by unemployment."

Depression produces "ungovernable children" and "runaways." Unemployment makes adults "ungovernable" and this spirit passes to the children. They run away from home to escape the crowding, irritability, and bad treatment suffered from adults. I have gone with probation officers to the homes of children brought into court for running away. I am certain that I should have run away from such a home. Any healthy-minded child would.

Probation officers have gone over with me the cases on probation at the time and the majority tend to be children of the poor, many of them out of work at the time. This is in line with the best researches on the causes of delinquency and of crimes committed by youth. Most delinquents and youthful criminals, even in prosperity, come from homes afflicted with poverty and more or less unemployment.

The boys and girls hardest hit by the depression are from sixteen to nineteen. Many of them are in a desperate plight. The public welfare office in some cities does not help unmarried persons, in others it gives them a mere pittance, for instance, $2.50 a week in one large city. Unmarried men are not given work relief because there is not enough for the married man. How then can these boys live? One city has established a municipal lodging house where youths and men are given two meals a day and where they must lodge, that is, no money is given for lodgings outside. Here assemble the derelicts from the four quarters of the city, as well as the unemployed of every occupation, old and young, and they sleep on cots placed close together, a hundred in a room. In other cities they flop on the floor of the public lodging houses. As one goes through a great pen of this kind one cannot blame youths for not wanting to sleep and eat there. One large city has not made any systematic provision at all for boys or unmarried men. The boys try desperately to get work but there is nothing to do. They collect junk and sell it. The people put their rubbish out in cans at night and in the morning there is almost nothing left. The boys come with push carts and take everything—bottles, newspapers, everything except the ashes. But this keeps only a few of them busy. They sleep where they can. The family welfare society gives some of them meal tickets. But they have no money for clothes, shoes and other necessities. The wonder is that more of them do not steal. Recently that city has been having an epidemic of burglaries.

The girls sixteen to nineteen also are hard hit but many get positions as domestics working in homes for their board and room and two or three dollars a week. These girls have no money for recreation and nowhere to go in their leisure hours, which makes the company of any available young man a welcome diversion. This situation has an unfortunate effect on sex morality. What these boys and girls need is recreational centers.

The depression not only has caused crime but also has made it more difficult to find work for prisoners who have qualified for parole, which prevents the discharge of prisoners,[2] and has increased the difficulty of those on parole keeping their jobs or finding new work. This of course makes it more difficult for them to keep their parole. For instance, some years before the depression a boy of twenty-one with several other boys jumped into an auto and drove around the city, finally leaving the car where the owner later found it. Evidently there was no intention to take it as his own. For this boyish prank he was sentenced to ten years in prison. After serving five years he was released on parole, got a job and did well but was laid off because of the depression. He could not get other work and was in a precarious condition because the public welfare office of the city had made it a rule to give no relief to any unmarried person without a family. But the boy's aunt took him in and her budget was slightly increased. Many boys on parole are not so fortunate.

It is impossible statistically to demonstrate the effects of

---

[2] Testimony of J. P. Murphy before the United States Senate Committee on Unemployment Relief, Dec., 1932, p. 50.

unemployment and our welfare practices on delinquency. In some cities there has been a significant increase of court cases during the depression. But the statistics do not enlighten us as to the causes of the delinquencies. They give only the kinds, that is, the legal classifications. They throw no light on the relation of delinquency to unemployment. Furthermore, the statistics of court cases in a certain city may not show any increase and still delinquency may be on the increase in that city. For instance, in one city a child welfare society took charge of children who, up to that time, were cared for by the court, so the court records showed a decrease in cases, though a careful study of all records showed that delinquency was on the increase in that city. But how much we do not know. In another city the police followed the policy of dealing with delinquents summarily instead of taking them into court, because the police saw the conditions of which delinquents were victims during a depression and hesitated to subject them to the humiliation of a court action. So there was no increase in court cases but there was an increase in delinquency, how much we cannot tell. It is evident then that statistics do not even give an accurate idea of the amount of delinquency in the cities; and they tell nothing about causes.[3]

The question is raised as to who is responsible for the delinquency arising from unemployment and the welfare practices. The Public Welfare Law of New York provides that the public welfare commissioner is to investigate complaints made to his office of the delinquency of a child, is to bring such a case when necessary before the children's court and to receive as a public charge any child discharged to his care by a court. Welfare officials are enjoined to coöperate with the children's court and with any private agency for the improvement of social conditions affecting the well-being of children.[4] What is needed, then, is local communities that aim

---

[3] The responsibility for improving statistics on delinquency and other child welfare problems rests with the local public and their representatives. Much has been done by the Children's Bureau of the United States Department of Labor in directing statistical reporting. See Breckenridge, *Public Welfare Administration*, pp. 751-52.

[4] Sections 80, 106.

to effectuate the law by holding their welfare offices and courts up to a performance that is in accord with the intent and provisions of the law. If children are paying for the depression by a sacrifice of morality and by an increase in delinquency, it is because the communities are not insisting on the improvement of social conditions and on the effective treatment of delinquency enjoined by the law.

The actual situation in most communities is something like this: A family which finds one of its children annoying tries to get rid of the nuisance by letting the child roam the streets or urging the responsibility of the school. The school teachers insist that the unruly boy ought not to be in school. Even if the city has a social worker whose function it is to do case work with such boys, the school often has not enough interest to tell the social worker about the boy. So he may be expelled from school. By this time he may be a delinquent. If now the citizens are told that delinquents are increasing in the city they say: "Send them to the reform school." The attitude is to get them out of the city. When a newspaper editor in a certain city was being urged to back a movement for boys' clubs because it would lessen the county expense of delinquencies he said: "But the city won't get the money we save the county." All he was interested in was the city. When another citizen was told that a certain efficient probation officer was keeping several boys from being sent to the state reform school he said: "But the county does not have to pay for boys sent to the reform school." The state, not the county, would bear the expense and he had no particular interest in diminishing state expenses. So there is a lack of interest beyond one's own primary group. The parent does not think of the trouble caused a school by letting a boy grow up selfish in his family relations; the school teacher does not think of what she is doing to the city by merely trying to get rid of a troublesome pupil; the city does not consider the burden it foists on the county by failing to take preventive measures against delinquency in the city; the county does not consider the expense and social menace to the state that is involved in the increase of young criminals in state institutions. Disregard for the child himself and narrow social intelligence prevent the community's realizing its enlarging obligations.

What is needed, then, is the education of the community along these lines. How is this education to be given? There ought to be classes in sociology in the public schools and a program of adult education in sociology in every city. Editors, clergymen, and civic leaders ought to equip themselves to contribute to this education as opportunity offers. Social workers ought to give more time to education. They often fail to be of service in this connection because they are apt to be more interested in getting public opinion behind them in something they want to bring to pass than in educating public opinion. This something may be wise and practicable, but in urging it they often show a perplexing lack of frankness about the larger situation of which it is a part, which repels men and women who are in the habit of doing only what they have well considered. There are in most urban localities and in most counties some people who are capable of interest in social welfare, and social workers of initiative will create opportunities for such people to learn for themselves what they need to know in order to support social work.

PART II

PUBLIC AND PRIVATE WELFARE IN ACTION

CHAPTER IX

PUBLIC RELIEF IN HOMES

THE UNITES STATES CHILDREN'S BUREAU has estimated that 72 per cent of the money raised for relief in 1930 in seventy large cities of the country was raised by taxation and only 28 per cent by voluntary contributions. In 1931 and 1932, public relief was very much more in excess of private. Are the public welfare offices functioning in a way to reduce to a minimum the disastrous effects of unemployment? Are the relief funds adequate and is relief economically and efficiently administered? Is the public office able to do the welfare work associated with its relieving function?

Under the Public Welfare Law passed in 1929, which superceded the old Poor Law in force up to that time, New York is one of the most advanced states in the country in public welfare work.[1] This is especially true of its public relief in homes. We therefore shall center on New York with the assumption that other states will eventually develop their public welfare in somewhat the same direction. Furthermore, we may assume that a critical account of relief in New York, if taken as indicating conditions more widely, will not over-emphasize the short-comings in other states.

A New York State Commission on Unemployment Problems, which was appointed to investigate the needs created by the depression, studied the administration of public relief in the fifty-nine cities of the state outside of New York City and reported in January, 1931, that only a few cities made any attempt to base public home relief on the actual needs of the applicant. The report cited one city which made home visits largely for the "spiritual uplift" of the families and limited

---

[1] Huston, *Social Welfare Laws of the Forty-eight States.*

expenditures for food to four dollars a week, no matter how large the family. The report continued: "A grocery order of about four dollars a week, regardless of the size of the family, is the practice in about half of the cities of the state." "Coal is usually given in amounts varying from one-quarter to one-half ton a month." Here is a starvation and a freezing ration for children in half the cities of the state. The report stated further that rent was paid only to save families from eviction and in some cases not then. Few public welfare offices provided any clothing or paid for light or electricity. All this, the Commission pointed out, was contrary to the Public Welfare Law of the State. The Law provides: "It shall be the duty of public welfare officials, in so far as funds are available for that purpose, to provide adequately for those unable to maintain themselves"; and "it shall be the duty of the board of supervisors of a county, the town board of a town and the appropriating body of a city to make adequate appropriations."[2]

The Commission's report related to the latter part of 1930. Relief was still more inadequate in 1931 because the available funds had to be distributed among a greater number of unemployed families. What this means in terms of personal hardship may be illustrated by the case of a family of father, mother and six children. The father, an industrious and capable workman, could not get work and the family were entirely dependent on the $5 a week earned by a daughter of eighteen. Eventually, in May, 1930, they were given $9 a week of relief the first week, $8 the second week, $7 the third week and $6 the fourth week. A baby was born the second week and weighed nine pounds. The next week it had dropped to seven because, as asserted by social workers who knew the case intimately, the mother had lost her milk and it was not being properly fed. The family was half starved. A year later, in May, 1931, the father was still out of work but their relief was reduced to $5 a week. The only other income of the family was the $5 earned by the girl.

The inadequacy of local relief supplemented by private funds

---

[2] Sections 43 and 77.

was evident to those who understood the situation and in 1931 New York, under the leadership of Governor Roosevelt, enacted a law which provided for a Temporary Emergency Relief Administration to administer a special state relief fund.[3] New Jersey, Rhode Island, Wisconsin, Illinois, and Pennsylvania later enacted similar laws. The Temporary Emergency Relief Administration issued schedules of minimum food allowances for families of various numbers of children and made the rule that only offices which approximated to this standard would be given the refund by the state of forty per cent of their expenditures for home relief.[4] The food requirements were in excess of what most public welfare offices had been giving but were barely adequate. The coal allowance of half a ton a month was merely to keep people from freezing. Clothing was not specified as to amount and some offices have given only shoes and rubbers to children. As to rents, the public welfare office was not required to pay rent to keep a family from being evicted but it could not leave a family without a habitation. One must be provided. Gas and electricity in many homes have been turned off and medical care has been deficient. The administration has tried to raise this standard. The requirements as to food, coal, investigation of cases, and other procedures have been enforced by an administrative staff including the best social workers, but it is a question as to how far they have been able to bring the public welfare offices up to their minimum standard of adequate relief in the matter of food alone, to say nothing of other necessities. There has, therefore, been much unrelieved need among the unemployed in New York, even though it has a Temporary Emergency Relief Administration with broad and unusual powers of control. These powers have been used to persuade and teach rather than to force localities up to a higher standard. This policy of education is the only possible

---

[3] Laws of New York, Chapter 798, passed Sept. 23, 1931; Chapter 567, passed March 31, 1932. Temporary Emergency Relief Administration, Rules Concerning Home Relief: Rules Concerning Work Relief.

[4] Thus there is no reimbursement for institutional relief, for veterans' relief, for old age relief and for widows' allowances.

policy because localities can withdraw from under the state relief administration and depend on their own funds.

The central figures in the administration of relief are the town, county and city welfare officials. The tenure of these officials is subject to the vicissitudes of party government. Their degree of competency depends on what kind of a man or woman happens to hold the office at the time—generally no special training is thought to be necessary. This lack of training and of special ability for a task requiring it is one of the weak spots in public welfare work in New York. Though some officials are fine examples of good judgment and devotion to the needs of the unemployed, it is rare to find one who is efficient according to a standard which such a man would require in his own business. He may be efficient in his own business but this is not his business and he is not trained for it. Nor are his investigators usually trained welfare workers.

Yet the Public Welfare Law requires not only relief but constructive welfare work, which can be given only by a trained staff. The office is required to give such treatment as may restore the needy "to a condition of self-support." The office shall not require people to be destitute as a condition of receiving aid but shall "give such service to those liable to become destitute as may prevent the necessity of their becoming public charges." "As far as possible families shall be kept together, and they shall not be separated for reasons of poverty alone." "Whenever a public welfare official receives an application for relief, or is informed that a person is in need of care, an investigation and record shall be made of the circumstances of such person." Relief shall be continued as long as necessary, and those relieved shall be visited at least once a month. Especially shall the office investigate cases of destitute children and give relief in a way to prevent the separation of children from their parents, and take measures on behalf of neglected children. "It shall be the duty of every public welfare official to render assistance and coöperation within his jurisdictional powers to children's courts, boards of child welfare and all other governmental agencies concerned with the welfare of persons under his jurisdiction. Every public welfare official shall also coöperate whenever possible with any private agency whose object is the relief and care of persons in need or the improvement of social conditions."[5] Thus the law outlines a comprehensive welfare program, involving a complicated interlacing of relations and functions. It places an official under a legal obligation actively to work for the improvement of social conditions and to coöperate with other welfare organizations to this end. Yet a man appointed public welfare commissioner in a large city recently confessed that "I know nothing about this job." Nor was his staff very well trained, and this at a time when the administration of his office was the keystone in the arrangements for meeting a great emergency in that city. The welfare office, with rare exceptions, is still a place merely for giving relief, not for constructive welfare work.

Any resident of a town or city may apply for aid at the office in that town or city but the public welfare official decides whether or not the applicant is in need of relief and whether he or she is legally entitled to relief from that office. The best practice is that of requiring a home owner to raise by mortgage all that he can on his home and to spend this before he gets relief. He is not required to sell his home because that would involve a financial sacrifice, owing to the slump in real estate prices. Furthermore, it is as economical to give a man money to pay interest on a mortgage as to give him money to pay rent, as he would have to do if he gave up his house. As to his inability to pay his taxes, he cannot be deprived of property for non-payment of taxes for several years. An owner of an auto must give up his license plates to the commissioner and, if he has been paying installments on his car, he must cease this. The owner of a car may not be required to sell but must cease spending any money on it. Money can be spent only for necessities. People are not required to sell household goods, personal belongings or tools or farm animals.

In many cases the best practice is not followed and a man is required to sell farm animals, tools, even an auto used in his work. In some cases this would not be unjust. It depends

---

[5] Sections 77-80, 105.

on the individual case. Under the more rigorous officials a man is required to sell a house for what he can get and to use up the money. One who will not do so is worse off than one who is entirely destitute. For instance, a man who had a house mortgaged for all he could borrow on it, and judgments against him for $500 which he could not pay, and no relatives or friends to whom he could turn could get no help from the public welfare office because he was not entirely destitute. He could get no private relief either, because the funds were exhausted—even medical attendance, though his boy was seriously ill. He was worse off than if he had owned nothing.

The essential problem in public welfare is the problem of control. The public welfare commissioner is important but there must be some power to select him; and some power advises and directs and in the last analysis controls him. On the nature of that controlling power will depend in good part his efficiency. Consequently the significant changes in the practice of public welfare have followed changes in the controlling power.

The problem of control is discussed in Chapters X and XI. In New York the town officer is appointed by the town board and the funds at his disposal are provided by the board. He is usually advised and controlled by the supervisor of the town. The county commissioner is elected but is dependent on the funds voted by the county board of supervisors. Though elected he is dependent on the local politicians for nomination. The city commissioner is in most cases appointed either by the mayor or city manager or by a board appointed by the mayor. There is a variety of other methods of choice. If appointed, the public welfare official feels dependent for direction on the person or persons who appointed him. Whether elected or appointed he feels that he must stand in with the politicians of his party. They in turn look to members of the propertied classes for campaign contributions and for "moral support," inasmuch as the mere connection of a man of large property with a political party gives its candidates increased influence in the minds of the voters. The propertied classes, therefore, exercise an influence over politicians that is out of all proportion to their numbers.

The members of the appropriating boards theoretically represent all classes of their districts but they are especially in sympathy with property owners and most of them are property owners; wherefore they naturally have felt the losses of property owners during the depression more than the losses that wage-earners have suffered. Furthermore, they are not in contact with the needy unemployed. The public welfare official in contact with the needy is himself powerless to meet the needs unless funds have been voted. Those who have power to produce or withhold funds never see the needs. The conclusion is that the non-propertied classes should be more advantageously represented on the appropriating boards than they are. They are entitled to a more sympathetic hearing than they get, if only because of their losses as wage earners during unemployment.[6]

With this brief delineation of the public welfare scene and of the extremely important limitations[7] imposed on public welfare officials, we turn to the behavior of these central figures. In discussing their work we must make it explicit that, as in every other vocation so here, there are incompetent and competent men. If we give more attention to the former than to the latter, it should be remembered that we are inquiring why the effects of the depression are so terrible in spite of apparently sincere efforts toward relief. In the preceding chapters we have said that the community has failed to assume its full measure of responsibility for enforcing the Public Welfare Law. In this chapter and the next we are centering on the public welfare officials and those who control them.

Incompetent Welfare Officers

The mark of an incompetent official is the inclination to proceed by mechanical rule of thumb, to adopt a mechanical

---

[6] Chapter IV.

[7] Breckenridge, *Family Welfare Work in a Metropolitan Community*, p. 6.

eligibility test—the applicant must be "worthy" and destitute—and then adhere to this with dogmatic consistency. Beyond this, relief is indiscriminate. That is the old way. The
new way is to investigate applications for aid and decide each
case on its own merits and under an intelligent interpretation
of the Public Welfare Law. The rule of thumb attitude is a
refuge before the chaos of unemployment. A commissioner often
will adhere to his rules so meticulously that his treatment of
applicants is ridiculous. To investigate, to modify rules according to the results of investigations is a mental tax he cannot
stand. The rule of thumb attitude usually involves a tendency
to be rigorous or "hard boiled" rather than humane. He puts
"economy" on behalf of the controlling propertied classes before relief of the unemployed. This attitude appears in the
official's handling of a great variety of situations. For instance,
an applicant for relief is sometimes found to be carrying an
insurance policy. Now whether he should be compelled to cash
in and use up the money before getting relief depends entirely
on the individual case. In some cases possibly he should, in
others not. But some officials make this an arbitrary policy:

Commissioner Baker regularly compels an unemployed man to
cash in on his policy. For instance, Edward Terry, who had always
had good employment but was thrown out of work during the depression, carried a $900 policy and had already paid the premium
up to 1933. Nevertheless he was told that he must cash in the
entire policy before he would get any relief. So he lost the year's
premium and got only about $120. Instead of being told to cash
in a part of the policy and use this money to pay the premiums on
the other part, or instead of stopping premiums and having so much
paid up insurance, he had to give up all of that little nest egg
which he was cherishing as the one provision he could make for
his wife and family in case of his death. He must cash in and spend
every cent and appear before Commissioner Baker without a nickel
in his jeans and publicly declare himself a pauper, without money,
without friends or relatives who could help or any visible means
of support, before he could get a cent of relief. Baker is thus
following the doctrine of the old Poor Law that a man must
publicly declare himself destitute before he can get relief. The
majority of these men who must so declare have been industrious
all their lives, exemplary citizens, many of them small property

owners, and are now reduced to penury through no fault of their own.

This making paupers of honest and industrious unemployed is expressly contrary to the Public Welfare Law which, as we have said, provides that the office shall help those liable to become destitute, not merely those who are destitute. Under the law an official can pay a life insurance premium or do anything else that an intelligent and humane person would do. We should add that there are public welfare officials both in large and small cities and in towns and counties who condemn, as unreservedly as we do, this compelling a man to be destitute before he can get relief. Even officials who for other reasons could hardly be classed as competent will not stand for the destitution doctrine. But there are numbers who follow it in the administration of their office.

The rigorous and mechanical attitude makes constructive work impossible because it disregards the psychology of applicants for relief. Note, for instance, the effect of the treatment of Edward Terry. He said: "Well, I've done with saving. There goes my nest egg." While he held on to his insurance he could get no relief and was worse off than John Gilman who had been too thriftless ever to take out any insurance. After letting the insurance go he was just where John was. The thrift and morale of thousands will be permanently broken by the depression and this moral deterioration will continue in their children.

Another way in which the psychology of applicants is ignored is in connection with fraud. There are doubtless numbers of people on the books of the welfare office of a great city who are frauds. But the real fraud must be distinguished from the person who is technically guilty of fraud but entirely different in his psychology. For instance, here is a man who has saved $50 and has declared that he has nothing in order to get relief, and yet he is not bent on cheating the office. That is not his motive at all. He is merely uncertain about what lies just around the corner and so he clings to his little hoard of $50. If business men are uncertain and, with all the resources they have, hoard money during a depression, how much more uncertain and apprehensive is a man who has nothing but $50 and his two hands and not the slightest expectation of an opportunity to use them to feed his family. Do we wonder, then, that Dan clung to his $50 and tried to get a living from the welfare office? He did not know how long the office would help him. I am not arguing that we should ignore the frauds but that the public welfare office should thoroughly investigate every case and wisely discriminate between the motives of those found to be practicing fraud.

Some public welfare officials do make such a discrimination. In fact, what I have just written was told me by an official of a large city, and a few days later another manager in the office of another large city spoke in the same vein. But, as these men pointed out, it is one thing for an official so to discriminate and another thing to be able to steer the course of justice in accordance with the discrimination. Fraud is fraud and, though the discerning welfare official may discriminate in individual cases, to the courts law is law. So the courts are apt to punish without paying much attention to these psychological differences. "And," added one of these officials, "the public reads the account in the paper and exclaims, 'Ah, another fraud!' without knowing anything about the circumstances."

There is not enough discrimination between men who will not work on work relief jobs because they are lazy and men who will not work because they cannot. Here is a man who has tuberculosis, and whose children have tuberculosis, doing relief work in a marsh because he dare not protest. Here is another man with tuberculosis who seemed to be a lazy worker and finally quit the job and was haled into court for unwillingness to work and support his family, when the reason for his apparent laziness was that he had tuberculosis—the records showed that he had. Some officials are too ready indiscriminately to condemn as loafers all men who do not appear on the work relief job offered them. Other officials attempt to understand the physical condition of applicants for work relief. One large city employs a physician to make physical examinations at the public welfare office and the results of these are consulted in assigning work.

The unemployed suffer from uncertainty as to the future, and the public welfare official often appears deliberately to try to increase this anxiety under the belief that thus he will incite them to try to get work, though there is no work to be had. One can see that this behavior is a reaction to conditions of the prosperous past, when men out of work might be suspected of being unemployed through some fault of their own, and not because of lack of opportunity. Some officials characteristically assume, also, that applicants are trying to beat the office, so they indiscriminately grill everybody. Here is a case where an investigator decided that a family of man and wife and seven undernourished children needed $8 a week. The welfare official called in the mother and made her think she had wrongfully impressed the investigator and might get nothing at all and then asked if $5 a week would not be enough. She, scared speechless at the thought of getting nothing, assented. Then he turned on the investigator and rebuked her for her extravagance and later told this incident to his political associates as showing how much more he knew than investigators and how zealous he was to "save the town money." Evidently he had not the slightest interest in the seven half-starved children.

Something more than a rigorous attitude is required to avoid waste in relief and really save the town money. The community must require intelligence of public welfare officials:

Sam Blandsmiler is commissioner of public welfare in a certain city. He climbed up through various offices to the dizzy height of county sheriff, jailer of a few criminals, then started on his downward career and finally landed in the office of city welfare commissioner, arbiter of the fate of hundreds of families of the unemployed. He had been dispensing relief without any investigation of applicants, giving as the spirit moved, that is, according to the cleverness of the applicant in displaying a flattering submission, had a weakness for attractive widows and apparently enjoyed using the people's money to satisfy various phases of his egoism. One widow had two sons employed and could herself have worked but preferred to work the commissioner. In the spring of 1931 he had already spent two-thirds of his appropriation for that year. But not until this wasteful administration of his office had been going

on for two years did an investigation get underway to inform the
city of the well-to-do what he had been doing with his funds.

During the first two years of the depression, public welfare
officials in many cities had not yet admitted that an emergency
existed but maintained toward the unemployed who applied for
relief the traditional attitude towards the poor. This attitude
is described in the story below of Hiram Grimshaw. After two
years of unemployment it was seen that an emergency existed
and this attitude began to weaken. Welfare officials were floundering before a situation for which they were totally unprepared. The old attitude has not by any means disappeared
but it has been to some degree modified by the requirements
and constructive program of the Temporary Emergency Relief Administration. Where public welfare officials are hopelessly at sea, this Administration has saved the situation. Here
is the story of a floundering official:

Oldie Shriver, town welfare officer, with five hundred families on
his books and a pistol in his pocket, threatened by hungry men
and women, has found himself stalled with an antiquated relief
machine and no funds to make it go. As one contemplates Oldie,
safely shut in there in his inner office from the throng of the
unemployed, as helpless before the problem of budgeting his families as a boy would be in the wiring of a house for electricity, one
is conscious that this is the land of the free and the home of the
politician. Oldie is saying to the social worker who has been designated to assist him: "Oh I don't feel well. I don't feel well *at all*.
My nerves have gone back on me. I've got to get away. I'm glad
you've come before I go. Now I want to talk with you and if you
do just as I say you'll get along all right." So this is one of the
captains of our great American unemployment relief. No wonder
he wants a vacation. As we survey the wreckage of the economic
system that drifts into his office we wonder what is happening in
other nations, if America really leads the world in efficiency.
During the ensuing weeks the social worker brings order out of
chaos, as far as is possible with inadequate funds, and one is impressed with the immense service being rendered by the Temporary
Emergency Relief Administration. When we consider what would
have happened without it, we do not need to justify it by extravagant claims of success.

Hiram Grimshaw was until recently commissioner of public welfare in a large city. He is a grim product of the honest past. If

his clerk brought him a column of figures with the suggestion that it was not necessary to add them, as the work had been done by the adding machine, he replied, "I'll add them just the same." He hewed to the line of an ancient principle, that relief must not be sufficient to enable families "on the town" to live as well as the poorest independent family, the idea being that a family in need is in some way to blame for it. His policy was to keep applicants away from the office as long as possible by a reputation for being hard-boiled, to keep them waiting if they came, to postpone action after he had seen them, to rebuff and humiliate and so goad them into helping themselves, as if they had not already worn away sole leather trying to find work. Applicants who had gone without food for a day or more were sometimes compelled to sit in the waiting room from nine oclock until four and then might be told that he could not see them that day. In this attitude the commissioner was supported by politicians and leading citizens. One of the members of the city council declared that every city should have a whipping post and that a man who did not support his family should be whipped.

This apparent desire to discipline the jobless man, as if he did not want to work, has resulted in more than one tragedy in that city. Robert Ward had a wife and five children. He lost the job he had had for several years and could not get work. He mortgaged his house and lived on the money until he could not borrow any more. Then he got credit at the grocery store until he could get no more. When he applied for relief his application blank showed that he owned a house but that it was heavily mortgaged. The commissioner did not think he was properly poor. He was told that the office would look into his case. It was just *his* case. The commissioner did not consider that five of the next generation of Americans also were involved. Robert was told to apply at the bank for a loan. It was refused and he told the commissioner. Nothing was done. Finally, when he visited the commissioner a fourth time he was told that they would send somebody to investigate his case. Nobody came. About six weeks after he first applied for relief he drowned himself in the lake. The family got relief. The newspaper merely reported that he jumped into the lake while despondent. The commissioner removed the record of this case from his official records. The outcome of this case is unusual but the treatment is representative of the stupid way in which the unemployed have been dealt with in some cities.

Sophie Dombroncke of this city, a twelve year old girl interpreting for her parents, said, "Father asked for help last week but didn't get any grocery order. There wasn't any food left in the house so he went to get fishes." He was arrested for fishing without a license and was sent to jail without his family being notified. They learned of it when Sophie came to notify the police that father was lost. Later he was tried, convicted and sentenced to pay a fine of $25, "to stand committed until the fine is paid," that is, for 25 days. This was his first offense. Later he was released through the efforts of interested citizens. Thus was burned into the soul of sensitive Sophie her first lesson in criminal justice. She was taught by the case method.

Here again some of the circumstances of the case are peculiar but many cases, like this one, show thoughtlessness not only of public welfare officials but also of judges. Take the cases of children of needy families arrested and put on probation for picking up coal on the railroad track. Should not the judge go further and send these children's parents to the commissioner for relief? These little children can feel a sense of injustice as well as adults and they never forget it. Is it wise to foster in the next generation of America this sense of the injustice of government?

Commissioners who think of the unemployed as just shiftless are unjust to the great mass of laborers in the modern city. What the unemployed want is work not charity. We have irrefutable evidences of this. For instance, in Hiram's own city the city council voted a sum of money to give work to the unemployed. They would call the bluff of these hundreds of men who professed to want jobs. Men with families could have work. Eight hundred men registered for work. There was work for less than a hundred. They jammed Hiram's waiting room all day. They hummed and pounded the wall. He dared not appear and tell them that there were no jobs. Denial of food and shelter never aroused men like that. What they wanted was work.

Hiram was imbued with certain attitudes that have survived from the past. First, he desired to make a record for economy for his department, so his emphasis was on money saved rather than work done. Though his departmental budget provided for two investigators, he employed only one, to show his intent on rigid economy. The result was that once families got on his relief list, he could not continue to supervise them, so they might draw relief when they no longer needed it. Therefore he tried to keep them off his list, and if they got on gave an inadequate, traditional dole, and often arbitrarily diminished this week by week. Another attitude that moved Hiram is expressed in the belief that all money raised for relief should be expended as relief. He failed to see that an expert staff would diminish waste. It is true of other cities that families continue to receive relief after it should be discontinued. Most of them have been rebuffed and humiliated by the office. They feel that there is no fairness in its policy, so getting relief becomes a game of getting all you can. A trained and seasoned staff would change this situation by developing in the unemployed a different attitude to the public welfare office.

INCOMPETENCE DUE TO CONSERVATISM

These various attitudes of which Hiram is a victim have survived from the old rural poormaster days (the word "master" is significant). Our relief system dates back to the agricultural era when cities were smaller, the population was less migratory, and the poor were known to the community. A man let out by one employer could go to another. We have passed into an industrial era of great corporations with much technological unemployment even in prosperity, and a depression paralizes business generally. But men out of work are still treated as they were in the old days when laziness was more apt to be the cause of unemployment than today. For instance, here is a well-to-do supervisor who is saying, "We are spending too much money and we shall have to cut down on this poor relief." An industrious farm laborer's family is living in a shack with the windows boarded up for lack of glass and the roof leaking, but the supervisor insists that this family will have to remain where it is. "And we'll have to cut out the county nurse," he asserts. The nurse's business is to take care of "such families" and so her services are not really necessary. In this attitude to the dependent the supervisor has the weight of tradition behind him. On the other hand there is a more progressive sentiment in that community and the question is: how can this sentiment be stimulated to function against him. Obviously a progressive attitude must be strengthened in the communities, and we hope this will take place as the people come to understand the Public Welfare Law and learn about the defects of their own public welfare administration.

The people generally are not conscious that a new public welfare system has been set up in New York. Their attitudes are still set in the narrow lines of the old dole system. The new system may exist legally, but it is not psychologically established and in operation.

The old American dole system was not deliberately set up to meet the conditions then existing. It was originally copied from England. But England has gone on to a system of state unemployment insurance adapted to modern industrial conditions, while we are facing those conditions with various adaptations of the old agricultural machinery. We fail to recognize that the unemployed are a class distinct from those who require charity. We lump the needy all together and aim to care for them, without much discrimination, under practices copied from Old England with its landlord and tenant order.

The attitudes which in England actuated a landlord class in dealing with a class of more or less contemned tenants were, with the law, transferred to this country and actuated the independent farmers in their treatment of the poor. So the man whom they selected to look after the poor was accustomed to think more of economy, for the sake of the independent, than of the needs of the poor. He was wont to give a meagre dole and often was so harsh and humiliating in his treatment of the poor that their pride was wounded to the quick. He was essentially a poor master. The result was that charity was not sought except by families "on their beam ends" and not then unless they were broken in health or courage. These attitudes to the poor and of the poor toward receiving relief are widely prevalent today, are part and parcel of our rural heritage, and cannot be understood from any other point of view.[8]

INCOMPETENCE IN RURAL AREAS

Especially in the rural districts, therefore, may we expect to find the traditional attitude to the poor. And as a matter

---

[8] Williams, *Our Rural Heritage,* Ch. XIII; Williams, *The Expansion of Rural Life,* pp. 147-51.

of fact we do find it there, though some officers are getting away from it. Here is an officer who boasted that he "had only six needy cases in the town last year." As a matter of fact there were several times that number, but either they were rebuffed or they kept away from him altogether because they did not want to be humiliated and still probably get no help. A wife about to be delivered agreed with her husband that they would not ask the officer for a doctor's help but that she would try to go through it without a doctor. After she had endured twenty-four hours labor he went to the village to ask a doctor to come. The doctor got the baby dead and the wife, after months, is still in the hospital. Was that officer a financial asset to the town in that case?

In some towns officers are so inconsiderate that men just home from the insane asylum or the tuberculosis sanatorium are forced into any kind of a job so that they eventually have to return to the hospital or sanatorium, whereas a little consideration would help these unfortunates gradually to improve their earning capacity until they again were able to support their families. Is this policy *profitable* for the town— to put it on no higher plane? If officers cannot see how they should handle a case for the financial interest of their own town, of course they will not sense the interest of the state. Here is a problem boy of twelve, denied a health and psychological examination by a pennywise county commissioner, who is proved pound foolish after the boy is finally sent to an institution when he might have been cured by treatment given in time. Now he must be supported by the state for a term of years.

LACK OF PREVENTIVE CARE

A welfare official will boast of some little way in which he has saved the town money when he cannot see the ways in which he is piling up expense for county and state, and the taxpayers are too indifferent to inquire. Probably the greatest waste in the aggregate which can be laid to officials, both in the rural parts and the cities, is the failure to give preventive relief, that is, a little medical attention in time to prevent a serious illness, or a little mental hygiene treatment in time to prevent a mental hospital case, or a little care of a wayward girl in time to prevent her becoming an unmarried mother or being sent to a reformatory. In any one of these cases the cost of the preventive treatment would be but a few dollars compared to the hundreds that will be spent because of the lack of it.

Not only is there a lack of preventive care but the way in which applicants are treated sometimes spreads disease. We find cases like this: The husband, industrious, well-educated, skilled as a workman and a man of good habits, now twenty-seven, is tubercular. He went to a sanatorium at twenty-two, improved and came back home and went to work. Now, while the inspector is at his home, he is coughing constantly. Yet this family is advised to give up its home in order to save rent, fuel, electricity and gas and to move in with another family, and this would have been done had not interested people intervened. The wife looks tubercular but never has been examined. One child born in May, 1931, died at birth. Why is not the man in a sanatorium? He feels that he must be looking for work and nobody suggests that he go back to the sanatorium.

Waste is due also to lack of proper investigation of applicants. Welfare officials often lack the training to give them insight into just what investigation is required in each case, and they also lack initiative to make investigations.[9] For instance, an official will accept a statement that an auto belongs to an applicant's brother instead of checking the plate at the office and finding that it belongs to the applicant himself. He gives an applicant the traditional dole from November to March but does no case work with the family from March to November in order that they may learn so to use their earnings that they will need less relief and possibly none at all. The

---

[9] The same was recently found to be true in the State of Pennsylvania. Says Frankel: "There is seldom an inquiry into the particular circumstances leading to the necessity for public relief and an attempt to find out the underlying difficulties the family or individual is facing, in order to set up a workable plan for the immediate treatment and future rehabilitation. The investigation is seldom carried beyond perfunctory interviews with the members of the family in the home, although the neighbors seem to be one of the most fruitful sources of information and often the deciding factor whether or not relief should be given." Frankel, *Poor Relief in Pennsylvania*, State Department of Welfare, Bulletin 21, 1925, pp. 58-59.

welfare official's job is one of diagnosis, which most of them cannot do; and when they hire investigators these are usually chosen for local reasons and are not trained for their work.

THE HARD-BOILED OFFICE

A large city welfare department is both an intensive and an extensive enterprise. There is the commissioner of public welfare and under him the director of home relief and supervisors of other divisions which generally speaking are about as follows: old age relief, child welfare, hospital relief, out of town relief and, in some cities, a division that has charge of applications for payment of rent and another of applications for payment of gas and light. In addition there may be a nutritionist, a legal advisor, a head bookkeeper or auditor, investigators, stenographers, clerks and others. The Commissioner is the guiding spirit of the whole enterprise. As one director expressed it, "A hard-boiled commissioner will get the whole force hard-boiled. It isn't altogether a matter of compulsion. They just begin to feel and act as he does." Now the commissioner, and deputy commissioner if there is one, are not in actual contact with applicants for relief. They cannot appreciate the needs. I have brought certain cases of failure to attend to needs to the personal attention of these men and they would not believe what was said until actually shown. They do not want to be bothered with these family situations. The people in actual contact with applicants and the investigators who see the home conditions have so many cases to handle and are so powerless to meet needs adequately that they develop the cynical, defensive attitude that enables them to escape the poignancy of the situations. There are investigators who are too human to do this, others are under supervisors who are sympathetic and they are kept human by this influence. One official remarked to me that even in an office hard-boiled from the commissioner down, "if you know how to present your case, and have taken time to investigate all the little things so that they can't stick you, you can get what you want, maybe. The trouble with the commissioner is that he never sees the homes. I say, 'Come down with me to that man's home and see how they are living.' You have to fight for your client." This man added that most cases get a superficial investigation or none at all and a snap judgment. Sometimes when a humane commissioner succeeds a hard-boiled one, the home relief director will continue hard-boiled. He thinks that thus he is pleasing the politicians above the commissioner. The commissioner may have to over-rule him and so run the risk of incurring the distrust of the politicians.

INCOMPETENCE AND POLITICS

Officials cannot be considered apart from the political situation in which they function. They are one aspect of it. The well-meaning official often is uncertain as between two contrary influences, between his political affiliations and whatever intelligent public interest in relief may exist in the community. He may have to take orders from political associates who interfere with his administrative efficiency. For instance, in one city the commissioner was compelled by politicians to give grocery orders on stores on an "eligible list." He declared that he could save his city thousands of dollars annually if he were permitted to give orders where these would be filled least expensively. Under the law of course he had the right to give orders where he pleased and the interfernce was not legal. But he had to bow to it because he got his appointment as the gift of the party in power. Consequently he must issue orders on the designated stores, even if the recipient of the order must pass a store where she could have got a sack of flour for much less than at the store on which the order was issued. Worse than this, sometimes these stores did not sell vegetables. A mother who was told by the public health nurse that she must provide vegetables for her children replied that the store which her order was on did not sell them. She would have to take dried herring instead. The commissioner when asked to give his order on another store explained that he could not do so. This is not the place to explain what is behind such dictation. It is contrary to the public interest and of course is kept secret.

Public interest is most readily aroused in connection with

conspicuous waste in giving relief. Six main causes of waste may be mentioned: first, giving relief to those who do not need it but who can influence the official by flattery or some other seductive appeal; second, keeping a person on the relief list after the need has passed; third, giving too much relief; fourth, giving the wrong kind of relief, for instance, making a rule that only chestnut coal can be given in relief orders when this coal falls through the grates of furnaces in which it is used, or bringing a farmer groceries when he has plenty of food in the cellar and what he needs is shoes; fifth, giving too little relief—this may be worse than none at all because it may convey the idea that the person is being helped and so prevent him from getting adequate relief; sixth, giving relief expensively, as by orders on high-priced stores. In one city the waste became so apparent that certain taxpayers were about to start a citizens' suit against the public welfare office but were stopped by other leading citizens who argued that to expose the inefficiency of the office would hurt their own political party.

Lack of Coöperation Between Public and Private Offices

One of the weakest spots in welfare work is the lack of coöperation between public and private welfare agencies. The traditional policy of private agencies, a policy no longer tenable, is to take the cases which require family case work and leave mere relief cases to the public office. But family case work may involve giving relief, in some cases more relief than the private society can give. So private and public societies have been in more or less constant conflict over questions of relief. The private society is exasperated by the inadequacy of relief or waste of funds by the public office, and the public office shouts back that the private office is "too scientific" or "not practical." In both villages and cities often there is merely haphazard coöperation or none at all. Sometimes the public welfare official will have nothing to do with the private society, will not tell the society what families he is relieving, and, in cases where this is known, will not tell how much he is giving. No one knows what records the official keeps, if any. When he

goes out of office he sometimes destroys whatever records he
may have kept.

This failure of the public welfare official to coöperate is
contrary to the express provisions of the Public Welfare Law.
It is a cause of vast waste in relief. For instance, a social
worker of a children's bureau had worked on a number of
cases for a long time and was bringing the families to the
point where they could intelligently care for their children.
This involved giving some clothing and medical relief. Then
the community chest decided that this bureau could no longer
give relief. It must be given, if at all, by the public welfare
office. So the bureau handed these cases over to the public
welfare office which neglected them. The families slipped back
to where they were at first and so the many hours spent by
the bureau on these cases were of no avail. This waste from
lack of coöperation extends through our whole welfare system
and, in the aggregate, must be enormous. Another source of
waste is the failure of judges of children's courts to follow the
recommendations of social workers who have carefully investigated cases and instead to decide on legalistic lines. For instance
a social worker had as a client a delinquent boy of ten, living
in an impossible home, and had worked with this family off
and on for two years. She had brought the case to the point
where a foster home of a certain kind was the only solution
of the problem. But the judge sent the boy to an orphan
asylum, which was not the right kind of a place for such a boy,
and from which he repeatedly ran away. Finally he was returned to his home and continued his delinquencies. Eventually
he was sent to a reform school and apparently is on the way
to become a confirmed criminal. All that social worker's efforts came to naught for lack of coöperation. Her time spent
on the case, representing a good many dollars, was wasted.
This is not saying that the social worker is always in the right.
But the selection of a home for a boy merely from the point
of view of legal requirements is not apt to be wise. Children's
cases are to be regarded not as legal adjudications but as
social adjustments. Sometimes a judge will coöperate for some
time with the clinical and social workers who work out his

cases, then go off on the legalistic tangent for awhile, then back again to coöperation.

These various lines of waste through lack of coöperation will be diminished only as positions requiring a knowledge of social work come to be occupied by those who have been trained in social work. One of the functions of a Council of Social Agencies is to bring about this coöperation. But we find a lack of it in cities where such councils are functioning as well as anywhere. The two examples of lack of coöperation above given are taken from such cities.

INCOMPETENCE PROTECTED BY SECRECY

The incompetent public welfare official is protected in his incompetence by the fact that his records are strictly private. This is a necessary measure, for otherwise Tom Jones, disgruntled against James Smith, would have a right to find out all the records might disclose about James Smith. On the other hand, citizens who may wish to learn what is being done in order to correct abuses are denied access to the records.[10] These are open to the State Department of Social Welfare and to the Temporary Emergency Relief Administration, both of which are so inadequately staffed as to be unable effectively to supervise the city, county and town officials of the state. However, if the public welfare office had an advisory committee, as suggested later, this committee, either as a whole or through some designated member, would have access to the records, and a strong committee would quite effectively remove any protection given by secrecy to waste or other inefficiency.

COMPETENT PUBLIC WELFARE OFFICIALS

Competent officials are found in some towns, counties and cities. The incompetent distrust state supervision—that is one aspect of their incompetency—while the competent are interested in suggestions and go half way in meeting the desire

---

[10] Section 155 of the Public Welfare Law provides that all information relating to a person receiving relief obtained by any officer or employee in the course of his work is to be regarded as confidential. However, a commissioner, in his discretion, on being shown that the public welfare will be promoted, may authorize the giving of information.

of the state supervisors to be of service. The competent are the kind of men who like to do a job well and feel that it is never so well done but that it might be done better:

John Wellington is commissioner of public welfare of a county which contains one village of some eight thousand inhabitants with a large factory population out of work and another village of forty-five hundred. He has lived his whole life in the county which he has served now twelve years as commissioner. He takes his job as seriously as the old time craftsman took his trade. He knows the Public Welfare Law and is bent on administering his office according to the full intent of the law. He investigates each case and decides each on its own merits. He does not require an applicant to be entirely destitute, emphasizes adequate relief, interprets adequacy according to the best practice of the time, centers on the welfare of children and knows the best practice in that work. He coöperates intelligently with the State Department of Social Welfare and with private relief agencies. He appears before the board of supervisors, explains clearly why they must pass the budget as submitted and gets the appropriation asked though it may be larger than before. The supervisors know him to be a man who weighs his words. They know that, whichever party elects its candidates, he has always been elected; that he keeps his eagle eye on all his town welfare officers and, while urging them to give adequate relief, at the same time examines their accounts and detects any extravagant relief and any misuse of funds. They know that he enforces the provision of the law which requires any person who has had relief to repay the amount he has been given, within a period of ten years back, when he is again able to work, and that he gets from estates what the deceased owed because of relief.[11] They know that he does not wait for a needy man to come to him but seeks out one who has lost his job, helps him to get another and advises against sacrificing tools or household goods and against continuing expensive habits formed in prosperity.

In spite of his efficiency, however, one of the supervisors has announced himself a candidate against John in the fall primaries and there are rumors that the party organization intends to retire him because "he has given too much relief." If this is so and if he is beaten in the primaries, he can run on an independent ticket, looking to those whom he has helped to stand by him (this happened in a neighboring county and the independent commissioner was elected and next time was nominated by his party); or John can retire with the satisfaction that at least he "never bowed to anybody."

---

[11] Section 128 of the Public Welfare Law.

Only those who know a competent public welfare commissioner intimately can realize how difficult it is to be competent in such an office. He is the center of a conflict which has developed as the depression has become acute. The thousands of unemployed had expected to get work in the spring of 1932 but jobs were as scarce as ever. As for the well-to-do, stocks were lower and rents and other income more uncertain. So there was an increasing pressure on the city administration to diminish relief in order to lower taxes and, on the other hand, increasing threats from the city of the unemployed. To reassure taxpayers the city administration must constantly make gestures, which, however, inevitably irritated the unemployed. Then, not to turn these thousands of voters against the administration, the odium must be directed against some agency and the public welfare office was the natural "goat." So the competent public welfare commissioner found himself the victim of political deceit and trickery, and if he resigned, that move would merely seem to confirm the impression about him that had been conveyed. For instance, a city administration published newspaper stories of fraudulent applicants for relief who had been hunted down and fined or imprisoned, and of the per capita cost of feeding the unemployed reduced to a few cents a day. This constant reiteration of frauds punished and of lowered cost of feeding the unemployed pleased the well-to-do but irritated the unemployed. They resented being thought of as frauds when most of them were not. They resented the constant boasting about the cheapness of their diet. The administration sought to ward off resentment by making unpopular measures seem to emanate from the public welfare office. The commissioner stood this because of his sense of responsibility for doing a vital service for the unemployed. Hardest of all to stand was the fact that his old friends believed what they read, shook their heads and said, "H——— is not the man we thought he was."

As a result of the publicity given the public welfare department as an avenue of alleged unnecessary disbursement of public funds, other departments can get their hands into the public treasury unnoticed. While a certain department might reasonably reduce its expenditures, a large appropriation goes through, much of it "gravy" for certain politicians. Or a department discharges a large number of low paid employees, which is advertised as an economy and the public applauds; then most of these soon appear on the books of the public welfare office as recipients of relief, which increases the disbursements of that department. So the office and the commissioner become the object of a public odium that ought to strike elsewhere. Is it any wonder that a competent man will not readily accept such an office? But the point is that a competent man does accept such an office, that he sticks, that he gathers a staff of competent social workers around him and that he gradually improves every branch of administration of his office. So in spite of all the facts we have recounted, we can make the assertion, based on facts, that competence is possible, even in a position held by a political appointee and closely related on all sides to gross incompetence.

PUBLIC WELFARE OFFICIALS REPRESENT COMMUNITY SENTIMENT

In the last analysis incompetence is chargeable to the inertia of the intelligent people of the community. The majority of public welfare officials in New York doubtless are well intentioned and honest men. They administer their office just about as the average citizen would administer it. But they are functioning in communities where the well-to-do are not interested in public welfare but have recently become "tax conscious," that is, inclined to support cuts in public expenditures without much consideration of what the effects will be. Furthermore, the public does not discriminate as it should between the unemployed or otherwise unfortunate and the lazy and dissolute poor. Then, too, there is the tendency to regard foreign families of certain nationalities as more or less undeserving just because they are "foreigners."[12] These "foreigners" include not only those not born in this country

---

[12] Williams, *The Expansion of Rural Life*, pp. 40, 52-54, 157, 278.

but all those whose speech or manners or relationships suggest foreign ancestry. Public welfare officials often share the prevailing indifference to, and contempt for the poor and the prejudice against foreigners. These attitudes militate against any interest in constructive welfare work.

TAXATION UNJUST

"The development of the public agency cannot be considered aside from the question of the source of support. The heaviest need for relief falls naturally to the communities which are highly industrialized. Frequently the industry is located outside the city from which it draws its labor, because of the lower rates of taxation, yet during the period of unemployment the responsibility for the unemployed workmen falls upon the city relief agency. Taxes are frequently laid primarily upon property owners rather than upon those who have received large financial returns from business and industry. Many cities and counties are finding it difficult to secure sufficient funds or credit to meet the demands which are placed upon them.

"The general property tax upon which a large number of local communities depend for support of government appeared in many counties during the primitive stage of their economic development and, as Professor Seligman has written, the nature of the general property tax 'is such that it is more suitable to a simple and undeveloped economic organization than to one in which elaborate and complicated differentiation of wealth and methods of protection have appeared.'[13] During the past twenty years there has been an interest among tax commissions and students of government in changing our tax systems. Where the states or local governments have modified their tax system more nearly to meet present-day developments, they have to a degree been better able to meet the needs than in communities where they still rely upon the old form of taxation. However, still further changes are indicated which

---

[13] Seligman, *Essays in Taxation,* 9th ed., Ch. II.

will place less of the tax burden on the low income population."[14]

Resources for relief could be increased by diminishing waste in relief but more tax funds are needed. Lack of funds forces on the appropriating boards a policy of extreme economy and the public welfare official bears the brunt of it all. Is it any wonder that conscientious men hesitate before taking such a job? Under the pressure the official is driven to compromise with whatever good impulses he has. A newly elected city official remarked rather proudly, "I'm getting hardboiled," as if that was the main qualification of a good official. He meant that he was getting callous to the needs, in response to the pressure to economize. An official must become objective in his attitude and so save himself from emotional wear and tear,[15] but this does not mean becoming indifferent to the needs of the client in order to serve the interest of taxpayers. Some officials acquire a hard, peremptory exterior, even to acquaintances not involved in their situations, which, however, passes when they go out of office. Hiram used to say, "I try so to administer my office that every night my conscience will be clear." God pity Hiram if he succeeded. I do not think he did. Probably most officials have a conscience. Such men find it difficult to be welfare officials under American methods.

What we need is a system under which men and women of sympathy and training can administer the office according to the best practice of scientific social work. These administrators will have to devise a technique to make those who appropriate the funds see the needs as they do. And the appropriating boards will have to "heave" for a just system of taxation for welfare work.

---

[14] Porter, *A Study of Nine Public Relief Agencies*, July, 1932, p. 34 (published by Family Welfare Association of America).

[15] Lee and Kenworthy, *Mental Hygiene and Social Work*, p. 236.

CHAPTER X

THE SUPERVISION AND CONTROL OF LOCAL PUBLIC HOME RELIEF ADMINISTRATION

THE ONLY CONTROL over local public welfare officials in the field of home relief, other than public opinion, is that exercised by the New York State Department of Social Welfare[1] and the Temporary Emergency Relief Administration. This Administration is intended to be temporary[2] so a short statement will suffice, after which we shall discuss the State Department. The Administration's powers are given it for the purpose of administering the state relief fund and of supervising the home relief dispensed by the city and county public welfare offices that come under its jurisdiction[3] and the work relief given by the local work bureaus. It has supervision and control of the local home relief and work relief.[4] If any city or county public welfare commissioner "shall violate any rule made by the administration, or in the judgment of the administration shall be inefficient or remiss in the performance of his duties, the administration may transfer all the powers, functions, and duties of such city commissioner or county commissioner with respect to home relief to the local (work) bureau."[5] That is, the commissioner can be discharged as an agent of the Administration but would continue to exercise his other functions. Also the Administration can withhold from the city or county office the forty per cent reimbursement for relief given by the state. So it has two important and unusual means of control, control of funds and power to discharge a commissioner.

---

[1] Section 138 of the Public Welfare Law.
[2] Laws of New York, Chapter 798, Section 3.
[3] Laws of New York, Chapter 567, Section 35.
[4] Laws of New York, Chapter 798, Section 9; Chapter 567, Section 7.
[5] Laws of New York, Chapter 798, Section 12.

The Emergency Administration has made possible the systematic planning of unemployment relief on a state-wide scale. It has been able to concentrate state funds at points of greatest need, to install efficient directors of relief at these points and to set in motion experimental relief methods that localities left to themselves could not have attempted. It has acted like a general staff over a far flung front, keeping informed of the needs at every point and distributing forces here and there as the emergency required.

The State Department of Social Welfare has no such powers of control. In the field of home relief it is mainly supervisory and advisory.[6] It is directed to investigate the condition of persons seeking public aid and to devise measures for their relief, which makes it the agency for receiving complaints from aggrieved applicants in welfare districts throughout the State; to supervise the work of public welfare officials and advise them in the performance of their duties; to promote a uniform system of records; and to collect information about public relief throughout the state.[7] The executive details of this vast undertaking are carried on chiefly by a Director and two assistants of the Bureau of Home Relief, which is in one of the six divisions of the Department, the Division of Child Welfare. These three people have the supervision of some 116 city and county public welfare offices and over 1,000 town offices. Obviously only a few of these offices can be visited each year, to say nothing of seeing them often enough and studying them carefully enough to make supervision effective. The task is a colossal one and impossible of performance by the three people hired by the state for this purpose. In addition, these three people handle a large percentage of all complaints made to the Department and the state executives by persons who feel aggrieved because they have not been relieved in their distress. These three people must investigate all these complaints sufficiently to find what there is to them and then take up those that seem to have some basis with the public welfare

---

[6] For a description of the constitution, powers, functions, and relations of the State Department of Social Welfare see Bulletin No. 1, "Social Welfare Brevities," May 1, 1932.

[7] Public Welfare Law, Sections 138, 139.

officials in whose jurisdictions they occur. Here is another task that requires a large force of supervisors. The lack of adequate supervision in the field in turn results in the department being insufficiently informed of the conditions it is supposed to supervise.[8]

It is a question as to how far the State Department can go in enforcing its recommendations, that is, whether it could impeach a public welfare official and try to secure his removal. Its control over officials apparently rests largely on their own desire to win the commendation of the Department or to avoid the publicity of an investigation the results of which could be made public by the Department.

The Bureau of Home Relief has, therefore, been able only to touch the fringe of the possibilities in its field. There are undoubtedly a considerable number of public welfare offices which would welcome advice and assistance. Conditions in most of them could certainly be altered for the better if the Bureau had an adequate staff. The three members are constantly visiting offices throughout the state and, in spite of the changing personnel of the public welfare offices, owing to the vicissitudes of party government, they are gradually improving the administration in some localities. They are doing something else which is perhaps more important just now, that is, gathering a body of information which will indicate what changes in the present administration of relief are necessary before there can be any marked improvement in public welfare administration. But the facilities for securing this information are inadequate.[9]

RELIEF UNSYSTEMATIC

In spite of the state supervision and control, therefore, our welfare administration is in the highest degree unsystematic. It is not a system but a survival projected into the present out of conditions of the past that no longer exist. The practice of officials is whimsical and inconsistent, in spite of all the

---

[8] This is true not only in New York State but throughout the country. Read Breckinridge, *Public Welfare Administration*, p. 559.

[9] This is true also in other states. See Porter, *A Study of Nine Public Agencies*, p. 36.

Temporary Emergency Relief Administration can do to prevent
it. One finds one family getting far less than the standard allowance for food and another family getting more per capita
(not more than the standard allowance), both families equally
deserving and equally destitute. For instance, in April, 1932,
in a large city which is getting the refund, I found, within
the short period of half an hour, a family of man, wife and
ten children getting a grocery order of $5.90 a week, two
quarts of milk a day, one-half ton of coal a month and shoes
for the children, this family living in a home which had been
stripped of furniture and with gas and electricity turned off
and no rent paid; another family of man, wife and seven
children getting $6.75 a week, two quarts of milk a day,
one-half ton of coal a month and no rent paid; another
family of man, wife and one child getting $5 a week, one quart
of milk a day, one-half ton of coal a month and rent paid.
None of these families had any resources or any help from
any other source. The lack of consistency is apparent, and
would be more evident if I had time to go into a discussion
of these three families. Furthermore, the first family mentioned,
which was receiving the lowest per capita relief, was about
to lose its home for non-payment of taxes.

There are various reasons for the inconsistent and unjust
differences in relief. Without the aid of efficient investigators
the official is influenced by the manner of the applicant as he
or she appears at the office, which may have nothing to do
with the needs in the case. The family may be of a political
or sectarian affiliation that pleases or displeases the official
or may have a reputation which commends or condemns it in
his mind. The head of the family may impress the investigator
or official favorably or unfavorably. These aspects of the case
are irrelevant to the question of need. The needs of the children
often seem to make little impression. More important for the
family than real need, in many cases, is its ability to enlist
some influential politician to bring pressure to bear on the
office.

Private welfare offices only perpetuate this chaotic system
by supplementing relief in families that have been slighted.

They should not try to make good the failures of the public welfare office but should let the administration stand or fall on its merits.

The wide difference in the fortunes of the unemployed under our welfare practices fosters a deep sense of injustice among those who fare ill. Many families which are too proud to endure the humiliation of applying at the office get nothing at all. Then there is the senseless practice of diminishing the relief given week by week, for no other reason than as a threat to remind the family that the breadwinner must find work. This merely increases the anxiety at a time when no work is to be had. And in some cases relief is suddenly stopped altogether, because the ire of the officer has been stirred by some episode. This chaotic situation has been somewhat smoothed out under the supervision of the Temporary Emergency Relief Administration, the supervisors of which lay down rules for commissioners who are found to be erratic, but there are still variations in the practice of the same official, and there are wide variations in the practices of different officials.

RURAL PUBLIC WELFARE ADMINISTRATION

Under the Public Welfare Law needy families which have a settlement in a town are given home relief from town funds, except in a few counties that have the county system. The law enjoins that the town board shall make adequate appropriations but this is apt to be ignored. Some towns, and cities as well, carry over a deficit every year though this is illegal, and the result is that the welfare officer always is faced with this deficit which discourages adequate relief. Furthermore the town officer often is appointed because of his own need and is apt to be jealous of anybody to whom he has to give relief. He feels that he is as entitled to it as his neighbor who applies for relief, but fails to consider that he is getting his in the form of the salary as town officer. He is restrained not only by his jealousy but also by his position under the supervisor of the town who is the local political leader. The supervisor is mainly intent on keeping taxes down, not by intelligently eliminating waste in relief but by skimping the appropriation at the disposal of the town officer. If now the county commissioner, in his capacity as overseer of town officers, enjoins adequate relief in county cases handled by town officers, he has the slipshod methods of the town officers to contend with, and his legal authority often has less weight than the extra-legal authority of the local political leader. Furthermore, most county commissioners have to play the game with the local political leaders in order to get nominated and elected. Therefore, though the county commissioner is not appointed by the board of supervisors but elected, he is, unless an unusually strong personality, under their control.

RECOMMENDATIONS

The question of necessary changes in the administration of public relief is the subject of so much difference of opinion and heated controversy among experts in this field that what we can say in a few paragraphs is bound to be unsatisfactory and it might be better to say nothing at all. But that would leave the reader with the impression that nothing is to be done about the situation. Therefore, without implying that the improvement of public relief is to be sought merely by changes in administrative machinery, we shall venture certain suggestions. These will be criticised as not of national application—and they are not intended to be; and as not going far enough—and they are not thorough-going from the standpoint of the constructive political scientist but are offered merely as certain next steps for states like New York.

First, we should abandon the principle of the town as the administrative unit and substitute the county and the city. This can be done in New York under the present law. It would have two main effects. First, it would enable richer towns to share the burden of the poverty of poor towns, which, of course, the richer do not want to do. Second, it would enable the county commissioner to provide himself with a trained staff to do the welfare work throughout the entire county. This group would replace the present politically chosen town officers.[10]

---

[10] Porter, *A Study of Nine Public Relief Agencies*, p. 34.

Our suggestion of a county instead of a town unit therefore involves the second suggestion that only men and women should be appointed to the staff of the commissioner who are trained social workers, and that their professional education and training should be certified, say, by the State Department of Education. We must look forward to the day when, if the locality cannot furnish people with the necessary professional and technical qualifications, these can be chosen from outside.

We are moved to recommend the appointment of trained social workers for two reasons: First, as any person knows who has read Miss Porter's pamphlet, *The Organization and Administration of Public Relief Agencies*,[11] only a trained person can do the work as well as we hope it will eventually be done. Second, one urban county in New York and one city have in each case appointed a social worker as public welfare commissioner and those offices have attained a high standard of efficiency. Whether this proves that the same could be done elsewhere, without other reforms, is a question that requires a detailed study of conditions in that county, and that city, which cannot be undertaken here.

This question of "other reforms" raises the question of the method of choosing the county commissioner. Should not he or she be selected under a merit system from a list of eligibles submitted by state authorities?

The next suggestion relates to state aid. Should not this be made a permanent feature of the Public Welfare Law? This would make the principle of equalization above referred to state-wide. Furthermore, the counties and cities would have to attain a certain standard of welfare work in order to get state aid, that is, provided the state supervisory body was efficient. However, can the high quality of the personnel of the present Temporary Emergency Relief Administration be maintained after the depression? It would be possible only under certain conditions, which are: that adequate funds for ad-

---

[11] This guidance report was prepared at the request of the President's Organization on Unemployment Relief and can be obtained by writing to the Family Welfare Association of America, 130 East 22d St., New York City.

ministration be provided and that the State department to which this administration is entrusted permit the necessary initiative and the maintenance of professional standards. The number of social workers employed would have to be sufficient to make state aid really effective in maintaining a reasonable standard of welfare work, and these men and women would have to be well paid. After efficient state supervision was provided as a permanent organization, time would be required to work out a well defined set of principles in accordance with which its work was to be done. On the working out of these principles would depend both its effective coöperation with other state departments and the degree in which its service could be professionalized.[12]

THE ADVISORY COMMITTEE AND THE ADMINISTRATIVE BOARD

Effective public welfare administration requires the support of intelligent local public opinion. Another suggestion is, therefore, in order. If the local public welfare agency is headed by a paid director, he should have an unpaid advisory committee to represent the citizens of the community in their relation to the agency and to interpret the work of the agency to the community. If the agency is headed by an unpaid administrative board, which appoints and controls the director, then an advisory committee is unnecessary. The argument against this latter form of organization is that it sets up a board between the chief executive of the city or county and the department head, and this decentralized responsibility is unwise especially where the chief executive is an expert city manager. But, given the prevailing form of city and county government, the weight of opinion in the field of social welfare is in favor of the administrative board. The members have overlapping terms to give them greater independence of the appointing official and not only appoint the director, unless he is appointed under some merit system, and hold him accountable, with power to dismiss him, but also determine policies, have general direction of the work of the agency and repre-

---

[12] This is a principle of general application in public welfare administration. See Breckinridge, *Public Welfare Administration*, p. 560.

sent the citizens in relation to it. Effective citizen participation may be secured under either an advisory committee or an administrative board.[13] Without this participation, any interest of a community in its welfare official's activities is apt to take the form of calling him to account either for inadequate relief in this or that family or for spending too much money. An official thus criticised is apt to develop a chronic defensive attitude, which interferes with his peace of mind and efficiency. If now, instead of public opinion being sporadically active and always without a full appreciation of a situation, the public is represented by an advisory committee or an administrative board to which citizens make their complaints, and this committee or board regularly discusses these with the commissioner, he will regard them as something to consider, instead of something to take on the jaw.

No mere form of organization will insure citizen participation. The advisory or administrative body needs an enlightened and progressive community behind it to make it effective. We know boards, appointed by the mayor, that are merely means used by the mayor of rewarding his political associates. If none of these want the unpaid office of member of the board, the mayor appoints certain respectable citizens through whom he can control the appointment and the activities of the public welfare commissioner. The board is merely a cats-paw of the political powers.

The advisory or administrative body would act as the publicity agent of the public welfare office. Wise publicity is an indispensable requisite for the improvement of public welfare. Something may be accomplished by gathering officials into state, national and local associations which hold conferences for the discussion of their problems. But when these officials return home they need an incentive to live up to the aspirations stirred at conferences, and no incentive is so effective as the desire for the approval and esteem of their fellow townsmen. But if there is no publicity, if the thinking people know nothing of the work of the welfare office, the official is

---

[13] Porter, *The Organization and Administration of Public Relief Agencies,* pp. 7-9.

shut in with his own political clique and subjected only to their approval or disapproval. Their influence is not such as to incite him to maintain high standards of administration. Sometimes he can so manipulate the political situation as to carry out his policies and not jeopardize his position or the organization he has built up. Even so he has no sense of security. In the long run the only guarantee of effective public welfare administration lies in the backing of the intelligent people of the community. Without this a state administration of home relief is thwarted in its efforts to improve local conditions and is apt to degenerate into an ineffective and expensive bureaucracy.

The advisory committee is opposed by political demagogues, whose egoism has been concentrated by office-holding and political aspirations. Particularly is this true of mayors, who realize that they are by law given large authority over city departments. This "authority vested in me" makes a certain type of man emotionally unpoised and intent on maintaining the last ounce of his authority. A mayor of a large New York city told the public welfare commissioner: "I don't want you to organize an advisory committee. I will not have anything standing between me and your department, like the board of education." The board of education of this city had successfully opposed the mayor when he wanted to interfere in the affairs of the schools. As one watches the transformation of a mayor newly elected to office—and an elective office seems to inflate a man more than an appointive office—one realizes that the psychological effects of democracy are not wholly good. The feverish impulse to enlarge and maintain authority, especially in a democracy where the competition for office is so keen, stirs an eagerness to see one's name in the paper and to be everywhere conspicuous. Success in winning popularity sometimes turns the head of the mayor, or of the county executive, to the point where the only approach to him is through flattery. One must make him feel that the idea originated with him, in order to gain his support in following out the idea. Now the mayor knows that an advisory committee is intended to originate ideas and to carry them out. He does not want to be thwarted, and an egoistic mayor wants to convey the impression that all wisdom flows from him. Hence his opposition to the advisory committee. We mention this tendency to egoism among officials as an obstacle that often must be overcome before an advisory committee can be started at all; and, after it is started, the committee will have to reckon with it in directing the welfare department. The point is that the progress of democracy lies in centering authority in expert managers and unpaid boards so as to render innocuous the egoism of an official whom political exigencies have elevated to office. As we have shown, a public welfare department in a large city is an extensive organization requiring as expert operation as a business corporation. And, in addition, there is necessary such a sense of social responsibility as not many public welfare commissioners themselves have adequately shown. Hence the need of an advisory committee to protect such commissioners from their own egoism and from that of officials to whom they are subordinate.

The advisory committee or administrative board would emphasize planning in public welfare. It would represent the continuing body in local public welfare administration while the commissioner would change according to political exigencies. The emphasis is placed on planning in all progressive business, and in professional and educational work, as well as social welfare. Says Miss Porter of her study of nine public relief agencies throughout the country: "It is apparent from the agencies studied that progress in the public welfare field has been made only when there has been outstanding leadership in the community. This has varied in the different communities from centralized leadership of a few to broad social planning. . . . The leadership in the nine communities has varied in its effectiveness but it is apparent that only through thoughtful planning can desirable results be reached. Real planning leads to integration rather than domination; and by this sort of thoughtful leadership seemingly insurmountable obstacles can be overcome."[14]

---

[14] Porter, *A Study of Nine Public Relief Agencies*, p. 37.

CHAPTER XI

TRENDS AND CONFLICTS IN PUBLIC HOME RELIEF ADMINISTRATION

THERE ARE TWO approaches to an understanding of trends in public welfare, one through the writings of leaders in this line of work, the other by an investigation of welfare practices. In a country where public welfare administration is highly centralized, the writings of leaders would be of greater importance than where administration is highly localized, as is home relief and child care in America. There it is of first importance to know the local practice. The most relevant data, in the last analysis, are data of behavior—what officials actually do and how what they do affects their clients. Wherefore, in this book we have centered on welfare practices.

Ideas and projects, laws and procedures are to be judged from their effects on the welfare of the people. The pleasure of making plans, the admiration of a smooth-running organization is such that administrators tend to forget that plans are made, an organization is run only to get results, and stands or falls, according to the results it does get. Too often the necessity of showing results leads only to extravagant claims of success.[1] Where these are not made, ineffective administration may be allowed to go on, with the plea that the project is sound and some day the means may be provided to make it effective. For instance, one of the four field workers of the Department of Mental Hygiene of a great state recently said, "What vexes me beyond measure is to have to go from city to city and just start the cures of all these children that

---

[1] Professor Glueck has proved this to be true of the administration of penal institutions, and we need the same kind of checking of other lines of public welfare. See his *500 Criminal Careers*, pp. 4–7.

are brought to the clinics without having time to carry on the treatment and complete the cures." Consider the folly and waste of a system where the working force is so inadequate that cures can be merely started.[2] Would not some of our mental hygienists say that we are still in the childish stage of development of personality in which we love to have projects, to talk about them, to pass laws, to start things, without putting them through to a stage where they will stand a scientific checking up?

The approach to an understanding of the local practice in public welfare administration in America begins with an appreciation of our faith in the individual. Although among the socially superior there always has been a tendency to emphasize "heredity," because that belief implies that those socially superior are also personally superior, the rank and file of Americans have had an abiding faith in the potentialities of the common man. This has fostered a devotion to education as the process of making good those potentialities. Education in turn has been identified with the work of the school. "As a consequence the faith in education becomes a faith in the school, and the school is looked upon as a worker of miracles."[3] From the first, certain classes of children were excluded from those who were the objects of this faith—the dependent, defective, and delinquent. Their deficiency was ascribed to "poor heredity" and public care of them was largely a make-shift. Then began modern child welfare work and the faith in the individual was extended to those on the borderline of social deficiency. In some cities the beginning of advanced child welfare work is definitely connected with work for school children.[4] Welfare work has proved that many socially deficient children are such not because as individuals they differ from other children in heredity, but because they were made so by home influences and neighborhood conditions. The extension of faith in education to children of the once

---

[2] In addition to the four regular field workers, members of the staffs of several of the state hospitals do some work in the clinics.
[3] Counts, *The American Road to Culture*, pp. 16-17.
[4] Chaper XV.

ignored classes is reflected in the change in institutions for socially deficient children from houses of refuge to state training schools or industrial schools, and in the change from institutional to foster home care. In addition to these changes which imply an effort to include socially deficient children in the educational program, the juvenile court also is becoming less a judicial and more an educational institution.[5]

The term, public welfare, thus differs from the traditional charity by implying a kind of educational process whereby rehabilitation is hoped for. Public welfare differs from public education in that it signifies social welfare work by the government for the socially deficient, as contrasted with an educational program that applies to all. However, while this distinction may be made abstractly, the most skillful mental hygienists find social deficiencies very widely distributed among school children. These and other social deficiencies imply that both the social organization to which adjustment must be made and the adjusting individual are factors that require attention and treatment to make good the deficiency. Therefore, though public welfare and education imply two different functions of government, and are clearly enough distinguished where the government has the custody of the socially deficient, these functions often merge into each other and are administered through the same institution, for instance, through the schools, where the visiting teacher administers public welfare and the other teachers carry on the conventional education. These visiting teachers are fine artists in mental hygiene treatment. The public welfare official relieves the homes of economic stress while these teachers bring relief from mental stresses and strains. The spread of the visiting teacher movement is an expression of the trend toward preventive public welfare work through a fine discrimination of potential social deficiency in children.

The laws of over half the states of the Union show some evidence at least of penetration by the new conceptions of public welfare, particularly in their provisions for welfare work for

[5] See the chapter on Trends in Public Welfare by Howard W. Odum in the forthcoming report of the Research Committee on Social Trends.

children.[6] This has come about through the influence of social workers in the public and private fields, who have been consulted in the formulation of new laws and indeed have been the prime movers for those laws and sometimes have drafted them. But the old attitudes to the socially deficient persist everywhere, even among the most "intelligent" people of the community. College graduates often do not know the difference between "charity" and "public welfare." In fact, one often hears social workers themselves talking the old jargon.

The trend toward public, as contrasted with private welfare is seen in the vast increase in expenditures for public welfare during the last quarter century, and in the reliance on the government in emergencies, as compared with the reliance on private contributions in the past.[7] Thus is our "rugged individualism" gradually giving way before a realization of governmental responsibility for the devastation wrought by economic changes before which men are powerless.

The development of public welfare is due to three main causes: first, modern industry; second, democratic government; third, the development of mental hygiene. Modern industry has increased insecurity for the mass of wage-earners, and public welfare is intended to take care of the ravages to health and personality that result from this sense of insecurity and from material needs. Democratic government has extended governmental functions from the traditional protection from invasion and internal disorder to insurance against some of the forms of insecurity. Mental hygiene has revealed a whole brood of insecurities from which children suffer: financial insecurity, insecurity because of friction which imperils the home, and insecurity because of some personal defect that interferes with the child's adjustment in the school or makes him shrink from community contacts. The growing conception of the ravages to which insecurity subjects the personality is causing public welfare to be recognized as a matter not of charity but, as Governor Roosevelt expressed it, "as a matter of social duty."

The Public Welfare Law of New York was passed in April,

---

[6] Huston, *The Social Welfare Laws of the Forty-eight States.*
[7] Odum, *Trends in Public Welfare.*

1929, and the unemployment that culminated in the depression began to be evident about that time, while the financial crash that heralded the depression came in October, 1929. Consequently, the constructive welfare work contemplated by the law was very soon overshadowed by emergency relief. The emphasis in local public welfare administration has been placed on relief, and, up to the establishment of the Temporary Emergency Relief Administration, the lines of the old Poor Law were followed rather than the policies expressed in the new law. Furthermore, public relief has eclipsed private so that the private agencies, which have especially emphasized welfare work, have spoken with diminishing authority. On the other hand, the Bureau of Home Relief of the State Department of Social Welfare and the Temporary Emergency Relief Administration have been cognizant of the significance of the new law, as contrasted with the old Poor Law. So there has been more or less difference of opinion in regard to administration as between the state supervising agencies on the one hand and the local public welfare offices on the other. The public welfare offices are tied up with local politics. Local political organizations are parts of the state political organizations which, in turn, have power to make or unmake the Temporary Emergency Relief Administration and to affect the work of the State Department. This complicated circle of influence and authority is fraught with manifold conflict situations.

The conflict is essentially one between the archaic methods of local relief in homes and the new methods which the state administration is seeking to have put into practice. It seems to be true not only in New York but generally, as Professor Breckinridge puts it, "that in the field of service in which the state institution or the state agency is the appropriate authority, reasonable progress has been made in efficiency and in adequacy of service; whereas in those fields in which reliance is still placed on the local unit, retardation, archaic methods and great unevenness in service still prevails. The almshouse, outdoor relief, and the county jail remain with few exceptions the despair of the social worker and of the public welfare official."[8]

In New York within the last year there has taken place what may prove to be a permanent change in the control of public welfare resulting in a marked change in its administration. As in business, we distinguish between the control of business, which ought to be vested in wage earners and consumers as well as owners, and the administration of business, which ought to be carried on by experts under this control,[9] so in public welfare we distinguish betwen the control of it, which ought to be vested ultimately in all classes of society, not merely in propertied classes, and the administration of public welfare, which ought to be carried on by experts. As we have seen in New York the State Department of Social Welfare was given little administrative power but the Temporary Emergency Relief Administration was given great power. The Emergency Administration represents expert social work practice. The social workers that carry it on are intent on relief of need and so do not share the emotional states either of the propertied classes or of the unemployed. Their attitude is objective. They have set a standard budget that does not satisfy many of the unemployed, who want what they want, nor does it satisfy the propertied classes who want expenditures cut to the bone. There is, then, a conflict between the liberals in welfare work and the local boards, made up largely of representatives of propertied classes, which have heretofore wielded the control in public welfare.

We must keep in mind another conflict situation, that is, the recently repealed Poor Law, with which the attitudes not only of the local public welfare offices but also of local sentiment are still largely articulated, and, in conflict with this, the new Public Welfare Law and the emergency law. The Public Welfare Law was conceived by forward-looking workers in the

---

[8] Breckinridge, *Public Welfare Administration*, p. 4.

[9] Slichter, *Modern Economic Society*, pp. 887-88; Mitchell, *A Preface to Economics*, p. 499.

public and private fields and was set up as an ideal gradually
to be given administrative reality as communities were educated
up to it and as their representatives in the public welfare and
closely related offices (mayor, supervisor) were inducted into
its conceptions. There is, therefore, a conflict between those
moved by attitudes rooted in the past and those motivated
by the enlarging purpose for the future. Let us look at some
phases of this conflict.

Chapter IX raised the question whether the public welfare
office efficiently administers relief and is able to do the constructive work associated in the new law with its relieving function. Only people with a social viewpoint can comprehend the
new law. Consequently, only these people would raise such a
question at all. The significance of the present situation in
New York is that these people are now brought face to face,
as supervisors of relief administration, with local officials many
of whom never have conceived a social point of view but react
in the traditional individualistic manner. Public welfare officials
in name only, they continue to be superintendents or overseers
of the poor as of old. One phase of the conflict is, then, the
conflict between the individually and the socially minded. The
socially minded are objectively centered on the needy, and
everything done is evaluated according to its effectiveness as
constructive relief. The individualistic are thinking primarily
of their own interests, either of economy or personal advancement or some other personal interest, and they have the traditional attitudes to the needy. For instance, they require an
applicant to be practically destitute, while the socially minded
official takes measures to prevent the applicant becoming destitute. They are blind to that provision of the law which requires the public welfare official actively to coöperate with other
welfare agencies, public and private, and to that provision
which requires them to be active for "the improvement of social
conditions," while a socially minded executive is intent on
these aspects of his legal obligations.

Another conflict is that between professionally trained social
workers and rule-of-thumb executives, that is, people who
make motions without any keen interest in what the motion

is intended to achieve, or without much thought as to whether it is calculated to achieve anything at all. For instance, a complaint of an applicant for relief may be attended to with a view to bestowing justice where it is due or to passing the complaint along as a matter of routine and forgetting it. Rule-of-thumb executives raise no question at all about the efficiency of relief and the possibility of associating with it various lines of social welfare work, while to trained social workers, failure to raise such questions is a confession of failure to realize the very nature of the work which the Public Welfare Law requires them to do. The trend in public welfare work seems to be toward increasing conflict between socially minded workers and rule-of-thumb officials. However, once having framed a law requiring a socially minded administration of welfare work, though backward steps may be taken, the trend in that direction seems bound to go on. The vastness and the urgency of relief and welfare problems require the utmost intelligence in handling them. This will become evident and the local communities will be forced to learn more about the law and about their own welfare work. Meanwhile we must expect increasing conflict and try to give it publicity and interpret it in order that the communities may learn what it is all about and may appreciate the importance of the outcome.

This awakening of communities is much more pronounced at certain points within the state than at others, depending on the local situation. For instance, in one city where the inefficiency of the public welfare office had become notorious, at a favorable moment the incumbent was replaced by one of the ablest social workers in the country, possibly to forestall an investigation of the office, the idea being that the new incumbent would remove all suspicions of any further inefficiency and the citizens would be willing to let by-gones be by-gones; or the Temporary Emergency Relief Administration may have influenced this appointment. At any rate, because of the local situation a sudden change was brought about from one extreme of public welfare administration to the other. In another city the inefficient public welfare official was allowed to continue in office but, through the influence of the Emergency Administration, an efficient social worker was installed who tactfully checkmated him into the position of a rubber stamp, ran the office efficiently and let him take the credit. In still another city, where the rule of the dominant political party has for some time been disputed by a strong insurgent movement in its own ranks, the public welfare office has not become so inefficient that it has been necessary to "kick it upstairs," nor has it been discreetly transformed, but a radical experiment is being tried there by the State Administration with the coöperation of the local authorities. Here again the local political situation as a whole has affected the quality of public welfare administration and determined in a measure the method of attack. So we go from one city to another and find a different political situation in every one, requiring different tactics in public welfare. But in all the cities the great catastrophe has given public relief an importance it never before has had. Thoughtful citizens are beginning to realize that their only hope is in socially minded welfare executives with a background of professional training. However, these thoughtful citizens have not as yet got enough influence behind their idea to free a public welfare official of his political bonds. He is reminded of his political obligations when the time comes to make campaign contributions, even though he does not belong to the party in power. He must make his bow with a contribution at least. And he must make it in other ways also.

Another aspect of the conflict between the old and the new attaches to the emphasis of the new law on home relief as compared with that of the old on institutional relief. This is due to the new law's emphasis on constructive treatment as contrasted with mere poor relief. Families are to be kept together as long as possible: "They shall not be separated for reasons of poverty alone," nor, as the law implies, for reasons of economy alone. A further extension of the welfare principle is the provision of work relief (as in the law creating the Temporary Emergency Relief Administration). As against this emphasis on home relief and work relief, the first impulse of some welfare officials schooled in the old Poor Law, when depression and the emergency came, was to turn as many needy families as possible to the county home.

A third conflict arises over the importance given the care of children in the new Public Welfare Law. Under the old law children were merely attaches of a poor family. The new law recognizes the various children's agencies of proved worth in the community and enjoins the public welfare official to co-operate with these and not only this but himself to engage in various lines of welfare work for the children under his charge —health work, mental hygiene work, juvenile court work. On the one hand, then, we have incompetent public welfare officials who have not yet come to a realization of this aspect of their duties under the law and, on the other hand, those who understand the new obligations and the state supervisors who aim to instruct the officials and their communities in these new meanings of the law.

A fourth conflict arises out of the powers of supervision and control entrusted to the State Department and the Temporary Emergency Relief Administration. Most public welfare officials still think of themselves as answerable only to some local politician, as was the case in the old days with the superintendents and overseers of the poor. Since these local politicians collectively constitute, with state politicians, the party organizations that control the legislature, which, in turn, in many ways affects the fortunes of the State Department, it follows that the representatives of that Department who deal with local officials, and who often find themselves in conflict with the local politicians that have heretofore controlled the officials, must tread warily. Merely giving a State Department and an Emergency Administration supervisory and controlling power over local welfare officials has not by any means taken the welfare offices out of political control.

A fifth conflict arises out of the dependence of the public welfare office on other agencies for funds. This dependence shows the difficulty of making progress in one line of public administration while another is still set in the grooves of the past. The enforcement of the new Public Welfare Law is tied up with other old laws still unchanged, among them the tax laws. As we go deeper into the circle of conflict situations we come to the conflict over taxation between the well-to-do who are anxious to conserve their own goods and those who want to have put into effect the full implications of the Public Welfare Law. The well-to-do, in turn, are divided into conflicting groups—real estate owners who feel that the singling out of real estate for taxation is unjust, security owners who do not want to be taxed more than they are, and salaried men who do not want to be taxed any more. So we find the same situation noted by Plato so long ago, the division of the community into well-to-do and poor and the division of the well-to-do into groups and of poor into groups, all more or less in conflict. Outside of all this, as far as possible, stand those who have the law's conception of public welfare at heart, with the desire of turning all conflicts to the account of the public welfare program that has been moved, seconded and passed by the representatives of all the communities of the State in the legislature assembled.

These trends and the conflicts they involve between the old and the new are seen not only in the State of New York but in other states where conceptions of public welfare are functioning. In all there are the socially minded and the rule-of-thumb workers, those who are still inclined toward the old institutional care as against the new constructive home treatment, those who still regard children merely as members of a family rather than as distinct personalities with problems of their own, and those who stand for the old local isolation and control as against the new state supervision. In the great industrial states the conflicts between the old and the new attitudes may be more varied, though not by any means are they more intense or vital than in the rural states. Rural social workers who have won their spurs as county workers in New York go to western states as state supervisors of county work and there fight their battles over again with county judges and other politicians who want the people to continue to feel that all good things flow from them, and who therefore, distrust these experts because they suspect them of knowing more than they do about welfare work and so of being difficult to control. But by a more mature use of the same strategy with which they made some headway in the face of the traditional decentralized public welfare administration in New York, they achieve more striking results in the West where local traditions are not so strong.

The two main trends in public welfare work, toward centralized supervision by experts and toward a finer discrimination of needs of the socially deficient that are entitled to recognition by public officials, are spreading through the country. As to the first trend, the preceding chapers have shown the evils of local administration with little state supervision. The attitude against state supervision, the distrust of it in New York is expressed by local officials in various ways. The prevailing idea has been that "these state people don't know as much about our local conditions as we do." They may be useful in interpreting a point of law but their ideas about relief do not fit our local conditions. It has been impossible as yet for the State Department of Social Welfare to assemble public welfare officials in certain centers for short courses of instruction but they have been brought to conferences and advised in their own localities. The trend toward centralization is thus a trend toward more intelligent direction of public welfare work. The trend toward finer discrimination is seen for instance, in the budgeting of families to be relieved and in the beginning of welfare work for children in offices staffed with one or more expert workers. Discrimination of needs is encouraged by giving publicity both to crude public welfare administration and to examples of fine leadership in this field.

CHAPTER XII

THE WORK OF PRIVATE WELFARE AGENCIES

THE MOST IMPORTANT private welfare agencies are the nursing agencies, the children's agencies, and the family welfare societies.

The Red Cross nursing agencies are supported by the community chest or by contributions of citizens. The nurses are called into homes where the family cannot employ a private nurse. The nurse makes regular visits and charges a small fee for each visit. If the family is unable to pay the fee, it pays according to its ability. If it cannot pay anything, the nursing is given free, and the patient receives the same care as one who pays. If the condition of the patient requires it, the nurse does bedside nursing.

During the depression the demand for nurses has greatly increased, in some cities is twice as great as before, and much of this is for free service. At the same time, one-half or more of the agencies of the country have suffered a reduction of appropriations. One effect of the inadequate service is that, while families need to be taught now, more than ever, the fundamentals of proper diet and care of the health, this part of the program has had to be given up because of the increasing need for nursing service. The inability to do this preventive work is especially disastrous to children. Nurses have not time to follow up cases of under-nourished children until the public welfare department has been persuaded to improve the diet. In a few cities nutrition committees have been organized to do this but not generally.

The emergency has caused a more effective coöperation between visiting nurses who specialize in physical treatment and psychiatric social workers who center on the mental health.

The professional attitude of a nurse is one of taking orders from a doctor and giving orders to a patient in bed. But when she becomes a visiting nurse she goes from door to door and, as one of them says, "the nurse who has not learned the technique of making friends with a watch-dog never gets inside the door of many of her homes." Once inside she must make friends with old and young. These conditions make the visiting nurse a kind of social worker. The forced coöperation in the great emergency has shown the nurse what an advantage it is to understand the emotions of people, and has taught her to appreciate the emotional conditions that interfere with the curative effect of purely physical measures of relief. And it has shown the psychiatric social worker how important it is to consider the purely physical conditions of existence. Nurses are coming to feel that they need to know not only psychiatric nursing for the care of the mentally diseased but also mental hygiene, that is, ways of treating more or less simple problems of personality, for the everyday practice of nursing.[1]

CHILDREN'S AGENCIES

The work of a children's agency differs from that of a family welfare society in this: the family society works with a family when its problem only incidentally involves a child, while the children's agency takes the case when the problem centers in some child. The more effective the social case work of the family society, the less apt are family situations to come to a point which require the attention of the children's agency. When they do, the care of a child, even its removal from parents and placement in a foster home, creates a family problem that requires the technique of the family agency. So the two societies work in very close relations.

A society that exists solely for the welfare of children is necessary because this involves a ready knowledge of the child protective and child labor laws, and of the technique and devious ways of approach whereby the police, the public welfare and other departments are to be enlisted in doing what must be done for the welfare of children. Furthermore, there

[1] Fox, "The Nurse and Psychiatric Work," *Survey*, Dec., 1931, p. 307.

are family situations where a case worker would err because she is not an expert in child problems. Then too the probation officers of the court cannot successfully care for certain kinds of children put on probation to them without expert advice, nor can a judge wisely decide what to do in many juvenile cases without the advice of a children's agency.

A children's agency is a center of enlightened ideas with respect to the physical and mental health of children in a surrounding darkness of traditional beliefs and prejudices. It usually employs experts for making physical and psychiatric examinations of children under sixteen, social workers to investigate the family conditions of dependent, neglected, and delinquent children and a child placing department. It may also have a child study department and a temporary home for children. It may give clothing, medical supplies and other relief, or may bring these needs to the attention of the public welfare office. Whether it is able to get the needs provided for depends on its personnel, on its social backing in the city and on the number of years during which it has been extending its work through the community. To bring a children's agency to a high degree of efficiency takes time.

FAMILY WELFARE SOCIETIES

These societies are found in many cities though not by any means in all. They almost invariably started as non-sectarian and later the Catholic and Jewish groups withdrew and formed separate organizations. In the small cities only the Protestant organization is financially strong enough to support a full-time paid worker and this worker does case work in all families regardless of sect. In the larger cities the Catholic and Jewish societies have paid workers who do case work with families of their own sect. Up to the time of the depression, the family welfare society had charge of the case work throughout the city. However advisable case work by a public welfare office might be, it was done very little.

The usual method of the case worker is "to establish such a relationship with the family, such a sympathetic and understanding relationship, as to be able to bring out the strengths within the family itself, its resourcefulness, with the aim of enabling the family to stand upon its own feet.

"That means, of course, that there are normally many families under the care of family welfare agencies which are not particularly in need of relief . . . normally anywhere from 80 to 50 per cent are receiving other types of service.

"Then, with the families requiring relief, those other services are outstanding. As far as relief is concerned, there is an attempt to weave it into those services merely as a part of them, and to . . . base it on the varying individual needs of the family. . . .

"Also a part of the normal operations of any family welfare agency is a very close coöperation with other agencies in the community in behalf of the families themselves. As an illustration, in a large proportion of the families there are serious health problems which may or may not arise from economic distress. In those instances there is a close coöperation with the health agency. . . . There is a close coöperation with recreational agencies where the recreational needs of children are concerned. . . . The whole fabric of social organization of the community enters into the picture; and it is a part of the normal function of an agency to make use of those community resources on behalf of the families."[2] Mr. Swift goes on to say that the depression forced these societies to accept many more families than they could do case work with. In some instances they had three times as many families in 1931 as in 1929, but even so they could take on only 40 to 70 per cent of the applicants. They could maintain relief and case work standards for only a small percentage of their clients, those with whom they had been doing constructive work for some time. So we see to what extent children of the unemployed have failed to have the services of the family society.

The family society is controlled by a board of trustees chosen, among other reasons, with a view to their ability to contribute money and enlist contributions necessary to carry on the work. Because of this control, the paid social worker

---

[2] Testimony of Mr. Swift before U. S. Senate Committee on Unemployment Relief, pp. 88-90.

or workers, who alone have direct contact with needy families, cannot speak out with entire freedom about working conditions, low wages and other economic causes of family troubles. Furthermore, the professional requirement of secrecy about the affairs of their families or "clients" may lead social workers to keep silence about conditions that require publicity if they are to be remedied. Of course the same is true of the medical, the nursing, the engineering and other professions.[3] Much as they may want to, social workers are not free to enlist interest and aid by making public specific cases and circumstances with names, places and dates, in order to prove the disastrous effects of the depression on parents and children.

The trustees of the family society come mostly from the city of the well-to-do and so cannot readily appreciate the problems before their social workers. The social worker tries to bridge this gulf by having a "case committee" made up of the well-to-do in which concrete family problems of the other city are presented for discussion. There is constantly an effort to bring new people into this inner circle, and out of this group are recruited the volunteers who, in emergencies, assist the social workers. But case work has necessarily become so technical that laymen cannot understand it other than superficially. The members of a case committee are apt to feel that they cannot advise on a case because they lack the equipment. On the other hand, if the members of the committee are doers of welfare work, not merely women of wealth and prestige, and are interested enough to attend meetings regularly, the discussions are bound to extend their knowledge of social work, as is evident from the questions they ask.[4] It is hoped that they will interpret social work to the community and the community's view of social work to the professional worker.

Mr. Walter West, executive secretary of the American Association of Social Workers, made a very interesting comment on the case committee in his testimony before the United States Senate Committee on Unemployment Relief: "We have

---

[3] Williams, *Principles of Social Psychology*, Chs. XVI-XVII; Atkins and associates, *Economic Behavior*, I, p. 437.

[4] Newmeyer, "A Case Committee under the Microscope," *Jewish Social Service Quarterly*, March, 1932, pp. 139-40.

. . . community chest budget committees and local city councils . . . who are asking that this and that and the other relief appropriation be cut down, and the way to keep getting your figure up is to organize . . . a case committee and bring illustrative cases before that committee, and then ask them what they would cut out of the relief figure, and of course they are always so appalled by the small amount of relief that is given that it works very well in getting an increase usually instead of a decrease in the amount."[5]

Interest in the work of the family society has been weakened for the time being by the imperative need of emergency relief. The attention of citizens has become centered on the public welfare office. The funds at the disposal of public welfare offices have greatly increased. So community chest committees have notified family societies and children's agencies that they must diminish relief to their clients and turn over cases requiring relief to the public offices. The suddenness with which many families were thus thrown on a public office unequipped for welfare work has resulted in extreme hardship to children. For instance, the children's agency of one city had been giving children under its care necessary clothing and medical care. This agency was notified by the "Chest" that it must cease giving any relief at all. So it was forced to turn over to the public office all those families in which children needed clothing or medical care, with recommendations as to what should be done in each case, though it was clear that the office, unequipped to render these services, would not do it. One result was that a child ill of nutritional anemia, who has been started on the road to recovery by the physician who was giving his services to the private society, died of neglect.

The family welfare society and the children's agency have been pioneers in the working out of social welfare standards and during the emergency these social workers have sincerely aimed to maintain these standards. In this they have fought more or less of a losing fight, and it has been with some bitterness of spirit that they have heard this fight interpreted by the lay public and by government officials as a struggle

---

[5] *Report of U. S. Senate Committee on Unemployment Relief*, p. 68.

to protect their own jobs. Our observation has been that, in the great majority of instances, the social worker's anxiety has not been primarily for his or her job but for getting a job well done. A large number of the professional social work group realize that, if social work should become public, there ultimately would be a place for them in public welfare work.

The passing of the relief-giving function of the family society, in some cities, has curtailed its case work because families that need case work of course do not apply for that but for relief. Therefore, as the rumor goes abroad that the private society is not the place to get relief, the movement of applicants is toward the public office. So it is natural that private workers should consider the ultimate effect of this trend. Some private societies have reacted to their solicitude by saying that they would prove their right to exist by doing what they could to make their standards effective in public welfare work. This of course is of prime importance. A children's bureau in one of our large cities handles one-third of the cases of problem children while two-thirds fall within the field of the public welfare office which until recently had done practically nothing for them. Shall the majority be sacrificed just because they do not fall within the program of the private society?

There is occasionally a private society that is inclined to hold aloof from the public office much as the impeccable citizen declares that "politics are rotten," when at the same time he is too self-righteous to mix in and do something about it. We have found two reasons for this attitude. One is the tendency of professionally trained people of a certain temperament to be on the defensive because they are over-conscious of the difference between themselves and the untrained. A susceptibility to inferiority or superiority feeling will exaggerate this defensive attitude. In people of this temperament scientific standards sometimes become so exacting as to make those who hold them intellectual aristocrats. Then, like other aristocrats, they may rationalize themselves into the belief that they are justified in thinking of the whole situation from the standpoint of their own self-preservation. This exclusive attitude among social workers is exceptional but, in some cases, there has been enough of it to make coöperation with the public office difficult. Another reason for the aloof attitude of some private societies is that their boards of trustees are aloof. One influential member of a private society gave as a reason for this opposition to the society's coöperating with the public office by doing case work with the families of applicants for relief that "if we get started in that, the public office is apt to get caught in something sooner or later and we'll be mixed up in it." There is no denying the fact that the public welfare office is bound up with municipal politics at present and those who habitually hold aloof from politics will have something of this attitude toward the public office.

The increase in the importance of public relief during recent years has raised the question of the place of the private society in our welfare administration. The weight of opinion seems to be that it has a permanent place.

Miss Edith Abbott observes that "the great advances in social work in the future must come through public rather than private agencies since only the public agencies can secure adequate funds for meeting modern standards."[6] This is true and still in the family welfare field there are lines of social work for which taxpayers will not pay, and which can be "sold" to contributors if the private society is alive in "selling" its program. For instance, case work is required in many family situations where the main problem is not financial at all but one of adjustment of member to member. This type of problem family is in evidence especially in prosperity when maladjustment is not masked under financial difficulties. These case work problems lead to others which the public office will not concern itself with, as when the case worker finds that one of the main troubles in a certain family is that a bright boy has had to leave school and go to work so that a scholarship must be secured to enable him to go back to school; or that a mother just home after an operation needs to be sent to a convalescent home. The private office will need to have funds

---

[6] Abbott, *Social Welfare and Professional Education*, p. 50.

for the relief incidental to case work, and should not be dependent on the public office for kinds of relief which taxpayers
will not support.

A second function of the private society is that of experimentation.[7] A good deal of the work for boys and girls now
regularly carried on by public agencies was once experimental
work of private societies, which would not have been taken over
by the public agencies unless its worth had first been proved.
The progress of welfare work will always require experimentation which the public office cannot carry on, if for no other
reason than its dependence on tax money.

A third reason for the importance of the private society is
its constant pressure on the public office toward more effective
relief work. The private society has proved to citizens the need
of investigation and case work and politicians are beginning to
realize that the public welfare department must be able to co-
operate with these informed citizens and with the private
society. If a private society did nothing else, its existence would
be justified. Because of its influence public welfare officials are
in some instances becoming impatient with their political tutel-
age. They realize that politicians know nothing about welfare
work. We are not saying that we can take the public welfare
office out of politics in the near future, any more than we can
take the police department out of politics. But the private
society is one of the most effective instruments for moving
the public office in that direction.[8]

An extended discussion of the relation of the public to the
private welfare office does not fall within the scope of this
book. Miss Porter, after a study of nine public relief agencies,
one of them in New York (Syracuse), says: "No definite conclusions can be arrived at as to the division of responsibility
between public and private agencies from the communities
studied; and there is an indication that since the depression
there is even a wider difference of opinion as to this division

---

[7] Porter, *A Study of Nine Public Relief Agencies*, p. 37.
[8] Probably the most effective instrument is the Council of Social Agencies,
where this is not dominated by financial interests that control the "Chest"
policy. See Kelso, "Banker Conrol of Community Chests," *Survey*, May
1, 1932.

than previously existed." She notes the main points in the division at Syracuse, which has been worked out by a Family Study Committee of public and private, lay and professional persons under the able leadership of the commissioner of public welfare, Frederick I. Daniels. Some of these points are: The public agency shall bear the heaviest part of the relief burden; it shall undertake those cases in which the capacity for self-support does not exist to any considerable measure; questions of insufficient family earnings and of property equity are to be worked out by a committee representing both public and private agencies; the private agencies shall concern themselves with the study and development of the means by which wholesome family life may not only be conserved but enriched.[9] This makes the private society a conserver of the family and of wholesome childhood, in which, as we have seen, the public welfare office has failed, in spite of its legal obligations.

The private family agency is dependent on voluntary contributions for support and it is necessary, therefore, for the public to know of its work. The public office also, as we have seen, needs intelligent public support. This raises the question of the means of education of the public. The most important means undoubtedly is the newspaper. We may, therefore, at this point, discuss that subject.

WHAT THE NEWSPAPERS HAVE DONE

The publicity that welfare work has received is not the kind most needed. Newspapers have written of relief projects under way and of funds being raised. They have not given the well-to-do an adequate picture of the real needs in the city of the poor nor any critical appraisal of the projects under way.

If a work project was started and some of those who were to be given work failed to appear, that was made much of in the papers without any intelligent comment as to why they did not come. If a family which had applied for relief was found to have $50 in the bank, the paper published this as

---

[9] Porter, *A Study of Nine Public Welfare Agencies*, pp. 30-31.

an indication of the frauds perpetrated by applicants for relief. It did not investigate the case and give extenuating circumstances that might come to light. Again, newspapers have been too apt to take the attitude of the well-to-do who are centered on economy. In one city the public welfare commissioner, known to social workers for his inadequate relief and unsocial point of view, boasted at the end of his fiscal year that he had turned over to another department several thousands of dollars of his relief fund. He was praised by the newspapers and the public for his economy, though social workers knew that he had half starved hundreds of the unemployed and their children.

Stories of money raised and of projects under way have various effects on the unemployed, and also on landlords, employers, and the public. First, note the unfavorable effects on the unemployed. Many families bestir themselves for their share of the funds. Relief agencies have reported that directly after a newspaper story of funds being raised the offices were thronged with applicants. These people in many cases had legitimate needs. But the cupidity of many was excited, and the story brought needy to the city from other places. This increased unworthy applications and made it more difficult for relief agenies to handle their cases. Many of those who applied quoted the papers and showed themselves familiar with the projects under way. Case work with deserving families was more difficult. They resisted the advice and plans of social workers where family coöperation was necessary because the family "knows that the money is there." On the other hand there were some favorable effects of the stories of funds raised. Many industrious poor, who were in a starving condition and morbid, were encouraged by reading of help coming. Proud and deserving poor who had been suffering in secret made known their wants. The influx of applicants enabled public health nurses to discover and remedy new health needs.

We turn to effects of news stories on landlords, employers, and the public generally. Landlords are sometimes incited to dispossess tenants because they think the city will pay the rent. Employers are encouraged to believe that they have no responsibility because the city will look after their workmen.

A social worker asked an employer for a contribution to help one of his workmen who had been with him for several years until he was let go with the closing of the plant. The employer remarked that the man must have resources because he had paid him twenty-three dollars a week for several years. The man had a family and the social worker explained that twenty-three dollars was barely enough to support a family, so he could not be expected to save. Thereupon the employer retorted, "Well, let Montgomery or some other up-lifter do it." Employers come to rely on the "up-lifters" who lead in raising funds. As to the effect on the public, stories about funds give publicity to the hard times, make people who still have sufficient income cautious about spending, and keep others complacent with the idea that everything is being done that can be done. So much talk about funds blinds people to the need of welfare work by making it appear that the situation calls for money only, whereas it requires the expert handling of a great variety of family and child problems.

Our American way of raising a considerable part of relief funds by private contributions necessarily involves a good deal of publicity and propaganda. The effect of this is thus described by one who took a leading part in raising the $7,000,000 spent for relief in Philadelphia up to January first, 1932: "By the first of the year, then, Philadelphia will have spent $7,000,000 for the unemployed. . . . Obviously, to arouse the giving public, the City Fathers, and our legislators to a realization of the tragedies in our midst, we were compelled to resort to considerable propaganda. The publicity given to the human interest stories led, in some quarters, to hysteria. That hysteria resulted in the creation of 75 bread lines and neighborhood relief societies. . . . Picture 'the American System,' with all the demoralizing features which we associate with the term 'dole,' as it supposedly exists in England— and bear in mind that in Philadelphia, at least, we had the situation under such control that we became the envy of other communities."[10]

---

[10] Billikopf, "What Have We Learned About Unemployment," *Proceedings of National Conference of Social Work*, 1931, Reprint.

What kind of publicity is needed? The well-to-do should learn just what the needs are and what public and private agencies are doing to meet them and what they are failing to do. If public welfare officials are crude in their dealings with the needy, if they have a stupid attitude to economize at any cost, if they take orders from politicians, this should be made public. Landlords and other creditors should be sufficiently informed as to conditions among unemployed families to realize their responsibility. The unemployed should be able to learn from the newspapers where the welfare offices are and what they are trying to do. The office should be represented as a place where wise counsel can be had and relief if necessary. Above all, the needs of children should be published, with typical cases of malnutrition and bad effects on behavior caused by insufficient relief.

There is sometimes a very special need of publicity, as when adequate relief funds are blocked by a little group which holds an influential position in the politics of the city, or when the constructive work of years is about to be wiped out by a stupid slashing of the budgets of public schools and social agencies. Such situations require an attempt at a quick education of the people through the press on the importance of the schools and social agencies.

As a way of getting such publicity it is suggested that the advisory committee of the public welfare office should have frequent conferences with a committee of the press and interpret the purpose of welfare work with concrete illustrations of how it is working out.

Effects of the Depression on Welfare Workers

This chapter would not be complete without a paragraph on the effects of the depression on family case workers, nurses, visiting teachers, clinical, and court workers. These people have come to realize the paramount importance of industrial conditions. Even before the depression, to more than one social worker the psychiatric approach to social work had become a sort of compensation for a sense of futility before thwarting industrial conditions. There was a tendency to take refuge in the intricacies of psychiatric technique before the difficulties presented by unemployment and the poverty of the family. But the compensation no longer compensates. While social workers are insisting more than ever on the psychiatric approach, the outstanding attitude at the moment is an emphasis on the necessity of greater economic security. As one person puts it, social workers have "a new faith in, and a new doubt about, the value of social work." They feel that "social workers as a group should actively engage in efforts to alter the economic system which is breeding the ills we seek to alleviate"; that "case work unaccompanied by concern for our social and economic structure is largely futile."

Social workers have a responsibility for pointing out the industrial causes of family difficulties for they know these better than anybody else. They have daily contact with the unemployed. Yet they are often prevented, because of their network of obligations and responsibilities, from telling what the conditions are. Obviously the way out is to tell some one who is in a position to take the responsibility for publicity and who has the good judgment to make it effective.

CHAPTER XIII

WHAT THE CHURCHES AND OTHER RELIGIOUS ASSOCIATIONS HAVE DONE

THE DEPRESSION has had these effects on the churches: their income has diminished; their traditional function of offering solace to poverty-stricken masses has been exercised to some extent; many churches have started new relief projects; churches have been subjected to cross currents of criticism because of their failure to do relief work and because of the relief work they have tried to do. The two last effects are true of churches which do relief work only in emergencies, not of those which have well established family welfare societies.[1]

Churches have differed as widely as public welfare offices in their helpfulness during the depression. A few churches, under rare leadership, have done excellent service. If we give less attention to these than to those of which this cannot be said, it is because we are particularly interested in the obstacles to intelligent and humane welfare and relief programs.

The Church has in times past offered solace in adversity. It still does. But this does not reach thousands of poor because they have not good enough clothes to go to church. Middle class families once prosperous have lost their incomes, cannot dress well and have ceased going to church. To many of them, when prosperity returns, their church life will remain a thing of the past. Children have ceased going to Sunday School and church clubs because their clothes are unfit. Some churches do not want children of the poor in their clubs. For instance, one of the most effective visiting teachers of a large city was

---

[1] We are not considering the welfare and relief work carried on through prosperity and depression by Jewish and Roman Catholic family welfare societies, financed in some cities by the community chest.

discharged because the board of education wanted to economize. She had formed a club of under-privileged boys which met in a school building, and this club had diminished delinquency in that section of the city. But the board of education would no longer allow the room lighted and heated for the meetings of these boys. So, before she went away, she asked two churches in the vicinity to take these boys into their clubs. The churches refused on the ground that their children belonged to a different social class and the classes did not mix. The solace and other benefits of some churches are, therefore, not for those who need them most.

There is another reason for the failure of the traditional solace to reach the people. Among the rural population of the past, adversity was mainly due to the weather and to sickness, accidents and other conditions that were thought to be beyond man's control. In the present industrial age the belief has spread abroad that depression is not inevitable, and one finds everywhere a resentment that will not quiesce into religious resignation. Attempts of clergymen so to handle it are resented, and many of them do not make the attempt. The economic order is so at variance with the teaching of Jesus that clergymen are beset with perplexities. For instance, John Haven, a church elder, was foreclosing a mortgage on Charles Foster, an industrious workman who had never missed his payments until the depression. Charles confronted John: "Jesus Christ wouldn't do this," he pleaded.

"What has that got to do with it!" exclaimed John.

"But my children will be thrown on the street!"

Neither had that anything to do with it. Dependent as the Church is on an economic order that is alien to the teachings of the founder of Christianity, many clergymen are inclined to escape into the traditional formulas. But people are impressed by the contraditions between what these imply and actual conditions. The poor cannot reconcile the teaching of brotherly love with the way in which their fellow church members, who apparently have plenty, deprive them of their homes or let them go half starved and scantily clad. We find this attitude widespread among adults and it passes to the children.

While the solace of the Church does not reach the people as universally as it once did, more of them are going to psychiatric clinics. Many of these are church members. The woman referred to in a preceding chapter, who had a nervous breakdown just after she had to diminish her contribution to the church, went to a psychiatrist for treatment.

The Church is connected with relief projects in several ways. Instead of each church caring for its own poor, as in former years, the members contribute to the community chest. In addition to this, however, many churches have their own relief projects. They offer gifts of money, food, clothing, toys, loans, and scholarships for school children who would otherwise have to leave school. They run employment bureaus and nurseries for children whose mothers must work. These efforts have helped to meet the criticism that the church as such is doing nothing for the needy. But churches which run these relief projects are sometimes criticised by social workers as superficial and tactless in investigation, and spasmodic and unsystematic in the assistance given. Their resources are uncertain and, it is said, often they undertake what they cannot carry through. They "spoil" some families and then leave them for the established agencies to handle. They fail to use the social service exchange or central index and so complicate relief administration. They duplicate relief and other agencies have difficulty in finding out these cases because the families are reticent. On the other hand, where a church undertakes some specific work, as providing scholarships for school children, or a club for under-privileged boys, or milk or medical care for families designated by the school nurse, the service is very valuable. In March, 1932 the Society of Friends was providing one meal a day for over 30,000 undernourished children in the soft coal regions of Pennsylvania and other states.

In addition to these valuable specific services the Church has a more important function than it is fulfilling in connection with unemployment and social welfare. While a few churches have been outspoken on behalf of the unemployed, most of those in the cities studied have not been as alive to their sufferings as they should have been. A leader in emergency relief

in a large city said: "Not a clergyman in this city has spoken
out loud enough to make himself heard against the malnutrition of children." How much have the people heard from the
clergy about the different ways in which the city of the poor
is paying for the depression? Facts like those cited in this
book are evident to any intelligent man who is interested enough
to inquire into the condition of the unemployed in his city.
The plain fact is that the well-to-do generally do not want to
hear how the unemployed are faring; the subject is unpleasant, and the recital would disturb the peace of a church service.
Yet we hear a good deal about the "church militant." Should
not such a church speak out concretely, not in general terms,
on the sufferings and the permanent injuries of the unemployed
and their families? Should it not actively coöperate with public
and private welfare agencies by attempting some education
of citizens in the work of the welfare organizations of the
city? With the many citizens attending services more or less
regularly and in a receptive frame of mind, the Church has
a rare opportunity for adult education along these important
lines.

The Church, like other institutions, has failed to realize the
interdependence of all institutions. It has been inclined to put
its own dogmas first. Traditionally it has regarded itself as
above all institutions. Rulers have been thought of as ruling
only by divine right. Later these political pretensions were
given up and the Church merely took for granted or essayed
to perpetuate with its blessing the economic and political order
within which it happened to exist, though recently prominent
individuals and small groups in various denominations, Catholic, Protestant and Jewish, have quite sharply criticised certain aspects of the economic and political order. But the order
itself, egocentric profit-seeking, has not been attacked as fun-
damentally contrary to religious principles. To this traditional conservatism of the Church is due its hesitancy at the
present time to speak out about the causes of unemployment,
and about the slowness of the government to realize the responsibility of the body politic for relieving need.

The Church's main concern always has been and still is with

the family and with marriage relations on which the welfare of the family was thought to depend. But, in the present situation, the Church has failed to do much for the disordered families described in Part I. One reason for this is that their predicament has in many instances led to situations with which the Church cannot cope because of an unfortunate dogmatism which unfits it to handle those problems. We may approach this subject by a comparison of the Church's attitude with that of the social worker. It is generally recognized that the attitudes of the social worker and the church worker to certain types of family situations are apt to be quite different. The social worker centers on relief of need. She is trained to see the need objectively and to diagnose and treat it. The church worker is apt to be less objective, to be diverted by conventional beliefs about behavior. This difference of attitude causes a conflict in viewpoint between church workers and social workers which only a real effort to see each other's point of view will resolve.[2] To illustrate:

A professional good man wanted to send a Christmas basket to some worthy family. The social worker gave him the name of a mother with four small children. The husband was out of work and they had taken a boarder, a friend of the husband's. The boarder

[2] "One of the outstanding revelations of modern science is that the implications of misconduct are frequently more pathological than moral. To a civilization schooled in the sanctity of moral principles as the foundation of human behavior, this discovery presents a formidable dilemma. After one has pinned his faith to the Ten Commandments and to a moral code derived from them and other authoritative sources, it is not easy to believe that lying, stealing, filial disrespect, profanity, and even sex misconduct are not necessarily to be censured on moral grounds. Frequently no doubt, they should be, and always they are socially undesirable forms of behavior. In the light of modern science, however, they should not be dealt with on moral grounds until they have been studied, analyzed and diagnosed in terms of their causative history. . . .

"Throughout our civilization we have been more interested in conduct than we have in human beings. . . . One who is given to the exercise of easy moral judgments in terms of conduct may find it difficult to withhold those judgments until after he has explored the origins of such conduct. A person in social work who finds it impossible to restrain his tendency to react to human conduct in terms of the traditional moral code before the facts are in, has not developed the degree of objectivity which the professional obligations of social work demand." Lee and Kenworthy, *Mental Hygiene and Social Work*, pp. 237-38.

was in and the husband out when the visitor called. The good man did not like the embarrassed behavior of the woman. As she introduced the boarder she was confused and perplexed by the thought of what was in the mind of so good a man. He went away questioning her morals and later reproached the social worker for sending him to such a home. The worker was not *certain* about the morals of the woman. Overwhelmed with relief work she had not been able to know the family intimately enough to be certain. So she could not be positive enough to reassure the good man. What the worker saw was a woman disheartened by months of privation and anxiety for her children. What he thought he saw was moral laxity. He was not interested in the children.

Our second illustration involves a more complicated situation. By way of approach we may say that very many families disordered by the depression are not merely victims of the depression itself but of a family maladjustment existing before and made more acute by the depression:

Mrs. Bigelow's marriage never had been happy. She had married an "available" young man of a family with which her own had always been on friendly terms. He was the conventional, crude type of fellow who appropriated his wife without much consideration because, to be sure, he owned her and she was his to appropriate. Of course, if she had any sense, she would take his view of marriage. Unfortunately she was refined and did not acquiesce in his ownership. She was somewhat artistic in little ways and longed for a creative life. For seventeen years she endured the relationship, largely for the sake of her young daughter, Jean, a beautiful, artistic child who, at sixteen, gave promise of an unusual talent in drawing. Then the stress of the depression brought their always precarious economic situation to one of dire need. This made the husband more unbearable than ever. Mrs. Bigelow decided to get a divorce. This long process, with what had preceded, so unnerved her, as well as her daughter, that they were not prepared for what followed. She was a member of a church. The members heard of the divorce and "cut her dead." The school girls snubbed Jean in the same way. Mrs. Bigelow had never dreamed that such an experience could have the effect on her that it did. She was completely broken and went into a nervous prostration. They had no means of a livelihood. Jean, also, was on the verge of a break-down. Mrs. Bigelow felt that if she could unburden her troubles to some understanding soul it would lighten her load and help her to recover her balance. She went to her pastor and wanted to tell him all the inside experience that had led up to the divorce. He would not listen to her. "You must work out all those things for yourself," he said.

"But doesn't this pertain to the spiritual life?" she pleaded. "I have tried, I have struggled. Once you preached on 'A Soul's Pilgrimage'."

"No, I cannot talk with you about it."

The real thought in his mind was that his parishioners, especially the most influential of them, were unalterably against Mrs. Bigelow. If he were sympathetic, it might go out that he had "taken her part" and he could not do that. Apparently he did not even think of the child, heart-broken because of her mother's plight.

Mrs. Bigelow went in despair to the social worker, who arranged for her to have the services of a psychiatrist. The doctor did his best but she was not much better. The social worker could see that one of the main causes of her suffering was the social ostracism. How could this be remedied? She brought the case to the attention of an understanding person of no small influence in the community. This person, defying social censure, took Mrs. Bigelow and her daughter on several trips, gave them a thoroughly good time, made them feel her genuine human sympathy, gave them some remunerative work to do. Their acute emotional condition passed and they eventually became more happy and recovered their balance.

These cures were affected without any psychoanalysis, just a few feedings of the milk of human kindness and the bestowal of a sense of security that came of a fine friendship and remunerative work. Is not this spiritual regeneration of the individual the traditional function of the Church? Can it afford to let any dogmatic beliefs stand between it and the fulfillment of this function?

Christianity originated as social work, did it not? Let one who knows the meaning both of Christianity and social work tell us: "In many ways the Master Teacher might illustrate the Master Social Worker. He not only went about doing good, but His goodness invariably found its objectives in the bettering of human fortunes, the strengthening of human relations, the pointing of human destiny. A single illustration of the method and scope which His efforts exemplified will be found in the cases of healing and social adjustment recorded. Of the thirty-six cases with which I have recently renewed a hurried acquaintance, no less than thirty-two were of the essence and spirit of social work. As I interpret them each was performed as a result of an actual need which expressed itself in concrete form and social relationship. . . . There was to Him no limitation of wealth or poverty, of clean or unclean, of happy or bereaved. The centurian or nobleman or widow—all alike were to Him great human cases calling for human adjustment. If sometimes He seemed to favor the poor, He never discriminated against the well-to-do or rich. One would search in vain to find a difference in method or spirit in His treatment of the widow's son, or the nobleman's first born. Always He saw the need; always He worked on this basis."[3]

OTHER RELIGIOUS ASSOCIATIONS

The Y. M. C. A. and the Y. W. C. A. have had a rare opportunity for service during the depression because the age class of the population hardest hit is the boys and girls of working age. These youth are through going to school but have not been able to get work. Furthermore in cities where public relief, including both home and work relief, is limited to married people, these unmarried youth are in a desperate situation. Both the Y. M. C. A. and the Y. W. C. A. have expanded their work to meet the emergency.[4] The Y. W. C. A. has done a good deal for unemployed women and girls without resources, as providing relief, employment, recreation and other services.[5] It has also tried to enlighten well-to-do women on conditions among the unemployed. Thus we read in a report of its industrial department on the education of "other women," that is, women of the well-to-do classes, in industrial problems:

---

[3] Odum, *Public Welfare and Social Work*, pp. 12-14.
[4] National Council of Young Men's Christian Associations, Statement Regarding the Activities of the Y. M. C. A.'s of the United States in Relation to the Problems of Unemployment, 1930 to March 1931. See also the special report of the Rochester, the Hartford and other city Y. M. C. A.'s.
[5] See the reports by the National Board of the Young Women's Christian Associations, especially "Ways in which Y. W. C. A.'s Have Met the Problem of Unemployment among the White Collar Group," "Young Women's Christian Ass'n., National Program in Time of Unemployment," "Ways in Which the Y. W. C. A. is Tackling Unemployment," Series on Social Consequences of Unemployment and Mobilization of Association Resources," Bulletins I-XIII; "Community Planning for Unemployed Women without Resources."

"Although the problems of the depression are for most industrial women workers an intensified form of problems that continually oppress them—low wages, long hours, under-employment or unemployment, general insecurity—these problems seemed brand new to large numbers of middle-class women." After saying that this education, involving difficult controversial questions, has been carried forward with some success, the report continues: "With these encouraging trends, however, must be mentioned frequent efforts at dictatorship by business interests. There are all too many instances of local boards succumbing to such dictatorship, either in the stress of a strike or in the atmosphere of fear and discouragement caused by the depression. Sometimes this has taken the form of soft-pedaling the industrial aspects of the program of the Industrial Department in deference to protests from business interests, sometimes the dismissal of an industrial secretary with whom a board does not feel quite comfortable even though unable to criticise her work . . . ; sometimes it has taken the form of ignoring or ostracising girls who have been active in labor organizations or in strenuous labor education within the Y. W. C. A.

"On the other hand there are notable examples of boards refusing to be dictated to, keeping an industrial secretary, for example, in the face of her being called 'communistic' by certain business interests; in another case deliberately choosing a small program on a reduced budget instead of a large budget by acceding to the opinion of the dominant community group."[6]

The Young Men's and Young Women's Christian Associations have traditionally been concerned with the regeneration of the individual. In these character building efforts the organizations are increasingly brought into conflict with economic institutions. The interdependence between all kinds of religious organizations and economic institutions has been demonstrated during the depression as never before and religious organizations cannot evade the problems thus raised.

---

[6] National Board of Young Women's Christian Associations, *Biennial Report of Industrial Department*, p. 12.

The practices of these associations vary widely. In many places they amount to no more than clubs for the young people of the middle classes; the less favored classes make up no part of their membership and, indeed, would not only not be welcomed but would be discouraged if they attempted to take part in them. Fortunately this situation does not exist everywhere, but it is so widely prevalent that the name "Christian" Association is often a complete misnomer. Strangely enough, the Y. W. C. A. is generally less subject to this criticism than the Y. M. C. A.

CHAPTER XIV

WHAT THE PUBLIC SCHOOLS HAVE DONE

THE DEPRESSION has affected the schools in several ways. It has increased the number of pupils in school.[1] Children who in prosperous years would have left school to go to work have remained because no work was to be had. The enrollment has increased chiefly in the high schools and in vocational classes, while that in continuation classes for employed youth has decreased because fewer children have left full-time day schools to work and to study in continuation schools.[2]

While many children have remained in school longer than they would have stayed in a period of prosperity, others have been taken out by their parents in the hope that they might find work. Some children have left school with the family needs as an excuse. Many families, demoralized by unemployment and hardship, are indifferent as to whether or not their children continue in school.

A second effect of the depression is that the attendance of children has been interfered with by lack of shoes and clothing, by illness due to inadequate food and warmth of the home and because they had no money to pay carfare to school, to buy lunches, books and other necessary things. Some city schools have given their teachers a visiting hour during which the teacher drives around in her car and looks up absent pupils.

A third effect is that, owing to many pupils being undernourished, irritable and quarrelsome, "discipline" has been more difficult.

---

[1] The enrollment of private schools has decreased, which is one reason for the increased enrollment in public schools. See Bureau of Jewish Social Research, "Supplementary Data on the Effect of Current Economic Conditions upon Jewish Social Work," June, 1931.

[2] National Education Association, *Childhood and the Depression*, pp. 24-25.

A fourth effect arises from the necessity the school is under of doing some relief work in order to improve the attendance and the morale of pupils. In one city the superintendent of schools proposed to the teachers to contribute a week's pay to a school relief fund. This was a gesture to prevent a general reduction in salaries and also was intended as a contribution to the general need which it was felt the teachers should make. In New York City the teachers contributed two or three per cent of their salaries. Says the *New York Times:* "Teachers and other employees are to detect and investigate need and extend immediate help. Thus the teachers are at once contributors to the huge charity fund, the social workers that discover and inquire into the poor pupils' wants, the direct disbursers of free lunches, shoes, and clothing, and also the bookkeepers and administrators of the funds."[3] In other cities the cost of meals and clothing has been paid by some other agency while the cost of administering the relief has been borne by the school.

The kind of relief given by the schools has depended on the most obvious needs. In one large city a teacher was putting a class through gymnastics and the lying down exercises raised bare soles of little feet to her surprised gaze. This school provided shoes. Where teachers have noticed the dull-eyed, listless behavior of children, the school has provided hot lunches. Philadelphia provided breakfasts in one hundred and twenty-eight school buildings. Other cities provided a noonday lunch. In some cities these meals were free to all needy pupils and there was a periodic checking to see that the children were really in need. In other cities the meals were for all pupils and only those unable to pay were served free. Many schools which do not provide free meals serve free milk. In cities where the schools do not furnish relief, teachers and school nurses report to the public welfare office observed needs of children and many cases of destitute families are thus brought to light.

Some city schools have provided only "pupil relief," others, family relief also. The chief criticism of pupil relief is that the method of giving it may humiliate sensitive children and cause hard feelings in their families. The blindness of some

---

[3] *New York Times,* Oct. 31, 1931, p. 3.

teachers, principals, and superintendents to the evil of inviting children to declare their poverty before others is surprising. Children should not be designated for relief before other children or sent to a general store for clothing or shoes. Another defect of pupil relief is that some children may not fare well in the distribution, while others display shabby clothes when they have better ones and so get more than their share. These shortcomings of pupil relief are more in evidence in large than in small cities, where lunches, shoes, and clothing have been given with very little waste or humiliation because the committee in charge has known the children personally and so has avoided being deceived by tricky families and has relieved needy children in a tactful way. In large cities family case work is more necessary and teachers cannot do it. As to family relief, it is said that in some cases principals and teachers have not been discriminating in the cases they referred to welfare agencies, and have been inclined to dictate to the agency and to expect immediate relief without case work. On the other hand, some public welfare departments are notoriously dilatory and inadequate in their relief, and family welfare societies have been unable to do their usual case work.

Relief giving is not a proper function of the school, but, in a great emergency, it seemed to the school authorities necessary. Where teachers raised a relief fund it was felt that the teachers should spend it and they did so through a committee chosen from their own number. Being entirely untrained in relief work, mistakes were made. One suprintendent ruled that clothing should be distributed to children from a central store and that children should call there for their clothing and shoes. There was little investigation of the needs of applicants. The spectacle of a great public institution dispensing shoes wholesale conveys the idea that all are entitled to what they can get. Furthermore, there have been instances of schools which got so absorbed in relief work that they neglected their function of education.

On the other hand we must not fail to consider the beneficial effect of this relief work on the teachers themselves. They have learned much in following the natural impulse to be of service in a crisis. Many of them have come to realize the importance of social case work and the vital necessity of more visiting teachers, in short, they have learned that welfare work with the families of their pupils is not their job. Another benefit is that teachers have had their first actual contact with the great economic problems before the country and the world. Before the depression needy children were to many teachers merely offspring of families that were just no good; the families were of a "poor heredity" and the children hopeless. For the first time in their lives they have been brought into contact with the industrial causes of poverty. These teachers come to me with the question, "What do you think of this machine age?" and then begin stories of capable and reliable workmen who were thrown out of work before the depression by the introduction of machinery and have had little work since, and of men for whom the depression has put an end to their working life because they are forty years of age and therefore too old ever again to hold a good job. This depression has afforded thousands of teachers a laboratory course in economics.

Will the effects of the depression stop there? Possibly. Heretofore, teachers have been, for the most part, members of the city of the well-to-do. They have had its mental attitude of aloofness. Naturally they find more rest in the sense of security, in the ease and pleasures of that city than in the insecure and barren homes of the city of the poor. Now that they have been awakened to conditions among the poor, will this prove to be any more than a temporary interest?

Nothing better proves the predominant influence of adults on children, as contrasted with the influence of their own associates, than the existence of the dual city. Among little children in the kindergarten there is no class feeling. They play together happily. Then the suggestions of adults begin to tell. One can observe the gradually growing class prejudice in boys and girls from seven or eight on. Even then they are beginning to rationalize it. Children of families of the well-to-do begin to think of children from the other end of town as "rough" or "dirty," whether they are or not. Teachers too often have the same prejudices, though many of them are outspoken in praise of a boy from the city of the poor who is "bright." In spite of this cross current, however, the class attitude more or less pervades the teaching body and supplements the home influences. These prejudices emanating from adults nullify any democratic feeling that might develop in children as a result of their intimate contact in the public schools. The democratic impulses of little children pass as they grow into the class attitudes acquired from parents, teachers and their social atmosphere generally.

While the school is not a nursery of democracy and cannot become such in an undemocratic community, there was, before the depression, a movement toward holding the school responsible for child welfare activities as well as for merely putting children through standardized instruction. The part the schools have taken in pupil and family relief seems to have accelerated this movement, temporarily at least. At the same time, just when the school is being given new functions, its financial support is being curtailed. "The situation faced by the schools may therefore be tersely expressed in these words: increasing responsibilities; static or decreasing resources."[4] An investigation made in 1931 revealed that, in 485 cities out of 1,461 reporting, teachers' salaries were being cut or the normal raises promised by the salary schedule were not being given.[5] Another kind of economy consists of reductions in school services. This practice is more widespread than the cutting of salaries and, in some schools, will sweep away educational features of great value, which have been worked out only after years of careful planning. Among these are classes designed to fit the school to the varying abilities and disabilities of boys and girls. Other unwise economies are the closing of night schools and of boys' clubs held in school buildings just when these are most needed, and the dismissal of visiting teachers and school nurses just when their work has become vital for the welfare of thousands of boys and girls. Real economy in education should be

---

[4] National Education Association, *Childhood and the Depression*, p. 6.
[5] *Ibid.*, p. 10.

sought at all times but this arbitrary and stupid elimination of the most valuable services which a school can render children shows clearly how children are paying for the depression.

The Public Welfare Law of New York provides for adequate and effective welfare work for children. That law should be enforced by those entrusted by the law with its enforcement. The school should not be obliged to do any relief work at all. Its welfare work should be in charge of a visiting teacher, who is a social worker and does no teaching except in the course of her contacts with pupils and their families who need her services. Her function is to interpret the needs of this or that pupil to the family, to the teachers, to the family welfare society, or the children's bureau, or the court or any other organization which provides for the particular need. She gives psychiatric social service, organizes clubs, and interprets to parents the significance and importance of the child's schooling. In an emergency she is the one who should bring the needs of children to the attention of the public welfare office and hold it responsible for proper relief.

The depression has stimulated schools to evaluate the various aspects of school work. To be sure boards of education have "cut the budget" often without raising essential questions, but in other cases there has been more serious thinking about education than in years before. The Progressive Education Association heard Professor Counts' challenge "Dare Progressive Education be Progressive?" and it will be interesting to see if the Association does anything toward arousing public and private schools to a sense of their enlarging obligations.[6]

The first step is to thrust forward the great principle of the interdependence of child welfare institutions and to emphasize the importance of the emotional development of children. Except in schools that have visiting teachers the more puzzling problems of behavior are beyond the power of the school to solve because teachers do not understand the emotional problems of children.[7] The understanding requires specialized knowl-

---

[6] Amidon, "Teachers Look at Education," *The Survey*, Apr. 15, 1932, pp. 78-79.

[7] "One of the greatest obstacles to the emotional adjustment of school children lies in the traditional administration of schools, both public and

edge which they never have acquired. The depression has increased the number of problem children and many examples of the failure of the school to deal successfully with them might be given. We shall give an example of one boy and one girl.

Jack Wickens was nine years of age when he began to steal. His father kept an amusement place of unsavory reputation and his mother was absorbed in social life. The children were neglected. Both parents were hot-tempered and erratic in their treatment of their children. Jack was a lovable boy but early developed an extreme sense of insecurity and his stealing was evidently an hysterical reaction to this mental condition and was also a response to that impulsive desire to have things which was so conspicuous in the behavior both of his father and mother. Without going into our long, pitiful record of Jack's case suffice it to say that in one year, when he was thirteen and fourteen, he was guilty of eleven burglaries and grand larcenies. These crimes were committed while he was on probation, and after he had escaped from the reform school where he had been committed.

Jack was a lovable boy. He seemed to try to behave in a way to be loved, as if to get from his teachers what he was denied at home. As the probation officer puts it, he was a "pet" of the teachers. But all they did was to pity him for his bad home and preach to him. That also was all the priest did, and all the court did, beyond putting him on probation. The probation officer did more. He tried to be a father to Jack, gave him some money to spend and really loved the boy. The one thing that boy needed was a good foster home. This was never provided by the court. So he continued to steal from nine years of age to fourteen when the court decided that the only thing to do was to send him to a reform school. The school teachers and the priest agreed that this was the only thing to do. Here we see the interdependence of child welfare institutions but an utterly unintelligent interdependence. They all agreed that he should be sent to a reform school, which was the worst thing that could be done with a boy of that type. Teachers may say that a problem boy of that kind is no concern of the school's. But he is in school, he is affected by the behavior of the teachers, and their opinions have weight with the

private. The requirements of the curriculum, traditional methods of discipline, the authoritative attitude of many teachers and principals, and the concentration of school attention on matters of scholarship are frequent causes of serious maladjustment in children." Lee and Kenworthy, *Mental Hygiene and Social Work*, p. 116. The authors state that this does not apply to all school authorities; that parents, teachers, principals, clergymen, employers, recreation leaders "show the same range from helpfulness to injury in their relationships to children."

court as to what should be done with him. This school system had no visiting teacher. From nine to fourteen this boy was a greater expense to the county, all things considered, than if he had been put in a foster home. So the necessity for economy during the depression was no argument against a foster home. The depression affected this case in that (1) Jack's family situation became worse as a result of the depression; (2) the need of economy was advanced as an argument against placing Jack in a foster home.

Belle Ramsey was an attractive high school girl whose father lost his position during the depression. Belle had been in the habit of dressing well but the finances of the family now prevented that. The high school dances continued, however, and Belle was in straits for a presentable dress. She was in love with Ben Minor and knew how proud Ben was of a well-dressed girl. One day she and her friend Maggie Raymond were admiring the gowns in Rutherford's. When no one was looking Belle snatched a gown and rolled it under her cloak. As she thought of it afterward, it did not seem as if she did this at all. It all happened so suddenly and without premediation. She had never stolen before. The theft was traced to her, the policeman came to her house, she had to confess, finally it "got around," and she stood disgraced in the eyes of her family and before the school. She was snubbed by many of her former friends. She was eyed askance by the teachers. One or two of them felt duty bound to talk to her. It was rumored that she was to be expelled. Worst of all, Ben broke with her. She developed a psychopathic condition and had to leave school. The thing that rankled with Belle was the injustice of all this ostracism. Here again we see the utter failure of the school to understand one of its own vital problems. School dances are a part of the school activities and the keen sense of inferiority that they stir in girls who cannot dress as well as others constitutes a school problem that is just as vital or more so than problems of standing in studies.

The emotional development of children and youth, as explained in Chapter I, determines the use they will be able to make of what they learn and of the intelligence they develop. Without mature character no mature use of learning is possible. If the integration of personality is made the purpose of education, the subject matter will have to include the child's social relationships because it is with these that his or her emotional life is bound up. This is especially true of family relations. The failure of the school to concern itself with emotional problems arising out of these relations has been evident during the depression. As was pointed out in Chapter VI, disordered family relations have been thrust before teachers as never before, but only those few schools that had visiting teachers could deal with these problems. An essential phase of the interdependence of child welfare institutions is this interdependence of the family and the school. But in explaining to a youth what is involved in his disordered family life, the teacher is carried inevitably into industrial relations. These too must be included in the subject matter of school education. And those relations are bound up with politics and the problems of citizenship. So the school is concerned with the entire web of life. This is already woven into the emotional life of children before they go to school and continues to mold them in spite of all the artificial restrictions of the school.

Integration of personality takes place in life's social setting, and this is also the arena in which the mature personality must act its part. Is the school yet conscious of these enlarging obligations? Can it be, as long as it is controlled by exclusive classes which are mainly interested in maintaining their social control?[8] How can the kind of education we have described be given except by mature, socially minded teachers who are not only trained but free to teach? I have not found any teachers who were entirely free to unravel with their pupils the tangle of industrial and political relations that have led to the disordered family life, the physical, mental and moral deterioration we have described in this book.

---

[8] Counts, *The American Road to Culture*, pp. 23, 38, 189-92; Counts, *The Social Composition of Boards of Education;* Counts, "Education— For What?" *New Republic,* May 18, 1932, pp. 12-13.

CHAPTER XV

THE DIFFUSION OF WELFARE PRACTICES

THE SOCIAL WELFARE agencies of a city are interested in what other cities are doing. New methods worked out in one city are discussed and copied in others, and so a city that is conspicuously successful in social welfare work comes to have a reputation in that section of the state. It has a more or less well defined culture area. This means merely that people in the area around that city get into the habit of looking to it for ideas and go there to consult the experts about the problems of their own communities.

A study of the diffusion of welfare practices from one city to another raises the question as to why the culture area concept is so little used in the study of modern communities. Probably one reason is that it involves such an analysis and comparison of communities as makes concealment of their identities impossible, and the analyses and comparisons always seem to communities to disparage them in some way or other. Studies like my *American Town*, or *The Expansion of Rural Life* and the Lynds' *Middletown* expose the authors to the disapproval of communities the members of which consider themselves entitled to keep their affairs private.

It is true that communities, like individuals, have a right to privacy. Because of a community's intimate knowledge of its own life, outsiders cannot understand that life as well as insiders. Any aspect of community behavior can be understood only in the light of a knowledge of the whole pattern, which is the possession only of those on the inside, and not necessarily of these. Only one who is capable of interpreting a good deal that remains unconscious to most insiders can understand it. Wherefore, any attempt of outsiders or of merely superficial insiders to portray the behavior of a community is bound to convey an impression that is not quite true or complete. A community has a right to privacy so far as such inadequate interpretations are concerned.

Has it the same right in case of an adequate, a true interpretation? What will such an interpretation do for a community? Will it not enable it more effectively to function as one of the family of communities that make up the state?

Nevertheless we must accept and face the fact that a community will resent any frank portrayal of its life, much as a family will. Communities, like families, have an impulse to cover up what other communities might not approve, even though other communities are guilty of the same practices. For communities, as well as for families, behavior is a good deal of a pose, and civic pride exerts social pressure on every member to carry out the pose in all of the accredited ways. Communities that are too inert to make an effort to eliminate civic evils thus often prefer to cover them up, and insist that nothing be said about them, and then pose as if these evils did not exist. This secretiveness is apt to result in social deterioration. No community has a right to privacy that results in deterioration. Because of the social stagnation that is apt to result from secrecy, we believe nothing is more important than thorough studies of communities.

The shortcomings of public welfare work described in the preceding chapters were, in many cases, possible only because of the secrecy customarily surrounding such work, and because the community as a whole felt secure in the secrecy that surrounded its treatment of its unemployed.

Communities should be studied not singly but as interacting groups. A community is both a center disseminating culture and a group to which culture is disseminated from another center. Some communities diffuse more and receive less than others. That is, communities, like individuals, act upon others or are acted upon.

Communities that are in advance of others disseminate their advanced culture beyond their own horizon to other communities far and wide. The area of dissemination varies for different aspects of the community's culture. It may diffuse educational ideas far and wide and be known only for that diffusion. Or it may diffuse one aspect of culture far and wide and another more narrowly. One city of New York diffuses certain esthetic aspects of culture over the known world, others over the states, others over a surrounding area of some fifty miles.

The auto and the radio have immensely extended culture areas and increased the variety of stimulations and ideas disseminated.

Social welfare methods spread from city to city like other aspects of culture. In so far as secrecy as to methods prevails, this diffusion is blocked. But the idea of secrecy itself is diffused, as we see when social workers of the different cities convey to one another their ideas of what information should be treated as confidential. Let us sketch briefly some aspects of this spread of welfare practices.

One cannot but be impressed by the differences between cities in social welfare work. Here is a large city where the public welfare office is advanced in some of its methods and behind in others. It has provided a large public boarding house where single men with a settlement in the city are lodged and fed. The city sent its public welfare official to a western city to get this idea. The idea was disseminated eastward to this city and thence to other large cities in its culture area. The child welfare work carried on by this city, its health and clinical work, nursery schools and child placing work also are superior. Its visiting teacher work is more advanced than in any city in the state. All these features of child welfare work have become known to surrounding cities and villages. The auto makes traveling to this city easy and the people engaged in this work are accessible and quick to discern the problems of outsiders. For instance, about fifty miles from this city is a smaller one which is beginning child welfare work. It stands midway between this large city in one direction and another large city fifty miles away in the opposite direction. In the new child welfare work this small city looks for suggestions to both cities but especially to the more advanced. So the methods of the more advanced are disseminated to this small city. Its culture spreads also to cities much larger than it is. A larger city is copying its visiting teacher work.

The small city does not copy from the more advanced city just because it is more advanced. It is interested for that reason but another factor is its own particular problem at the time. Thus, when the small city was recently face to face with the problem of the relation of private welfare agencies to the public agency, it found that the less advanced city had progressed farther in a solution of that problem than the more advanced, and so turned for the best ideas to the less advanced city.

The cities of the state generally have the prevailing type of political party organizations, the prevailing underworld, the prevailing relation between the dominant party organization and the underworld, and the prevailing control of police by "politics." But in the city with the more advanced child welfare work, the social workers are more outspoken against hampering political influences than in other cities. They are conscious that their city is advanced, that in virtue of this they are leaders in child welfare work, and this consciousness gives them an esprit de corps, an eagerness to assist one another, a readiness to be of service to people from other cities who seek suggestions for welfare work in their own cities. The city has thus become a dynamic center of dissemination of ideas about child welfare.

The advanced child welfare work of this city began in the public schools a quarter of a century ago. Certain extraordinary men and women advanced the idea that the school was made for the child and not the child for the school. They did not like to think of the school as a machine through which all children were to be molded and stamped as school products. Among these people were certain physicians, one of whom emphasized health work for weak children, another a flexible curriculum for retarded children. So the idea that the school was made for the child and not the child for the school expanded into this and that program on behalf of the pupils. But the schools were not free. They were part of a thwarting system. So the school had to be divorced from politics (as

far as a school system can be, with the power of appropriating
school funds still resting with politicians), and this was done
by various techniques, including new arrangements for the
election of the board of education and the extension to women
of the privilege of membership on the board. So a series of
ideas about child welfare grew into the culture of this city—
that the school exists for the child, that it must be free of
stupid interference, that health needs must be attended to,
that the curriculum must be flexible, that it must meet the
varying needs of children. These ideas and the associated
techniques and methods have diffused through the culture area
of this city wherever there have been individuals in touch with
the schools of their own community and capable of appropriating and applying the ideas, techniques and methods.

This appreciation by the school of the child as a functioning organism stirred other child welfare agencies. A judge of
the county court who had a sympathetic understanding of
children modified his court procedure for the rehabilitation
of the delinquent boy and girl and, in 1910, with the advice
of other experts, wrote the present juvenile court law of New
York State. In 1918 a committee of people, who had come to
believe that institutions should be made for the child and
not the child for institutions, organized to advance child welfare work. These people and those associated with them visited
Boston, New York, Philadelphia and Cleveland and used the
ideas acquired from these cities in constructive work in their
own city. Out of this wise guidance grew the present child
welfare program of the city.

Under the influence of their coöperating leaders the various
children's agencies of the city got beyond the policy of "splendid isolation." They began to realize the interdependence of
child welfare institutions and learned to discuss their problems
and to work out policies together; and so a policy which might
seem new and "somewhat radical" to some would be accepted
by all, with none thinking, "they are hitting me in this." Thus
they escaped the rivalrous or defensive attitude which child
welfare agencies are so apt to have one toward the other
and which interferes with the realization of their interde-

pendence. This coöperation of agencies prepared the way for a council of social agencies which was started in 1924.

The conception of institutions as living societal forms that grow and change, not inflexible arms that over-shoot society, has permeated the child welfare agencies. Social workers speak in praise of the schools with their flexible curricula which make possible coöperation between the schools and rehabilitation agencies. These growing institutions have disseminated techniques and methods through the culture area, and some of these, in some cities, have developed farther than in the culture center, and so better methods are disseminated back to the culture center. For instance, while the juvenile court of the culture center was a pioneer in advanced court work for children, another city now has a woman judge of the children's court who is a seasoned social worker of some twenty years experience, a kind of person who is superior to a lawyer as a children's judge.

Child welfare workers have a sense of responsibility to maintain the standards of the national professional organizations to which they belong. These national organizations thus have their own culture areas. It is this consciousness of standards even more than of achievements that gives workers their enthusiasm and their strength of conviction, and in this they differ from workers without such standards who have to be persuaded or driven to better work.

The very process of advance in child welfare work sets up an increasing strain between progressive agencies and reactionary political organizations, reactionary ecclesiastical organizations, reactionary business interests, and the conservatism due to the prevailing ignorance of social welfare work. These stresses and strains are bound to increase. But social mechanisms and traits of personality develop to meet them and these are disseminated throughout a cultural area. The progressive public welfare official forms an advisory council to gain community support for his policies, and also develops personal traits whereby he carries his political associates with him. His policies and his personality become known and are imitated far and wide. This great process of social invention and the diffusion of inventions is still in its infancy, but one cannot mingle with these inventors in this city and that and see the influence they have without realizing that it is a process to be reckoned with. The study of a culture center and of the diffusion of welfare practices is one of the most fascinating angles from which to consider social welfare work.

CHAPTER XVI

WHAT SHOULD BE DONE

THE WORD DEPRESSION signifies a slowing up or cessation of regular economic activities and a state of mind, that is, a mental depression resulting from inactivity and losses of profits, wages, salaries and an apprehension as to the future. This state of mind absorbs the individual, and one who would understand the situation must stand emotionally outside of it and face the realities. Unless one is thus emotionally outside and mature enough to face realities, one cannot possibly discern the salient points.

THE INSTITUTIONAL SETTING

The situation occurs within an institutional setting. Our economic system is one in which managers, representing absentee stockholders, and often under the dictation of absentee financial interests, control the activities of workers primarily for private profit. Great numbers of laborers are congregated in industrial centers where they are entirely dependent for a living on their jobs. Without jobs men cannot live and they have a will to live. When those in control fail to provide jobs, who then is responsible for the care of these workmen? Can we say that every employer is under obligation to provide his men jobs or take care of them, or that all are collectively responsible for providing jobs or care, that is, employers as a whole, all stockholders and bondholders, and all others who have any part in ownership of the instruments of production or who derive their living directly or indirectly from such ownership? Can we go even further than that and say that all of us, the whole body politic, are responsible for the existence of this system that has developed to the point where there are millions of workmen entirely dependent on their jobs? This may seem like spreading out the responsibility so widely that no one is responsible. But the economic system exists by sufferance of the body politic. Are we not all, therefore, responsible for those made dependent by it? And is not the obligation nationwide? Americans are one group. They so act in war and other emergencies. Nationwide unemployment is a national emergency. The taxing power of the states and the nation is the only effective means of carrying this responsibility.

This theoretical statement of social responsibility may commend itself as logically conclusive but in how far does it accord with the facts? It is impossible in one paragraph to answer this question. For a survey of the facts of economic responsibility at present the reader is referred to the recent notable textbook on economics by Professor Atkins of New York University and five associates. It appears that more than two-thirds of the national wealth is owned and managed by corporations. Since the invention of limited liability of stockholders, those aggressively in control of corporations have so shaped economic institutions as to enlarge their control and diminish that of stockholders until "the effective exercise of the power of ownership by the general run of stockholders in large corporations is very difficult, if not impossible."[1] "Divorced from control the owner-investor is a part of an undifferentiated mass of security holders. Whether he holds a contract which gives voting rights or one which gives non-voting rights, his part in the enterprise does not differ. He merely exercises his claim to his share of the earnings, if and when they are declared."[2] "It must not be inferred from the above discussion that there is any general complaint by stockholders of discrimination against them, or a demand to assert their power and reëstablish the ancient privileges of ownership. The investors are usually completely dissociated in interest from the corporation as a going enterprise. They are concerned simply with the future earning prospects of the corporation and with the effect that these prospects will have

---

[1] Atkins and associates, *Economic Behavior*, I, p. 149.
[2] *Ibid.*, pp. 164-65.

upon the value of their holdings."[3] "The owners of corporate
wealth are absentees in all senses of the term. They are absentees in residence; they are absentees in point of view of
positive contribution or participation in the government of
the corporation. They are merely recipients of income, active
only in seeking a shrewd shifting of their holdings for greater
speculative returns."[4] Inasmuch as the run of stockholders
have thus been retired to a position in which they feel no
responsibility for the management of what they own, can we
expect any feeling of responsibility for the care of the unemployed of the corporations in which they own stock? The
economic impotence of investors has in fact produced a general
sense of irresponsibility which is reflected in the political
lethargy of the times. Thus, in addition to the political submissiveness of the mass of workers noted in Chapter I as due
in part to the development of the great corporation, which
has forced them into a powerless and irresponsible position,
we have the political submissiveness of investors, resulting from
the same cause. Who *is* responsible in business? "Those who
own do not necessarily direct and manage. The risks of the
corporation as a going enterprise are not necessarily the personal risks of those who exercise governing power over the
enterprise. Managers and directors are in a position usually
to ascertain before the general public what the fate of a corporation is likely to be. Even though they may at the moment
own some considerable portion of the corporate securities,
they, as individuals, are able to sell out in advance. They may
grow rich even though managing a corporation faced with
prospective bankruptcy; deliberate or permissive mismanage-
ment may increase their personal fortunes. Fluctuating values
yield speculative harvests; the lure of gain may induce man-
agements to bring about fluctuating earnings."[5] "More than
two-thirds of our national wealth is owned by corporations.
They control at some point every process of economic life.
Their power is so great that many have wondered whether in

---

[3] *Ibid.*, p. 165.
[4] *Ibid.*, p. 166.
[5] *Ibid.*, p. 168.

time it might not overwhelm popular government. Yet in all this realm of power there is nowhere that sense of personal moral responsibility which is acknowledged between men and without which civilized human relationships would become utterly impossible."[6] As one reads this impressive description of interlocking irresponsibility, one wonders where responsibility for insuring regular employment under wholesome conditions can be placed and whether our economic system must not be so changed as to make possible an effective placing of responsibility in the economic realm before there can be any effective development of public welfare?

The defects of the economic order have been debated during the depression as never before. One of the most stirring discussions occurred at a meeting of the American Society of Mechanical Engineers between Mr. Flanders, vice president of the society, and Professor Wesley C. Mitchell. Said Professor Mitchell: "The social workers point out that there is a wide gap between average earnings and the cost of keeping a family of five physically fit. A vast number of American families on that showing are underfed, inadequately clothed, and poorly housed, even in a good business year like 1926. . . . The social workers are right in saying that the American population has vast unsatisfied needs, judged by the criterion of physical efficiency—not to speak of desires. Many billions of dollars must be added to our national wage income if we are to give a fair chance of physical and mental development to all our children. . . .

"Let me repeat Mr. Flanders' strong statement once more: " 'The engineer knows—all engineers know—that, if some omniscient dictator were installed as ruler of the United States they could provide for him raw material, machinery, and trained labor sufficient to flood, bury, and smother the population in such an avalanche of food, clothing, shelter, luxuries, and material refinements as no Utopian dreamer in his busiest slumbers has ever conceived.'

"Now, if Mr. Flanders is right, if you all know that it is feasible from the engineering viewpoint to abolish poverty,

---

[6] *Ibid.*, p. 170, quoting Garrett, *Civilization in the United States*, p. 411.

then you should present this stirring possibility to your fellow-
countrymen with all the force and persuasiveness in you. By
so doing, you could concentrate attention upon the need of
improving our economic machinery more effectively than any
other set of men. An emergency like the present time of
unemployment . . . puts many minds to work upon the task
of relief. You could do something finer: fix attention, not on
the mitigation of a temporary emergency, but on the attainment of a far higher permanent level of material comfort for
all mankind. Join your knowledge of the technical possibilities
of production with the social workers' demonstration of the
crying need of more food, more clothing, more shelter, more
of all the goods which minister to physical efficiency, and you
have an overwhelming case for inventing some way of enabling
the millions of families which need more goods to buy the
surplus products which are the nightmare of business men,
plus the additional goods which hover in your day dreams.
Mr. Flanders has said that we have a vast potential market
in needy American homes. The social workers' calculations
support that contention. If there are millions of needy American families, there are hundreds of millions of needy families
in foreign lands. All that is needed is to enable these families
to buy. But how can we do that? . . .

"Thus I come back at the end to Mr. Flanders' starting point.
Of course I have not solved the problem he sets to economists.
Nobody can solve that problem at present. I have merely tried
to make clear how many difficulties must be surmounted in
working out a solution and putting it into practice. The problem centers in the workings of a vast social machine. More
accurately put, it concerns the economic behavior of millions
of men. We must understand this behavior better than we do
now before we can have much confidence in any new schemes
we may invent. Plans which disregard the fixities and foibles
of human nature will not work. Mr. Flanders suggests that an
'omniscient dictator' might solve the problem. Thorstein Veblen
suggested a soviet of engineers. The Russians are trying a
committee of doctrinaire communists served by technicians.
All such schemes imply that we, the mass of mankind, shall

surrender to some higher authority our economic liberty to do whatever kind of work we can get a chance at, and to buy whatever kind of goods we can afford. Perhaps we should be better off in a material sense if we made that surrender. Perhaps we overvalue our present liberty of choice. In large part it is illusory, for many of our present choices are forced upon us by circumstances which we do not like. But we are accustomed to our present set of institutions. Getting us to change our habits for something better will involve re-education as well as invention. And re-education is a slow process."[7] Thus did Professor Mitchell urge the engineers to assume the responsibility of attacking the great problem of the attainment of a "higher permanent level of material comfort for all mankind." The point is to feel the responsibility seriously enough to do some thinking and to put thinking above personal selfish desires and group prejudices. An enlarging mind enlarges the sense of responsibility.

Characteristic of a mature personality is the capacity to comprehend and accept an enlarging responsibility. A mature college teacher considers his obligation to his college with its traditions and financial needs, but also his college's obligation, as an institution of learning and service, to promote the kind of learning that will develop among students a mature sense of social responsibility. And it may be said that the essential defect of school and college education is that it does not force these real problems of society on the student's attention, it does not force him (or her) to think but encourages wandering afield in irresponsible indulgence of intellectual tastes. This is called culture. The student is "tolerant" of every idea and serious about none. The ideas go into the mill of college talk with its conventional phrases. Education needs to be evaluated in the light of a mature conception of the enlarging obligations of school and college. A mature business manager likewise considers his obligations to the directors of his corporation but also his corporation's obligation to

---

[7] Mitchell, "Engineering, Economics, and the Problem of Social Well-Being—The Economist's View," *Mechanical Engineering*, Feb., 1931, pp. 109-10.

promote the welfare of those who work for it and of consumers and he aims to develop in those connected with the corporation this sense of responsibility. Prevailing social attitudes strike contrary to this social mindedness, especially the attitude to go with your group regardless of wider considerations. This is one of the fixities of human nature to which Professor Mitchell refers and it persists in men from boyhood and in women from girlhood. It is a survival of family and playmate life. Adult society is built upon this pattern. Go among the farmers of a countryside and you hear everywhere the same phrases about prohibition, depression, and other questions of the day. Among the people of a certain section of the city you hear the same sterotyped utterances. As bird cries to bird in the flock, as child calls to child at play, so adults find satisfaction in reiterating phrases of group sentiment and enjoy the literary turns that writers may give to these phrases. Candidates for political office phrase their utterances in a way to associate these sentiments of farmers and citizens with themselves and so win allegiance. Problems are not analyzed by candidates but merely played up with a view to invoking group sentiment and allegiance. So minds move in the circles of family utterances and community phrases. Responsibility implies a sense of real needs which disabuses the mind of mere phrases. How many people ever achieve the mature attitude in which they think sensibly of the real needs of their own family and community, to say nothing of looking beyond that horizon. They phrase their views on prohibition according to whether their set drinks or not. They phrase their way out of depression but still flounder in it.

The principal claim of a democratic state to superiority over other forms is that it enables any unfortunate section of the population to voice its needs and to win a share in available benefits through governmental action. Could anything be more evident than the failure of our democracy in this respect? The well-to-do classes have maintained that unemployment relief is a matter for local action. This is a mere evasion of responsibility. Many localities have not the requisite resources. The rationalizations of evasion show an ignorance of the elemental facts of economics. If the needy were given adequate food, clothing, shelter, fuel, it would help to quicken business activity because the wheels of industry would have to turn to produce all those goods. What else will start the wheels but an effective demand for goods? We are not saying that adequate relief alone would restore prosperity but that any increase of buying power among the unemployed would help. Yet, for many months prior to this writing (October, 1932) we saw just the opposite course of events. The standard of the unemployed masses dropped lower and lower, and the wheels of industry turned more and more slowly. Says Mr. Walter West, executive secretary of the American Association of Social Workers: "The human being . . . hangs on to life pretty hard and I think that what we do when we get short of relief funds is to take advantage of that and begin to pare down the amounts of relief and subtract little by little from the requirements for decent living."[8] This is not facing the situation. It is running away from it.

Evasion is seen not only in our own but in other countries. This failure honestly to accept sound economic principles has prolonged the depression. Says Mr. Hobson: "The monetary measures taken in the several countries for their own recovery do not betoken any clear grasp of the vital issue—namely, the putting of a larger volume and a larger proportion of the spending power in the hands of those who will spend it on consumption goods. For unless action is first stimulated in consumer markets, it is useless to offer abundant supplies of cheap bank credits or investment capital to industrial concerns. These latter cannot use more capital profitably unless they can have reasonable security that their enlarged outputs can be sold without further fall of prices. And this confidence they cannot get unless they know that the consuming public will have the wherewithal to purchase the increased supplies."[9]

When we say, therefore, that our democracy is a superior

---

[8] Testimony of Mr. West before the U. S. Senate Committee on Unemployment Relief, Dec. 1931, p. 71.

[9] Hobson, "The World's Economic Crisis," *The Nation*, July 20, 1932, pp. 53-54.

form of society because it insures a quick response to need throughout the nation, we are failing to consider that the social control in extraordinary times is the same as in ordinary times. Men have the same family centered habits, the same egocentric habits, and there is the same community of interest among those who control. Those of us who have followed the struggle to provide adequate federal, state and local relief realize only too well that, when it comes to the question of political control in the great emergency, the well-to-do classes have controlled and the less favored classes have suffered. On the other hand we find scattered throughout the country thousands of welfare workers who have a mature sense of social responsibility and who find some support in public sentiment, but they have little political power. They cannot finance newspapers or political campaigns or impress their communities personally as can men of financial power. So their fine discrimination of needs counts for little. The essential process of government still is the competition of aggressive particular interests for political control.[10] Dictatorship is advocated both by aggressive interests to strengthen their control and on the other hand, by those who want to curb these interests.[11] But how can those who advocate it for the latter reason be sure it will not serve the former?

Democracy implies an adequate sense of social responsibility and a recognition on the part of the dominant political class of needs which all men have in common. As a matter of fact all men are individuals like ourselves with a digestive, circulatory and nervous system, with a need of action and a need of rest, with a desire for security and for experiences that serve to integrate, rather than to disintegrate personality, and these needs cannot be realized except through a society with institutions kept fluid for that great end. The purpose of economic institutions is to provide food, clothing, shelter, and comforts in adequate and dependable quantities and institutions must be changed as required to achieve this purpose.[12]

---

[10] Williams, *The Foundations of Social Science*, Bk. II.

[11] Frankwood Williams, "Psychology in Dictatorship," *Survey*, May 1, 1932, p. 135.

[12] Chase, *A New Deal*, p. 22.

Public welfare expresses the principle of sympathetic recognition of needs and provision for them by governmental action, as contrasted with control of government by egocentric force. It is the democratic principle in government.

Back of the institutional situation as we have sketched it is the age-long conflict between the true spirit of science and that of our profit-seeking economic order. Let the case be stated by Frederick Soddy, Professor of Inorganic and Physical Chemistry at the University of Oxford and a Nobel Prize winner: "For many a decade now, owing primarily and indisputably to the intellectual achievements of a comparative handful of men of communistic and cloistral habit of thought, a steady shower of material benefits has been raining down upon humanity, and for these benefits men have fought in the traditional manner. . . . The strong have fed and grown fat upon a larger and ever larger share of the manna. Initial slight differences of strength and sagacity have become so emphasized by the virile stream that the more successful are becoming monstrously so, and the unsuccessful less and less able to secure a full meal than before the shower began. Already it savours of indelicacy and tactlessness to recall that the exploiters of all this wealth are not its creators; that the spirit of acquisitiveness which had ensured success to them, rather than to their immediate neighbors, is the antithesis of the spirit by which the wealth was won . . . let it not be forgotten that science is a communism, neither theoretical nor on paper, but actual and in practice. The results of those who labour in the fields of knowledge for its own sake are published freely and pooled in the general stock for the benefit of all. Common ownership of all its acquisitions is the breath of its life. Secrecy or individualism of any kind would destroy its fertility."[13]

Those scientists and thinkers who put intellectual achievement above money-making are, in our economic order, subordinate to profit seekers, in whom authority and control is vested.[14] The government also is predominantly under their

[13] Soddy, *Science and Life*.

[14] Williams, *Principles of Social Psychology*, Chs. V-VIII; Atkins and associates, *Economic Behavior*, I, Chs. I-XIV, XXV.

control and so the governmental policy is to seek first the prosperity of this class on the assumption that, if profits are made, the prosperity will in some way percolate to the professional and wage earning groups. Inevitably, therefore, the scientists and thinkers have not been called into the councils of the government on trade recovery. Says one of these thinkers, Robert D. Kohn, former president of the American Institute of Architects and now chairman of the National Committee for Trade Recovery, of the conference of business men called by President Hoover in August, 1932: "Of course there are in the group of business leaders now in national conference men of great ability, with generous instincts, but how can they lead the nation towards any worthy goal, tied as they are each of them to a particular self-interested group"? He illustrated this from the building industry in which, he said, "there has been a decade of perfect irresponsibility of a certain type of investment banker and speculative builder who have been interested only in their rake-off. . . . The real trouble lay in their outrageous indifference to the value of the projects they promoted in relation to the community as a whole, that is, the failure to see any more than the maximum profit to be obtained. . . .

"Where among the list of men called to the Washington conference are the real leaders of thought in our country, the men who have a vision of another state of affairs, the great teachers, those professional men who are truly professional because they have no masters but their conscience? Where are these men of vision by whom alone the course of our national economic life can be steered to a more worthy goal?"[15]

What Should be Done

After this survey of the situation we cannot be accused of a naïve optimism as we consider what should be done. We speak with due consideration of the setting in which the proposed procedures must be brought about.

First, we find the cause of this unprecedented depression in the new industrial revolution. Mechanical and other inventions

---

[15] *New York Times*, August 31, 1932.

and the driving of workmen have decreased the number of men required in industry per unit of product and this had caused widespread unemployment long before the depression.[16] Many of those employed suffered in reduced wages. The average manufacturing worker's yearly income dropped $55 between 1923 and 1928 and the average miner's $184 between 1922 and 1927. The only gains were in industries where organized labor was strong.[17] The basic cause of the depression was the enormous increase in productive capacity and the failure of distribution to give the masses the wherewithal to buy. The favored classes loaned huge sums abroad thus enabling our industries to sell abroad and continue for awhile the accelerated pace. Sales campaigns and installment buying instigated the masses to buy until the inevitable deflation came. This betrayal of the masses has been carried to its climax by lack of adequate relief during the depression until now their buying power is at the lowest ebb.

A group of eminent engineers which has for twelve years been studying the results of the new technology reports that "the adult population of this nation would have to work only four hours a day for four days a week to supply us with all our material needs." "The social system on this continent is being forced into a revision and revaluation of all its standards of value. The standards of the price system have been found wanting and an entirely new set of standards must be erected in order to deal with the physical conditions . . . created by the impact of technology on an old and outmoded social technique. America is witnessing the passing of the price system of production." "The United States is much nearer a complete industrial collapse, as a result of the events of the last three years, than the vast majority of its citizens realize. Our entrepreneurs and political leaders have believed so steadfastly and for so long that America is incapable of anything except a continuous onward rush to prosperity and ever-expanding development that they have been either blind to, or unaware of, the vast technological forces which have been steadily under-

---

[16] Henderson, *The Economic Consequences of Power Production.*
[17] Soule, *A Planned Society,* p. 25.

15

mining, particularly in the past two decades, our present haphazard industrial system of uncontrolled production, competition and distribution."[18]

What is to be done for the millions of victims of the unemployment situation thus forced upon us? There should be a
federal system of employment bureaus or labor exchanges
through which workmen could be moved from cities where a
surplus exists to cities where labor is needed. The states should
establish systems of unemployment insurance.[19] But above all
work must be provided. Unemployment insurance should provide work-relief and direct relief only where work-relief cannot
be provided. There is needed a nation-wide program of public
works, these to be increased and decreased according to the
degree of deflation or inflation at the time. A federal public
works agency should promote public works in the various
states, including works like housing, electrification and foresta-
tion which would be self-supporting if wisely managed, and
other works which would improve standards of life but would
not be self-supporting.[20] These works would be financed by
federal income and inheritance taxes, but would be carried
on in most cases, through state agencies. A huge public works
program would facilitate the establishment of state unemployment insurance systems by insuring work relief to the
able-bodied and so diminishing direct relief or the so-called
dole.

The Reconstruction Finance Corporation has been author-
ized to loan $300,000,000 to the states for direct relief of
destitution and $1,500,000,000 to states, counties, cities, or
in certain cases to private corporations, for "self-liquidating
public works," that is, enterprises to be devoted to public
use and which will earn an income. The appropriation for direct

---

[18] Parrish, "What is Technocracy?" *New Outlook*, November, 1932,
pp. 13, 14, 17. See also Dahberg, *Jobs, Machines and Capitalism.*

[19] For what is being done to provide unemployment insurance throughout
the world, see *Unemployment—Benefit Plans in the United States and
Unemployment Insurance in Foreign Countries*, U. S. Bureau of Labor
Statistics, Bulletin No. 544.

[20] Chase, *A New Deal*, pp. 224-229.

relief is much too small and has been grudgingly assigned, while millions of unemployed have suffered because of the delay. As to the appropriation for public works, ten weeks after Congress made the appropriation, though 243 applications for loans had been made, only three had been accepted and to none of these had the loans yet been made.[21] Greater competence in the unemployment relief of the federal government could be secured if it were administered by experts in public welfare. The public works program should be developed by one federal public works authority in which should be merged the various bodies existing at present and which should be made up of engineers who are cognizant of the economic break-down and of the necessity of public works as an economic measure.

There should also be, in each state, a state relief administration under which local public welfare administrations would budget families and certify them for work relief according to their needs. This has been done in New York under the Emergency Relief Administration. Though its usefulness has been curtailed by limited funds and by persistent opposition to its program on the part of egoistic forces in the cities and counties, nevertheless, through its support, public welfare offices have in various degrees improved their unemployment relief. One large city has secured a trained social worker as public welfare commissioner and an adequate trained staff. These people have formulated a public works program which is affording employment to the able-bodied men in the city who have been forced to seek public relief. Because the cost of relief is overwhelming to the still solvent citizens, each person or family applying for relief is strictly budgeted according to his exact minimum needs. The home relief department then certifies him for work according to his budget requirements and the man works each week the number of hours necessary to earn his budget. To assist him in making his funds go as far as possible, an agreement is made by the city with the retail grocers and milk dealers whereby they will sell to him upon

---

[21] Bliven, "Sabotage by the R. F. C.," *New Republic*, Oct., 12, 1932, p. 223.

proper identification his food at lower prices than to other patrons. Furthermore, a scientific relief diet has been worked out and many of the unemployed are voluntarily taking advantage of this balanced menu at the basic prices established by the coöperative arrangement between the grocers and the city. The work relief has been extended also to small home owners who are enabled to work out their over-due taxes, after mortgagors have agreed to delay foreclosures for a definite period.

The food relief is certified by nutritionists and social workers of the public welfare department as adequate to maintain health and growth and changes are made to avoid monotony. The food schedules, issued every two weeks, have contained twenty-five or more staple articles of food and in addition eight or ten necessary household commodities without food value. All adults receive the standard diet and only medical cases requiring extra nourishment are given special concessions in food. Infants and children through adolescence, and pregnant and nursing mothers and invalids receive fresh milk daily according to their needs. The person holding a grocery order is permitted to purchase from any one of a list of certified grocers and the recipient of relief is given the status of a regular cash customer so that the burden of providing courteous service and foods of good quality is thrown upon the grocer, if he wishes to hold his customer. The cost to the city per person per day, with the cost of fresh milk not included, averages ten cents. By this expert food relief this city has achieved a saving of $300,000 a year.

Rents are arbitrarily limited to a minimum, this being from five to six per cent of the property valuation, which covers city and county taxes with a small margin for other costs to the owner. Allowances for rents, as for food, are determined by an expert in this line of relief, and those certified for rent get the necessary work relief. Clothing and medical care are given directly as required. Allowances for heat, light and clothing are less adequate than for food and rent because of limited funds.

This office administers relief with an eye especially to the welfare of infants and children. Each child in the family of the applicant granted relief is furnished one quart of milk a day, orange or tomato juice and not less than six ounces of cod liver oil a week. A special effort is made to provide children with clothing and to furnish sufficient light and fuel to a family with children.

The weak spot in the relief work of cities who have attempted work relief is the lack of sufficient work relief and the uncertainty of its continuance. This is where the Reconstruction Finance Corporation has failed adequately to support the cities in their attempts at constructive relief.

The New York Emergency Relief Administration has officially designated the department of public welfare of this city as a "training school" for welfare administrators throughout the state.[22] The federal government should foster the growth of similar model public welfare departments in other states, especially in those which, if left to themselves, will not develop such advanced centers in many years.

We have described the achievements of one city under the Emergency Relief Administration in some detail because what one city can do is possible elsewhere. It could not have been done without the support of the Emergency Relief Administration. The federal government, by conditional grants of federal aid, could promote these efficient administrations in other states. Possibly there should be a permanent federal relief administration[23] to have charge of this conditional granting of relief, and with power to investigate and report, either on its own motion or at the request of Congress, whenever suffering in any state is not relieved by local authorities. A federal relief administration would take care of conditions which otherwise call for a Congressional investigation, which is difficult and sometimes impossible to bring about.[24]

---

[22] Department of Public Welfare of Syracuse, *The Syracuse Plan.*

[23] This might require a constitutional amendment.

[24] The commission appointed by Governor Sampson to investigate conditions among the unemployed miners of Harlan County, Kentucky, reported "conditions almost too horrible for belief." These conditions had existed for over a year, without any prospect of the state doing anything to improve them, and yet efforts made during all this time to bring about a Congres-

Under efficient relief administration this depression will teach several valuable lessons: first, that the consumption of the people can be directed in a way to avoid enormous waste and, at the same time, promote health and happiness; second, that the prevailing pessimism about governmental efficiency[25] is due not to an inevitable weakness of government but to the fact that only great crises make altruistic and expert leadership appear necessary for the salvation of the nation; third, that the federal government can coöperate with the states, and the states with the localities, to promote vast projects in public welfare. This will be one step toward the planned society that we need.

However, let us not ignore the difficulties immediately before us. In spite of the splendid achievements of the public welfare department described, under the leadership of the public welfare commissioner, Frederick I. Daniels, political vicissitudes might at any time destroy what has been accomplished. What is needed to give an experiment like this a more secure footing is that federal or state funds or a private foundation should carry it on as a demonstration plan for several years, emphasizing efficient relief, economy and the public works program as basic principles. By joining the work-relief to the public welfare department, the latter has a definite control of funds for all relief purposes; and this new instrument in public relief (work-relief) will more readily be taken over as one of the permanent features of public welfare.

At the same time we must remember that the most carefully developed program of work-relief does not by any means eliminate the evil effects of unemployment. It is merely a substitute for regular work. While an effort is made to provide employment suited to different capacities, for instance, office work for men not suited to manual work, this often is impossible. Men's bodies have become habituated to work of a certain

sional investigation and federal intervention were of no avail. The Red Cross cannot act effectively to relieve suffering in such situations because it is dependent on the employing class for contributions. See American Civil Liberties Union, The Kentucky Miners' Struggle; and Byars, Harlan County, Act of God? *The Nation*, June 15, 1932, 672.

[25] Pathfinding Committee of the Family Welfare Association of America, *Governmental Relief*, pp. 54-55.

general kind and many on work-relief jobs suffer hardship because the activities are beyond their powers. Furthermore, unemployment causes vast confusion and waste in the transference of men from private to public work. The economic system must be so planned that men can follow their regular pursuits with little interruption.

Long term planning is a matter not only for the federal government but for states and cities. Nor can the discussion of a planned society be limited to its economic aspects. The National Planning Board or National Economic Council of Chase, Beard, Soule and others, no matter how intelligent and courageous it might be, would have to make its recommendations to whatever kind of a Congress the body politic elected. Back of Congress is the body politic which must be regarded as ultimately responsible for any economic order we may have. This makes the struggle for social and political control the essential sociological process. Mr. Chase remarks that he has not "developed detailed specifications" for the political aspect of his program but he does not minimize its importance. Nor can the educational aspect of the program be ignored. There must be a progressive education beginning with the development of a free and socially-minded personality in very young children. Whatever other human rights there may be, every adult has a right to a childhood in which the foundations of physical and mental health and social-mindedness have been surely laid. Thus will boys and girls be prepared to achieve a secure and creative life; only such personalities can solve the problems of the new state.

INDEX